SIR HENRY KILLIGREW

ELIZABETHAN SOLDIER AND DIPLOMAT

SIR HENRY KILLIGREW

ELIZABETHAN SOLDIER AND DIPLOMAT

by

AMOS C. MILLER

with a Foreword by

A. L. ROWSE

LEICESTER UNIVERSITY PRESS
1963

Printed in the Netherlands by
Drukkerij Holland N.V., Amsterdam
for the Leicester University Press

TO J.

FOREWORD

BY A. L. ROWSE

THE Killigrews were the most variegated and fascinating of Cornish families during their comparatively brief floruit—which corresponded roughly with the tenure of the Tudors and Stuarts upon the English throne. What a spread of multifarious activities they covered and what arresting characters they threw up!

In Cornwall their hold depended largely on the governorship of Pendennis Castle, at the mouth of Falmouth harbour, a post which successive generations of them retained in spite of the ungoverned doings—amounting almost to piracy—of one or two heads of the family in the harbour and with the shipping in their care. At the centre of affairs the Killigrews were very much a Court family. William Killigrew, brother of the subject of this book, was groom of the Chamber to Elizabeth I for some forty years and must have known her as well as anyone. His son, Sir Robert, combined the captaincy of Pendennis with being Vice-Chamberlain to Queen Henrietta Maria and ambassador to the Netherlands. His son, another Sir William, also combined these offices, in his case the Queen being Charles II's unfortunate wife, Catherine of Braganza. No less than three members of the family wrote for the stage, the best known of them being the scapegrace crony of Charles II, Thomas Killigrew, who has a place in the history of Restoration drama, both for his plays and his prime part in building and directing Drury Lane Theatre.

In addition there was the usual complement of an Admiral, a Major-General, and—what was less characteristic in this highly secular family, much given to the enjoyment of life— a prebendary of Westminster and Master of the Savoy. The

Major-General was killed at the battle of Almanza; the last male heir of the senior line was killed in a tavern-fight at Penryn, on the hereditary Falmouth estuary. Naturally the Killigrews were Royalists to a man, and Sir Peter, knighted at the Restoration for his services, was better known as Peter the Post from his frequent missions as messenger from Charles I to Parliament during the Civil War. Even the women of the family were unusually gifted or had unusual fates. Young Anne Killigrew was drowned in the Queen's barge shooting London Bridge on the eve of the war; a younger Anne published her poems and had the felicity to be commemorated in a fine ode by Dryden, dedicated to her as "excellent in the two sister arts of poetry and painting".

All this stands in some contrast with the personality and career of Sir Henry Killigrew, a sober and upright Protestant inclining to Puritanism, immensely respectable, a virtuous and good man. Yet his public career was the most important of them all; he was the best servant of the state that the family produced.

Until Dr Miller's excellent book, little enough was known of Sir Henry; even to those of us versed in Elizabethan matters he was rather an impersonal figure. We knew of him as a skilled, professional diplomat, whom the Queen's government much relied on for difficult, testing missions abroad and in Scotland, and with the longest career of any in the foreign service, becoming professionalized—as Professor Garrett Mattingly has shown us in his masterly *Renaissance Diplomacy* —just at this time. Now, Dr Miller has rounded out the subject for us with admirable thoroughness: where previously we had but a figure, we now have a man.

We have good reason to be grateful to this young American scholar for his contribution to our joint historiography. He has got the Cornish background of the Killigrews accurately and well—and this is not easy for those who do not belong there. With the thoroughness that is a notably good quality of American historical scholarship, he has made conscientious explorations in the foreign archives as well as in England. He has mastered all the sources, and presents us the results of his prolonged researches in exemplary manner, well-written and clear, an intelligible and authentic picture of the Elizabethan diplomatic scene. The result is an excellent account of a representative Elizabethan—no romanticisation, but a portrait of the kind of man Elizabeth's government really relied on abroad as at home.

There are so many good subjects awaiting attention in English history, and few enough of our younger historians who perform their promise to attend to them. So let us hope that more young Americans will follow Dr Miller's example and enter this fertile and rewarding field. I not only commend his book but congratulate him on his achievement.

A. L. ROWSE

ACKNOWLEDGEMENTS

I WISH to acknowledge a special debt of gratitude to the late Professor Conyers Read of the University of Pennsylvania for suggesting the present study to me as well as the wider obligation which I, like all who have worked in the field of Tudor studies, owe to his splendid scholarship. I am indebted to Professors C. N. Howard, M. Curtiss, A. Lossky, and T. Brown of the University of California for their assistance and criticism when this work was originally undertaken as a doctoral dissertation. My thanks also to Professor E. L. Harbison of Princeton University for making available to me his notes on the Noailles correspondence in Paris.

Of the numerous other people whose comments and criticisms have suggested ways in which my work could be improved, the following merit particular mention: Dr A. L. Rowse of Oxford University who had the kindness to read the manuscript in full and whose advice has been of inestimable value on all aspects of this study, especially on sixteenth-century Cornish society on which he is the leading authority, and from which the subject of this biography sprang; Professor S. T. Bindoff, Sir John Neale, and Professor J. Hurstfield of the University of London who offered many helpful suggestions based upon their wide knowledge of the Tudor period; and members of the Institute of Historical Research where I read several chapters of my dissertation.

I should also like to express deep appreciation to my friend, Mr B. Carman Bickerton, formerly a graduate student of the University of London. Although a student of Imperial history, not directly concerned with the Tudor field, his observations had that indispensible quality of detachment which helped me to distinguish the forest from the trees. Finally, I must mention with gratitude the assistance given by Miss Carolyn Merion, graduate student in Tudor history of the University of London and, not least, my mother who read and criticized several of my chapters.   A.C.M.

CONTENTS

CHAPTER I

FAMILY BACKGROUND AND EARLY CAREER TO THE ACCESSION OF QUEEN ELIZABETH

SIR HENRY KILLIGREW had one of the most interesting and varied careers of any man in the Elizabethan age. His public life began in the reign of Edward VI when he was a servant of the Protestant leader, John Dudley, Duke of Northumberland, and it extended over a period of half a century almost to the death of Queen Elizabeth. During that time he found employment as a conspirator, secret agent, courtier, and diplomat. He was one of the few Englishmen of the sixteenth century who combined the profession of civilian diplomat with that of a soldier, a common enough type in continental countries, but one comparatively unknown in England.

Killigrew had a longer term of diplomatic activity than any other man in the English foreign service. Like William Cecil, Lord Burghley, and Sir Nicholas Throckmorton, two of Elizabeth's foremost servants, he worked for her even before her accession during the reign of Mary. At that time a Protestant exile, he undertook a secret mission into France under the direction of both Mary and her sister, the Princess Elizabeth. This episode is significant not only because it was Killigrew's first service for Elizabeth, but because it is the earliest recorded instance of her participation in the direction of English foreign affairs.

Immediately after Elizabeth's accession Killigrew was sent abroad on the first diplomatic mission of the new reign, an attempt to form an alliance with the Protestant princes of western Germany. Thereafter he became one of her most trusted and constantly used ambassadors. From the time she ascended the throne, with the exception of one ten-year break, he was almost continually employed as a diplomat until 1591. His missions carried him further afield than most men in the diplomatic service. During the course of his career Killigrew was in Italy, Scotland, France, Germany, and the Netherlands. He was, in fact, a perfect example of the astute, highly trained professional diplomats who served the English government during the sixteenth century.

In Elizabeth's reign he became a typical representative of the forward Protestant emissaries who filled many of the most important posts in her foreign service. Always working zealously for the furtherance of the Protestant cause, his assignments abroad and in Scotland brought him repeatedly to the very centre of the conflicts in which his country was engaged in the second half of the sixteenth century.

In 1559–60 Killigrew helped to foment civil war in France and to thwart the attempt of the French to reestablish their domination over Scotland. Two years later he acted as a secret agent and soldier in England's last determined effort to recover Calais from France. As ambassador to Scotland during a period of nearly three years following the Massacre of St Bartholomew in August, 1572, he worked successfully to consolidate a strong pro-English Protestant government under the Earl of Morton and to eliminate for a time the danger of Catholic conspiracy and foreign conquest. Thereafter, during the period 1585–91, as Councillor of State in the Netherlands, and as military advisor to Robert Devereux, Earl of Essex, in Normandy, he took part in England's new policy of open war to halt the threat of Spanish hegemony over western Europe.

At home Killigrew had an almost equally active career. In the reigns of Edward VI and Elizabeth he sat in the House of Commons as a borough representative from his native Cornwall. In the government he held the busy and lucrative post of Teller of the Exchequer. At court he appears to have gained some reputation in literary and artistic circles. He was related by marriage to the Lord Treasurer, William Cecil, and the Lord Keeper, Sir Nicholas Bacon. He was also a close friend of a number of other outstanding men in government service such as Robert Dudley, Earl of Leicester, the Queen's favourite, Sir Nicholas Throckmorton the ambassador—one of the most colourful figures of the age—and Sir Francis Walsingham, Elizabeth's great Secretary of State.

This work is a biographical study, an attempt to assess Killigrew as a diplomat, a Puritan sympathizer and forward Protestant, as a courtier, office holder, man of property, and, above all, as a human being. It is written in the belief that to understand such a man in the context of all his relationships affords a greater insight into the age in which he lived.

★　　　　　★　　　　　★

High on the western headland guarding the entrance to the Fal estuary stands Pendennis Castle, its central keep and embattled stone walls remaining today a durable reminder of the Tudor age in which they were built. Like St Mawes on the other side of Falmouth harbour, Pendennis was constructed about 1540 as one link in a series of fortifications along the south coast of England to protect the country against invasion. The land upon which the castle was built was leased from John Killigrew, Henry Killigrew's father, whom Henry VIII appointed as its first captain.[1]

Killigrew was a gentleman of substance and standing in Cornwall. His family came originally from the parish of St Erme, a few miles from Truro and had held land in the county as early as the reign of Henry III.[2] According to tradition the Killigrews were descended from an illegitimate offspring of

[1] Daphne Drake, *St Mawes and Pendennis castle* (H. M. Stationery Office), London, 1934, p. 5.

[2] William Hals, *The compleat history of Cornwall, general and parochial*, Truro, 1750, p. 126. (hereafter: Hals). P.R.O. Close Rolls, 5 Edward III, Part 1, (C. 54/150) (hereafter: C. 54).

Richard, Earl of Cornwall, the brother of Henry III.[1] Until the
end of the fourteenth century, however, they did not advance
from the status of typical, small Cornish gentry who, as the
Cornish historian, Richard Carew wrote: "could better vaunt
of their pedigree than their livelihood."[2] In 1385 one Simon
Killigrew married the heiress of Arwennack whose broad lands
extended from the Pendennis peninsula to the Helford river,
a distance of nearly five miles.[3] The family transferred its
residence to Arwennack and there drew profit from the
growing trade at Penryn.[4]

Like most of their fellow gentry the Killigrews grew rapidly
in wealth and influence during the sixteenth century benefiting
from the rising profits of land management, from grants of
church land and crown offices in reward for their services to

[1] Hals, p. 128. H. M. Jeffrey, "Two historical sketches of the Killigrew
family of Arwennack composed by Martin Lister Killigrew in 1737–8 and
known as the Killigrew manuscript," *Journal of the Royal Institution of
Cornwall* (December, 1887), vol. 9, p. 186. (hereafter: J.R.I.C.). A manuscript history of the Killigrews was written early in the eighteenth century
by Captain Martin Lister Killigrew who took the family name when he
married a female descendant of the Killigrews. His work was consulted by
several early historians of the county and published in part for the first time
in the *J.R.I.C.* in 1871. H. W. Worth, "Family of Killigrew," *J.R.I.C.*,
(April, 1871), vol. 6, pp. 268–82. The omitted portions of the manuscript
were subsequently added by H. M. Jeffrey in 1887. *J.R.I.C.* vol. 9, pp.
182–216. A bibliography of material on the Killigrew family is contained
in George Clement Boase and William Prideaux Courtney ed. *Bibliotheca
cornubiensis, a catalogue of the writings, both manuscript and printed of Cornishmen
and of works relating to the county of Cornwall with biographies, memoranda and
copious literary references*, vol. 1, pp. 287–297, vol. 3, pp. 1254–1259. See also:
Walter H. Tregellas, *Cornish worthies: sketches of some eminent Cornishmen
and their families*, vol. 1, London, 1893, pp. 115–195.
[2] Richard Carew of Anthony, *The Survey of Cornwall*, (F. E. Halliday
ed.), London, 1953, p. 136. (hereafter: Carew).
[3] *J.R.I.C.*, vol. 9, p. 187. J. L. Vivian ed. *Visitations of Cornwall, comprising
the Heralds' visitations of 1530, 1573 and 1620*, London, 1887, p. 267. (hereafter: Vivian, *Visitations of Cornwall*).
[4] Alfred Leslie Rowse, *Tudor Cornwall, portrait of a society*, London, 1941
p. 76. (hereafter: Rowse, *Tudor Cornwall*)

the Tudor monarchy. By marriage they became related to such important west country families as the Grenvilles, the Godolphins, the Trelawnys and the Treffrys.[1]

It was to the forceful personality of John Killigrew that the family owed its first rise to prominence in this period. His funeral brass can still be seen in the little village church of St Budock near Falmouth. He is portrayed thereon as a warrior, his body clad in armour. This representation affords a clue to the character of the man. Six times during the reigns of Henry VIII and Edward VI he appeared before the court of the Star Chamber in cases concerning violations of the King's peace[2]. On 26th January, 1530, for example, his neighbour, Thomas Glyn, charged that John and thirteen other "evil disposed persons... bearing swords, bucklers, and bows" unlawfully entered his property and dispossessed him of two horses and three oxen as well as of goods and other cattle.[3]

A terror to his neighbours in the countryside around Falmouth and later a notorious 'aider' of pirates, Killigrew had many characteristics of the west country free-booter. But he was also a capable and energetic representative of the Tudor gentry, of that class in whom, as Sir Thomas Smith wrote, "the prince putteth his special trust" for all the manifold judicial and administrative tasks of local government.[4] In addition to his post at Pendennis castle Killigrew was entrusted with a variety of civil responsibilities in Cornwall by Henry VIII and his three successors. Yet neither long years of government service nor old age itself lessened his contempt for authority. When about seventy years of age he threatened to

<hr>

[1] J. L. Vivian and Henry H. Drake ed., *The visitations of the county of Cornwall in the year 1620*, (publications of the Harleian Society, vol. 60) London, 1884, *passim*. (hereafter: *Visitations of Cornwall in 1620*).

[2] P.R.O. Star Chamber Proceedings, Henry VIII, vol. 14, f. 98; Bundle 20, f. 194; Bundle 30, f. 73. (hereafter: St. Ch. 2). P.R.O. St. Ch. 3, Edward VI, Bundle 2, f. 82; Bundle 3, f. 83; Bundle 6, f. 83; Bundle 7, f. 36.

[3] P.R.O. St. Ch. 2, vol. 14, f. 98.

[4] Sir Thomas Smith, *De republica Anglorum, a discourse on the commonwealth of England*, (L. Alston ed.), Cambridge, 1906, p. 88.

kill a Privy Council messenger who had come to Arwennack to recover 184 rubies which his son, Peter, had stolen. There was that in John's manner, as he uttered this threat, which left no doubt in the messenger's mind. He departed for London at once.[1]

John and his family were forward Protestants who belonged to that section of the Cornish gentry which most strongly supported and profited from the religious and social changes of the Reformation. Henry VIII, who well knew the wisdom of rewarding a loyal and able servant, instructed the Bishop and chapter of Exeter, in May, 1546, to lease to John Killigrew the manor of Penryn Foreign and Minster.[2] At court his brother, Benet, a groom of the Privy Chamber, was also picking up his share of the church land.[3]

John was undoubtedly a man of culture and taste, for the Killigrew manor, Arwennack, which he rebuilt in 1567, became known as the finest and most costly in Cornwall.[4] Situated within the crook of the Pendennis headland over-looking Falmouth harbour the manor contained a large ban-quetting hall, and the grounds upon which it stood were adorned by walled gardens, ponds, and an extensive park.[5] In his *Survey of Cornwall* Richard Carew gave an attractive picture of Arwennack as it appeared at the end of the sixteenth century. He wrote: "After the declining hill hath delivered you down from this castle (Pendennis) Arwennack entertaineth you with a pleasing view, for the same standeth so far within the haven's mouth that it is protected from the sea storms, and yet so near unto as it yieldeth a ready passage out; besides the cliff on which the house abutteth is steep enough to shoulder off the waves and the ground about it plain and large enough for recreation."[6]

[1] P.R.O. S.P. 15/14 f. 12.

[2] P.R.O. S. P. Henry VIII, Signatures by Stamp, (May, 1546), no. 63, (hereafter: P.R.O. S.P. 1).

[3] P.S. and Patent Rolls (July, 1540), g. 942 (121), (C. 66/695 f. 8, m. 30), (hereafter: P.R.O. C. 66).

[4] *J.R.I.C.*, vol. 9, p. 186.

[5] *Ibid.*, pp. 186–7.   [6] Carew, p. 226.

John Killigrew married Elizabeth, the daughter of James Trewinard of St Erth, a Cornish gentleman of ancient lineage. By her he had five daughters and five sons of whom Henry was the fourth.[1] There is no record of the date of his birth, but the evidence of his later career indicates that he was born between 1525 and 1530. Very likely he spent his childhood at his father's manor beside Falmouth harbor. Although Arwennack was not then the opulent mansion which it later became, a map of Falmouth drawn about 1544 shows the Killigrew residence to be an impressive place—a large castellated house protected by walls and turrets.[2]

Well placed socially as a son of a Cornish gentleman Henry grew up in agreeable circumstances at Falmouth with its equable climate and fine coastal scenery. Despite long absences at court and on diplomatic missions abroad the influence of his early Cornish environment never lost its effect on Killigrew's mind. He remained always a loyal Cornishman, devoted to his Cornish friends and relations, and keenly interested in the affairs of the county.

Life cannot have been easy in the western reaches of Cornwall during Killigrew's youth—even in the best of circumstances. Cornish society was clannish, conservative, and deeply attached to its ancient traditions. During the last ten years of Henry VIII's reign it was disturbed by the ecclesiastical reformation and the Dissolution. Quarrels over property, mutual depredations characteristic of an earlier social order were intensified by antagonisms that were the result of the new social and religious divisions. In this same period England was twice at war and its western coasts were frequently on the alert for possible invasion.[3]

It was in this atmosphere of insecurity that Henry and his brothers grew to manhood. From their manor—only a stone's

---

[1] Vivian, *Visitations*, p. 267.

[2] Daniel Lysons, *Magna Britannia, being a concise topographical account of the several counties of Great Britain* vol. 3, (Cornwall), London, 1814, p. 99.

[3] Rowse, *Tudor Cornwall*, pp. 246 ff.

throw from shore—they could see trading vessels of their own and other countries anchored in the harbour. Doubtless their ears were filled with tales of piracy and war on the seas. Even before the end of Henry VIII's reign Falmouth was a known resort for buccaneers.[1] In the winter of 1537 they may have looked on with other of the local gentry as a Spanish fleet pursued four French vessels all the way up the Fal estuary as far as Truro driving the flag ship aground.[2] Perhaps they shared the excitement of that October day five years later when their father set out for London as escort to the Spanish ambassador whose ship had just arrived in Falmouth.[3]

This hardy environment had an unmistakable influence on the characters of John, Thomas, and Peter, John Killigrew's three older sons. They inherited in full measure their father's taste for lawlessness and violence. As early as the reign of Edward VI Thomas and Peter had earned the reputation of being "notorious pirates."[4] In November, 1552, accompanied by another west country sea rover named Henry Strangeways, they captured two ships from a Flemish merchant fleet in the Channel. One of the ships was taken to the Scilly Isles where it was unloaded in full view of the inhabitants, and part of the merchandise, consisting of wool and wine, sold to the local populace who were eager to share in the rewards of piracy.[5]

Despite the protests of the Spanish ambassador and the efforts of the English government to apprehend them, they managed to evade arrest. Their escape was probably due, in part, to the fact that one of the officials in charge of the fortification and defence of the Scillys was John Killigrew the younger.[6] A few months later Thomas, Peter, and their friend, Strangeways, were haunting the coast of Ireland where they continued to loot foreign and English ships with a fine impartiality.[7] These

1 *Acts of the Privy Council*, vol. 1, pp. 170, 382, 468. (hereafter: *A.P.C.*).
2 P.R.O. S.P. 1/115 ff. 123–4.
3 *Calendar of State Papers, Spanish, 1542–3*, p. 159.
4 P.R.O. S.P. 68/11 f. 615.
5 *Calendar of State Papers, Spanish, 1550–2*, pp. 614–15.
6 *A. P. C. 1552–4*, p. 74.   7 *Ibid.*, p. 245.

escapades were only a prelude to the numerous acts of piracy committed by members of the Killigrew family in later years.

The response of Henry and his younger brother, William, to their Cornish upbringing, on the other hand, seems to have been almost entirely negative. In contrast to their brothers they became staid, conscientious government officials who devoted long and honourable careers to the service of their country.

The difference in temperament and character are especially striking in Henry's case. While his older brothers were reckless and spendthrift he was usually cautious and temperate in all his dealings. On many occasions during his life motives of patriotism, religious duty, or financial necessity prompted him to undertake dangerous and onerous tasks. But he had little of that spontaneous love of action and danger characteristic of the seafaring gentry. In later years he showed only a casual interest in the exploits of the great west country sea captains like Drake, Hawkins, and Frobisher. Given the choice, he would have preferred to live out his life as a country gentleman quietly watching over his family and property.

This contrast should not be pressed too far. Other features of his personality suggest that he owed something at least to his family environment. His fiery Protestant zeal may have been an inheritance from his family, and there was a certain streak of sternness, even ruthlessness in him which recalls that tough old soldier, his father. Perhaps the interest and ability he later showed in military affairs were first developed by the experience of seeing his father perform his duties at Pendennis Castle—supervising the repair of the walls, directing provision of the blockhouses with ordnance, shot and powder, and maintaining disciplined alertness among the garrison for the constant vigil against piracy and foreign invasion.[1]

It is unfortunate that so little is known of Killigrew's early years, but this is usual for people in the sixteenth century.

[1] There are frequent references to John Killigrew's activities at Pendennis Castle in the last years of the reign of Henry VIII. *A.P.C.*, vol. 1, pp. 170, 323, 349, 469.

Concerning the factors which influenced the formation of their characters, we are normally left to speculation. In some instances, however, such speculation may have a certain value. From what is known of the other members of Henry's family it is possible to suggest a fairly common psychological pattern. In a large family such as the Killigrews, where the father is a strong aggressive personality, the elder sons are likely to try to outdo him in the activities in which he excels.

The younger sons feel the pressure of this rivalry with the father less strongly. Towards them he is often less harsh and demanding, more willing to allow them to follow their own inclinations, and they enjoy a greater freedom to develop different capabilities. At the same time, being overshadowed by their more forceful elders, they frequently aquire a protective caution and reticence. This would be especially true in Henry's case because of his small stature. No doubt he found it safer and easier to achieve his ends by persuasion than by force. Life with a violent father and three turbulent elder brothers must have given him an excellent schooling in the wisdom of discretion. A better training for the future diplomat can hardly be imagined.

In the *Athenae Cantabrigienses* Thompson Cooper expresses the belief that Killigrew went to Cambridge, but no confirmation for this assertion exists in the records of the University.[1] Whatever its form there can be no doubt that he received an

[1] Charles Henry Cooper and Thompson Cooper, *Athenae Cantabrigienses*, vol. 2, 1586–1600, Cambridge, 1861, p. 345. The late Dr J. A. Venn, former editor of the *Alumni Cantabrigienses*, wrote to me that Killigrew was not a graduate of Cambridge, but that it was possible that he joined a College sometime prior to 1540–1 and perhaps kept a few terms. (College Admission Registers are not extant before this date.) Dr Venn said that local tradition was very strong at Cambridge and that Cooper may have made his surmise concerning Killigrew's residence at the University on this basis. Killigrew qualified for inclusion in Venn's *Alumni* only by reason of a benefaction which he made to Emmanuel College. J. A. Venn ed. *Alumni Cantabrigienses, a biographical list of all honors students, graduates and holders of office at the University of Cambridge from the earliest times to 1900*). Part 1, vol. 3, Cambridge, 1924, p. 16.

excellent education. The seventeenth-century biographer, David Lloyd, paid a glowing tribute to his learning and to the breadth of his literary and artistic attainments.[1] Perhaps Lloyd's statements are exaggerated, but there is no question that Killigrew was a man of considerable cultural achievement. His correspondence reveals a thorough knowledge of Latin and of classical literature. He also possessed a good command of foreign languages. He could speak and write Italian, and his fluency in the French tongue won the praise of the accomplished scholar and veteran diplomat, Sir Thomas Smith.[2]

Killigrew's educational background prepared him well for the career he was to follow. He took his first step towards entry into government service in the last years of the reign of Henry VIII when he became a gentleman servant in the household of John Dudley, Viscount Lisle. As a younger son in a large family it was natural that he should seek his fortune at court, and his uncle, Benet Killigrew, probably provided the backing necessary to obtain this appointment. Before his advancement to the King's Privy Chamber Benet had been a servant of Arthur Plantagenet, Viscount Lisle, John Dudley's step-father.[3] The first record of Henry Killigrew's presence in the Dudley household occurs in 1545 when the family visited the court at Greenwich.[4] He was about eighteen years of age at this time.

[1] David Lloyd, *The statesmen and favourites of England since the reformation, their prudence, policies, successes and miscarriages, advancements and falls during the reigns of Henry VIII, Edward VI, queen Mary, queen Elizabeth, king James I, and king Charles I*, second edition with additions, London, 1670, p. 586. (hereafter: Lloyd).

[2] In a letter to Sir William Petre and Sir William Cecil of November 1552, John Dudley, Duke of Northumberland, remarked that his servant, Killigrew, could "reasonably well expound Italian, both written and printed." P.R.O. State Papers, Foreign, Edward VI, (S.P. 68/10 f. 585). (hereafter: P.R.O. S.P. 68). In January, 1572, Smith wrote to Cecil that Killigrew had a better knowledge of the French tongue that he. P.R.O. State Papers, Foreign, Elizabeth, (S.P. 70/122 f. 13). (hereafter: P.R.O. S.P. 70).

[3] P.R.O. S.P. 1/137 ff. 104-5.

[4] Bodleian Library, Oxford, Western MS., 28996.

The accession of Edward VI two years later had a marked effect on Killigrew's personal fortunes. As member of a locally powerful west country family which warmly suported the new Protestant government he possessed some claim to favour, but the decisive factor in his advancement was his connection with the Dudleys. He obtained his first grants of office in the spring of 1552, shortly after his patron, John Dudley, now Duke of Northumberland, had secured complete ascendancy in the counsels of the King. In April, 1552, Killigrew was appointed harbour master of the Duchy of Cornwall, an office which had been vacated by the death of his uncle, Benet.[1] The following month he was made bailiff and collector of the rents for the manor of Helston in Cornwall.[2]

His association with the Dudleys brought him into contact with the brilliant group of scholars and politicians that gathered in the household of the young king. Lloyd says that Killigrew became the guardian of the younger Brandon. This must refer to Charles Brandon, the younger son of Charles Brandon, Duke of Suffolk and his last wife, Catherine Willoughby.[3] No evidence survives to substantiate Lloyd's statement, but the suggestion of Killigrew's connection with the strongly Protestant Duchess of Suffolk raises interesting possibilities concerning the early influences which determined his religious beliefs.

There is no reason to doubt that many of the friendships which affected Killigrew's future career were formed when he first entered court life in the reigns of Henry VIII and his son Edward. As a servant of Northumberland he was in close contact with the Duke's family, and it was perhaps at this time that he first gained the friendship of Northumberland's fifth son, Robert Dudley, whose devoted follower he was later to become in the reign of Elizabeth.

[1] Docquet Book of the Privy Council, 1550–3, B.M. Royal MSS., 18, CXXIV f. 199.
[2] P.R.O. Exchequer Augmentations Office, Miscellaneous Books, Enrolments of Leases, (P.R.O. E. 315) vol. 224, f. 221.
[3] Lloyd, p. 586.

In the circle around Edward VI Killigrew must certainly
have met his future brother-in-law, William Cecil, a rising
young politician attached to the household of the Duke of
Somerset and the irrepressible Sir Nicholas Throckmorton, a
boon companion of the young King. His acquaintances probably also included a number of distinguished men of learning
such as Sir Anthony Cooke, one of whose brilliant daughters
Killigrew would later marry, Roger Ascham, tutor to Edward
VI's sister, the Princess Elizabeth, and Thomas Wilson, author
of the *Arte of Rhetoric*, who was also an adherent of the Duke
of Northumberland.[1]

Killigrew may have received his introduction to the life of
diplomacy in the pleasant form of a grand tour. In his auto-
biographical *Travaile and Lief* Thomas Hoby mentions Killigrew's presence at Padua in January, 1549.[2] Like Hoby Killigrew was probably travelling on the continent to further his
knowledge of foreign languages in preparation for a diplomatic
career. Hoby was the younger brother of Sir Philip Hoby,
English ambassador at Brussels. Like Killigrew he belonged to
a forward Protestant family and was also to marry a daughter
of Sir Anthony Cooke. Hoby was nineteen years old   Killigrew, probably a few years older.[3]

Accompanied by another Englishman named Murphin these
two young men made a journey to Mantua and the Po valley.
Their trip was marked by one especially interesting incident.
They were given the opportunity to see Philip, the future King
of Spain, who was to become England's great antagonist in
later years. According to Hoby's account he, Killigrew, and

[1] In February, 1559, a councillor of the Elector Palatine wrote to
Killigrew asking him to extend greetings to his old friend, Ascham.
B. M. Cotton MSS., Galba B. XI, f. 193. In a letter to Sir Nicholas Throck-
morton of January, 1561, Wilson referred to Killigrew as his "dear friend."
P.R.O. S.P. 70/22 f. 604.

[2] Edward Powell ed., *The travels and life of Sir Thomas Hoby, Kt., of
Bisham Abbey written by himself, 1547–1564*, London, 1902, *Camden Miscellany*, vol. 10, p. 1. (hereafter: *Camden Miscellany*).

[3] *Ibid.*, pp. 3–1130.

Murphin set out from Padua on the 7th of January. On arriving at Mantua six days later they watched Prince Philip enter the city accompanied by a thousand horsemen, all of whom were clad in white. He was passing through Italy to visit his father, the Emperor Charles V, then living at Brussels.

After leaving Mantua the three Englishmen travelled by boat down the river Mincio and into the Po as far as Ferrara, returning to Padua by land. During the journey they stopped at a little village a few miles from Mantua where Virgil was born and saw the house where, according to the inhabitants of the country, the poet had lived as a shepherd. Nearby they also visited a residence of the Duke of Mantua called Marmoral which Hoby enthusiastically described as "a beautiful house of pleasure ... full of pleasant walks and fair gardens where the Duke has certain orange trees which he may remove from place to place." [1]

Aside from the Italian excursion there is no certain evidence that Killigrew was abroad during the reign of Edward VI. Lloyd says that Killigrew acted as an agent for Sir John Mason who was ambassador in both France and Germany at this time.[2] There is no information in Mason's surviving correspondence to support this assertion, but the nature of Killigrew's activities as an exile in Mary's reign and his friendship with Throckmorton and Sir Thomas Challoner, both of whom were charged with ambassadorial responsibilities under Edward VI, suggest that his diplomatic experience began at this time.

This conclusion is strengthened by a letter in the autumn of 1552 from the Duke of Northumberland to Sir William Cecil and Sir William Petre, the Secretaries of State. Northumberland informed them that Killigrew had just had a conversation with the secretary of the French ambassador and with an exiled French Protestant by the name of De Forge. He and De Forge had discussed the current war between France and the Empire, especially the state of the defences of Metz which was

[1] Ibid., p. 11.
[2] Lloyd, p. 587.

then under siege by Charles V.[1] The nature of their conversation indicates that he had personal familiarity with French and German affairs.

Killigrew sat as a member for Launceston in the last Parliament of Edward VI, probably as one of a group of personal adherents for whose election Northumberland had used his influence in order to gain support for his desperate bid to hold onto power in the now certain event of the King's death.[2] There is no information as to his attitude towards the unsuccessful attempt of his patron to alter the succession. Unlike many of Northumberland's erstwhile supporters, however, Killigrew did not desert his fallen master. Even after Northumberland's execution he remained a member of his household until its dissolution by Mary's government.[3]

On the other hand he was no martyr for lost causes. He did not follow the example of his friend, Thomas Wilson who, not only supported his patron to the last, but fled into exile after his fall from power.[4]

It is unfortunate that so little is known of Killigrew's actions at this juncture. Close association with that arch-schemer, Northumberland, must have afforded him a unique opportunity to gain an insight into the seamy underside of Tudor politics. One wonders, for example, how far he was privy to Northumberland's plan to deprive Mary of the succession and to place his son, Guilford Dudley, and Lady Jane Grey upon

[1] P.R.O. S.P. 68/10 f. 245.

[2] Brown Willis ed., *Notitia parliamentaria or a history of the counties, cities and boroughs in England and Wales. To which are subjoined lists of all the knights, citizens, and burgesses with an account of the Roman towns in every shire etc. with additions*, vol. 3, (2), London, 1716–50, p. 17. (hereafter: Willis).

[3] Northumberland's goods had been seized after his fall from power in July, 1553. His household was dissolved and payment of wages was made by Mary's government to servants who still remained in it. Killigrew was listed as one of these. P.R.O. Office of the Auditors of Land Revenue, Miscellaneous Books, .(LR. 2, vol. 18 f. 35, *et. sec.*)

[4] *The Dictionary of National Biography*, (Sidney Lee ed.), vol. 21, p. 604. (hereafter: D.N.B.)

the throne. The fact that Killigrew was acting as Northumberland's intermediary with the French ambassador's secretary in the autumn of 1552 suggests the possibility that he learned something of the Duke's attempt to secure French support for his coup d'état.

Killigrew, at any rate, did not become so far involved in the schemes of his patron as to incur punishment from Mary's government. Probably the most important effect of his association with Northumberland was to instill in his mind the prudent resolve, which he never afterwards forgot, to keep clear of factional intrigues at court.

Like most Protestants Killigrew and his family accepted the accession of Mary Tudor without open hostility. When, however, the Queen announced her intention to marry Prince Philip in the autumn of 1553 the national and religious antipathies of her Protestant subjects were aroused to fever pitch. Killigrew declared to an acquaintance that "England's ruin was working by the Spaniards," and his friend the colourful adventurer, Sir Peter Carew, tried to stir his fellow west countrymen to rebellion by warning them that if Philip came to England "the Spaniards would wish to do as they pleased and violate their daughters, which they ought not to suffer, but rather suffer death." [1]

Killigrew became deeply involved in the intrigues which led up to the insurrections of 1554 and was a close associate of leading figures in the conspiracies such as Peter Carew and Edward Randolph. Even before the outbreak of rebellion at the end of January he was in France secretly enlisting the support of the French government for the rebel cause. [2] After the collapse

[1] In May, 1588, writing to Sir Francis Walsingham, Killigrew recalled this comment which he had made to a Captain Borthwick who was also a Marian exile. P.R.O. S.P. 83/13 f. 265. On Borthwick see: Christina Hallowell Garrett, *The Marian exiles, a study in the origins of Elizabethan puritanism*, Cambridge, 1938, p. 101. *C.S.P. Spanish*, 1554–8, p. 83.

[2] Montmorency, the councillor of Henry II, wrote to Noailles, French ambassador at Mary's court, that an Englishman had appeared at Fontainebleau, late in December, 1554, and informed him that he represented eight

of the Western Rebellion he or one of his brothers helped its leader, Sir Peter Carew, escape in a boat from Weymouth.[1]

When Carew arrived in France he gathered around himself a band of English refugees, including a group of younger sons of the west country gentry. Among them were Henry and two of his older brothers, Peter and Thomas Killigrew. The plan of Carew and his friends was to invade England with the aid of French forces and depose Mary in favour of her sister, Elizabeth, and Edward Courtenay, Earl of Devon.[2]

While his brothers were roving the Channel in a French vessel plundering Spanish ships and looking for a chance to waylay Philip on his sea journey to England, Killigrew was at the court of Henry II negotiating on Courtenay's behalf. According to the report of a spy his "special work ... was to persuade all the Englishmen in France to follow Carew." [3] Soon afterwards Wyatt's rebellion ended in failure. Realizing the futility of his mission, Killigrew departed from the French court to rejoin Carew and his associates at Rouen.[4]

Aware of the present impossibility of overthrowing the English government and that further support for the rebels might result in war, the French King withdrew his bounty from

---

or ten English gentlemen. He offered to bring over to the French service eight or nine good warships. *Archives du Ministre des affaires étrangères,* Paris, vol. 9, f. 112. Professor E. H. Harbison, who has made an exhaustive study of the Noailles correspondence in Paris, believes that the Englishman, who made these offers to Montmorency, was one of the Killigrew brothers. Elmore Harris Harbison, *Rival ambassadors at the court of queen Mary,* (Princetown,) 1940, p. 117, footnote 23.

[1] P.R.O. State Papers, Domestic, Elizabeth, (S.P. 12/2 f. 18.) (hereafter: P.R.O. S.P. 12). John Vowell (otherwise Hooker), *The life of Sir Peter Carew, late of Mohonese, Otrey,* Middlehall, 1840, p. 180.

[2] Accounts of the activities of the Marian exiles in France are contained in Garret, *op. cit.,* and Allen Banks Hinds, *The making of the England of Elizabeth,* London, 1893.

[3] *C.S.P. Spanish, January to July, 1554,* p. 132.

[4] P.R.O. State Papers, Foreign, Mary, (S.P. 69/3 f. 187). (hereafter: P.R.O. S.P. 69).

the refugees. As a result many were left in a destitute condition. Some turned to thievery; others tried to win a pardon from their government, and of these not a few were ready to inform on their friends in order, as the English ambassador, Sir Nicholas Wotton quaintly phrased it, "to work their passage back to England." [1]

Killigrew does not appear to have participated in this dirty game—perhaps he did not feel driven to that extremity, for he may have received some measure of assistance from home. In the summer of 1556 John Killigrew was deprived of his office at Pendennis Castle, and with his eldest son, was summoned to London to face accusations of the utmost gravity. [2]

Many years later Henry's nephew, John Killigrew, recalled "My father and grandfather were charged with thirty points of treason, all founded on this that they being contrary at that time Protestants did keep my uncle Harry in the French court and did secretly succour and victual my uncles Peter and Thomas at sea." However, the charges remained unproven; the two Killigrews regained their freedom, and John's grandfather was restored to his post at Pendennis Castle. He added further: "... their innocence being established, they had in recompense 200 marks of their accuser..." [3]

At any rate, Killigrew shared the sufferings of the other exiles and the bitter realization that his actions were being exploited by the French for the ruin of his own country. For many of the refugees the time of their exile must have been a 'dark night of the soul.' Out of personal and political necessity most of them entered into treasonable conspiracy with the French government. Yet individual character also weighed in the balance to determine their actions. Some of the exiles were almost as willing to serve their French masters as they were to betray their accomplices to the English government. But

[1] P.R.O. S.P. 69/5 f. 252.

[2] *Calendar of State Papers, Venetian, 1556–7*, pp. 536, 571.

[3] *Hatfield Manuscripts of the most honorable marquis of Salisbury preserved at Hatfield House, Hertfordshire*, vol. 37, f. 8.

others, like Killigrew and his friend, Sir Nicholas Throckmorton, were influenced to a greater degree by religious and
patriotic motives. They had engaged in conspiracy and rebellion to free their countrymen from Spanish and Catholic rule,
not to subject them to an ancient and hated enemy. Yet, if
their plans were to succeed, or in some cases, merely to avoid
starvation, they had no choice but to turn to the French for
support. Their resentment against the French also had a very
human side. They found that Henry II and his ministers treated
them with the thinly veiled contempt reserved for foreign
traitors who are to be thrown aside when their usefulness is past.

An example of the sort of thing English exiles had to put up
with is given by the treatment Killigrew received when he
went to the French court at Rheims on Sir Peter Carew's
behalf in June, 1554, to announce the latter's wish to leave the
country. Deserted by his French allies, and now working hard
to obtain a pardon from the English government, Carew
decided to withdraw to Italy. Since he had previously promised
not to depart from France without the King's leave he sent
his friend, Killigrew, to secure the required permission. As
Henry II was absent from the court Killigrew delivered Carew's
message to the King's minister, Anne de Montmorency,
Constable of France.

Montmorency's reaction was characteristically ill-tempered
and caustic. He kept Killigrew cooling his heels at Rheims for
four days before giving a reply. He then subjected him to an
angry harangue on the inconstancy and bad faith of Englishmen in general and of Carew in particular who, he said, had
ungratefully requited the King's favour towards him. Finally
he sent Killigrew away with the answer that Carew might
leave the country if he wished.[1] One can well imagine the
feelings with which Killigrew received this lecture from a
Frenchman on the bad faith of his countrymen. Moreover,
this was by no means the last occasion on which he and Montmorency were to encounter one another on terms of hostility.

[1] P.R.O. S.P. 69/4 f. 243.

There can be no doubt about Killigrew's attitude towards the French. His brother, Peter, later declared that Henry had told him never to accept money from them but to live at liberty. He added that Henry had informed him that a French nobleman had once offered to intercede with the King to secure a pension for him, but that he had excused himself on the ground that his brothers had received nothing for their services.[1]

Personal necessity, however, may impose cruel choices and make it impossible for a man to follow the advice he gives others. At any rate, some time during the first year of his exile, Killigrew entered the service of a distinguished soldier by the name of François de Vendôme, Vidame of Chartres.[2]

He continued in this employment for the next two years, and it was perhaps then that he first learned the trade of a soldier fighting with the French against the armies of Spain and the Empire. Killigrew was by no means the only refugee who served as a mercenary. Driven to despair by poverty and idleness, a number of his compatriots talked of going to the wars in Italy—he himself may have taken part in the furious battles which raged up and down the Italian peninsula at this

[1] Peter Killigrew's confession. P.R.O. State Papers, Domestic, Mary, (S.P. 11/9 f. 24). (hereafter: P.R.O. S.P. 11). When Peter Killigrew was captured by an English naval force and sent to the Tower of London in August, 1556, he was forced to divulge not only his own activities as a pirate, but also what he knew concerning his brother, Henry, and other conspirators abroad. I believe that the information Peter gave concerning Henry's opinions, particularly with respect to the French, is probably accurate, for similar statements were attributed to him by the English spy, Martin Dare. "Examination of Martin Dare on the occasion of his going into France," P.R.O. S.P. 11/9 f. 59.

[2] Killigrew is first mentioned as being in the Vidame's service in October, 1554. Archives des affaires étrangères, vol. 10, f. 378. Peter Killigrew, in his confession, said of his brother, Henry: "His remaining hath always been with the Vidame." P.R.O. S.P. 11/9 f. 24. He did not, however, mention Henry's part in the Carew and Dudley conspiracies. For the Vidame of Chartres' career see: Leon De Bastard D'Estang, Vie de Jean de Ferrieres par un membre de la Société des Sciences historiques et naturelle de Lyons, Paris, 1856, pp. 23, 33–4, 56. (hereafter: Bastard).

time between French and Imperialist armies. It is certain, at
any rate, that cavalry units made up of English exiles were
recruited into the French army, for the Constable Montmorency was frequently troubled by reports of their depredations
against civilians when the military forces were out of action
or short of pay.[1]

Killigrew's military experience proved to be of great value
in later life.[2] Equally important to his subsequent career was
the contact with the Vidame of Chartres. The Vidame became
one of the early leaders of the Protestant movement in France,
and he was related not only to prominent members of the
Huguenot nobility such as the King of Navarre, Admiral
Coligny, and the Prince of Condé, but to Henry II of France.[3]
The associations which Killigrew established at this time among
leading men in French military and governing circles, through
his service with the Vidame of Chartres, were an invaluable
preparation for his long tour of diplomatic duty in France under
Elizabeth.

From the spring of 1554 to April, 1556, while serving under
the Vidame, Killigrew took no further part in the intrigues of
the English exiles. However, he kept in touch with his old
associates, Sir Peter Carew and Edward Randolph. Noailles,
the French ambassador in London, reported to the Constable
Montmorency on two occasions that Randolph had suggested
Killigrew as the ideal man to act as liaison agent between the
conspirators, Carew, and the French government in carrying
out plans for an invasion of England by the exiles abroad.[4]
Already Killigrew had established for himself a reputation for
skill in his profession, especially in the subterranean art of
secret diplomacy. This reputation stood him in good stead for

[1] *Archives des affaires étrangères*, vol. 10, f. 34, vol. 11, f. 291.
[2] In August, 1562, when requesting assignment to military service,
Killigrew reminded Robert Dudley that "all the misery of a soldier's life
is not unknown unto me." P.R.O. S.P. 70/40 f. 315.
[3] Bastard, p. 23.
[4] *Archives des affaires étrangères*, vol. 10, f. 270, vol. 9, f. 498.

the advancement of his career when Elizabeth ascended the throne three years later.

Killigrew was in France early in 1556 helping his brothers Peter and Thomas secure a grant of the French ship, Sacrette, in order to pursue their privateering operations against English and Spanish shipping. When this purpose had been achieved, however, he refused to sail with them. Instead he gave them a piece of characteristically sensible advice. According to Peter Killigrew's later testimony, Henry told them that if they had any good fortune to look well unto it in order that they might have enough to pay their debts and to obtain a pardon from the English government.[1] He probably knew his brothers well enough to doubt that this wise counsel would be taken.

Soon after his brothers sailed from Normandy Killigrew became involved in the Dudley conspiracy. An English spy reported that Killigrew was in Paris with Henry Dudley, Richard and Edmund Tremayne, and other refugees in April, 1556.[2] Dudley was a glib, unscrupulous knave, a cousin of Killigrew's old patron, the Duke of Northumberland, who had acted as the Duke's secret agent at the French court shortly before Edward VI's death to secure Henry II's support for Northumberland's plot to seize the English throne. The price which Dudley had been commissioned to offer for French backing was the delivery of Calais, the last remnant of English conquests during the Hundred Years War.

In March, 1556, Dudley was apprehended in another treasonable enterprise. He and a group of Protestant malcontents planned to seize the treasury and depose or assassinate Mary Tudor. When their designs were exposed Dudley and those of his followers who managed to escape arrest fled to the continent. For a second time the exiles turned to plans of invasion. With the help of the French they intended to make a landing at Portsmouth or the Isle of Wight. They believed that their arrival in England would raise a rebellion against Catholic

[1] P.R.O. S.P. 11/9 f. 24.
[2] P.R.O. S.P. 11/7 f. 59.

rule. In the execution of these plans their hopes again centered on Elizabeth and Courtenay. Dudley was also prepared to purchase French aid by the betrayal of Calais.[1] To loyal Englishmen, whether Protestant or Catholic, there could be no crime graver than this, and Dudley's treasonable connivance with the French King at this time was one of the factors which led to the city's capture by the Duke of Guise in January, 1558.[2]

There is no evidence that Killigrew had any part in the intrigues concerning Calais or that he had participated in the plans of Dudley and his adherants before their flight from England. After the rebels arrived in France, however, he placed his services as a diplomat at their disposal. About the end of May, evidently acting both for the exiles and the French government, Killigrew went to Ferrara, where Courtenay was living in exile, to persuade him to join the Protestant faction in France.

Nothing definite is known of Killigrew's dealings with Courtenay at Ferrara. However, Martin Dare, a spy of Sir Nicholas Wotton, the English ambassador in Paris, later testified that the Vidame of Chartres had sent a message to Courtenay which said that if he would come into France, he would provide him with 30,000 crowns and anything else he had at his disposal.[3]

During Edward VI's reign the Vidame had paid a visit to England, and had there gained the friendship of several members of the Protestant nobility.[4] From that time on he kept an interest in English affairs. He was therefore an obvious person to act the part of an intermediary between the French government and Courtenay, and it was equally natural that he should employ his servant, Killigrew, to carry his message.

[1] Harbison, pp. 270 ff.
[2] Garret, pp. 34, 148.
[3] P.R.O. S.P. 11/7 f. 59.
[4] The Vidame came to England in the spring of 1550 as a hostage pending fulfilment of the Treaty of Boulogne. On his activities at the court of Edward VI see: Hester W. Chapman, *The Last Tudor King, A study of Edward VI*, London, 1958, pp. 186–7.

According to Dare, Courtenay replied to the Vidame's communication by saying that it was not for him to enter into any king's realm upon his subject's promise.[1] If true, Dare's report casts a revealing light upon the attitude of the French government and that of Courtenay. Anxious to avoid direct involvement with the plans of the exiles, the French governement apparently chose to approach Courtenay by means of a request privately conveyed by one of its own subjects. Courtenay, on the other hand, was unwilling to commit himself to a risky enterprise without a direct offer from the French.

When Killigrew returned to Paris early in July, 1556, he spoke with a Captain Crayer, another of Wotton's spies. To Crayer he confidently declared: "I know as much of the Earl of Devon's mind as another, and he will be here at court very shortly."[2] Probably Killigrew's confidence was more assumed than real. He may well have known or suspected that Crayer was in Wotton's pay, and his words were perhaps deliberately framed with the intention of impressing his listener, and through him, the ambassador and the English government, with the power of the rebel faction in France.

Certainly even Killigrew's brief contact with Courtenay must have convinced him that little trust could be placed in this wayward youth. He lacked the stuff of which the successful conspirator is made, and there was little likelihood that he would leave the comparative safety of his Italian exile to share the hazards of Dudley's enterprise against England. At any rate, whatever hopes Killigrew and his friends had of Courtenay's cooperation were soon disappointed. He made no move to join them, and a few months later he died at Padua.[3]

The French, however, were already drawing away from the exiles out of fear of provoking war with England. Disillusioned and quarelling among themselves the rebels were forced to go into hiding in Normandy where they continued to nurse their hopes and grievances.[4]

[1] P.R.O. S.P. 11/7 f. 59.   [2] P.R.O. S.P. 69/9 f. 519.
[3] Garrett, p. 131.   [4] P.R.O. S.P. 69/9 f. 567. P.R.O. S.P. 11/7 f. 59.

Soon after his return from Italy Killigrew left Paris and went to Rouen with a number of the other exiles. At this time he again encountered his brothers, Peter and Thomas, at the nearby port of Havre where they were revictualling the Sacrette.

While he was talking with them aboard the ship Henry Dudley appeared on shore begging for a loan of money to relieve his penniless condition. All the exiles had come to hate him for his arrogance and dishonesty.[1] Killigrew may also have known something of his treasonable bargaining with the French over Calais.

Henry angrily declared to his brother, Peter, that if he were a rich man he would rather have spent a hundred crowns than that Dudley should come hither. He warned his brother not to meddle with him, adding that because of Dudley a large number in England were in great danger, and that all men had now deserted him. Concerning the intentions of the French Killigrew was equally bitter and explicit. The King, he said, planned to send over as many rebels as he could to incite revolution in England. When the realm was in poverty the French would seize their opportunity, and he predicted that they would launch an invasion by way of Scotland.[2] The information which Killigrew received at this time concerning the hostile designs of the French government against his country undoubtedly played a decisive part in determining his outlook and behaviour as a diplomat in the years immediately following his return from exile.

Not long after this conversation with his brother, Peter Killigrew's piratical career received an abrupt check. In August, 1556, an English naval squadron captured him after a sharp engagement off Portsmouth. Though compelled to suffer im-

[1] P.R.O. S.P. 11/9 f. 24.
[2] Ibid. Killigrew expressed himself even more strongly to Martin Dare. He told him that the French were unjust and untrue, that they would promise much and do little. If they did show any pleasure they would look to receive ten times as much in return and they were the worst natured men living. P.R.O. S.P. 11/7 f. 59.

prisonment and possibly torture in the Tower of London he ultimately obtained freedom and a pardon.[1] The following year, on the outbreak of war with France, he secured appointment as an officer in the Queen's navy.[2]

Henry was not so fortunate. Despite the intercession of Sir Nicholas Wotton, the English ambassador at Paris, he was unable to secure a pardon from his government.[3] In August, 1557, he was present at the Battle of St Quentin under circumstances which suggest that he was serving with the French army. A young Scotsman by the name of James Melville, one of Killigrew's closest friends, mentions seeing him at the town of La Fer a few miles from the battle field. Melville was serving under Anne de Montmorency, Constable of France, and shared in the rout of the French forces at the hands of the Anglo-Spanish army. He relates in his memoirs that he fled wounded to La Fer where he met Killigrew, who held his horse while he went into a barber's shop to have his wound dressed[4].

How Killigrew became involved in the fighting at St Quentin is unknown, but if he hoped to regain the favour of his government it was essential that he keep clear both of the French and of his former associates among the English rebels. There is no evidence that he took further part in the intrigues of Henry Dudley or in the plans of those mad-cap conspirators, Thomas and Robert Stafford, which led to an abortive landing on the Yorkshire coast in the spring of 1557. Perhaps to avoid compromising himself further by association with Dudley and the Staffords Killigrew left France and went to Germany. In the last year of Mary's reign he apparently lived for a time at Strasbourg, the residence of a considerable number

---

[1] *Calendar of State Papers, Venetian, 1556–7*, pp. 536, 571.

[2] List of officers of the Queen's army and navy in Advis, (8th May, 1557), *Archives du affaires étrangères*, vol. 13, f. 211. Harbison, p. 316, footnote 44.

[3] P.R.O. S.P. 69/9 f. 559.

[4] Sir James Melville of Halhill, *Memoirs of his own life*, (with an introduction by W. Mackensie), London, 1922, p. 24.

of English exiles including his future father-in-law, Sir Anthony Cooke.[1]

By this time he had regained the confidence of Mary's government sufficiently to be entrusted with a diplomatic mission into France. According to a memoir of his diplomatic services, which Killigrew wrote in 1573, a friend, Thomas Randolph, came to him with instructions from the Princess Elizabeth to undertake a journey into France.[2] Under what circumstances Randolph, formerly a Protestant exile, was able to get in touch with Elizabeth is not explained. Nor is any hint given of Killigrew's connection with her. It is unlikely that the two men were acting solely on the authority of the Queen's sister.

A more probable version of this episode is given in the briefer summary of Killigrew's services, which was also written in 1573 as a petition for the grant of the manor of Lanrake. This document states that Queen Mary sent Randolph to Killigrew in Germany in order to persuade him to undertake a diplomatic assignment. It adds that his journey to France was made with the knowledge and consent of the Queen's sister, Elizabeth.[3]

[1] Garrett, pp. 13, 34, 37–8.

[2] Leonard Howard, ed., *A collection of letters from the original manuscripts of many princes, great personages and statesmen together with some curious and scarce tracts and pieces of antiquity, religious, political and moral*, London, 1753, p. 184. (hereafter: Howard).

[3] B. M. Lansdowne MSS. 106, f. 31. In his biography of William Cecil, Lord Burghley, Dr Conyers Read expresses the opinion that Killigrew's memoir in Howard's *Letters* is a distorted version of the document in *Lansdowne 106*. I believe that this view is incorrect. The memoir is considerably longer, is written in the first person, and contains several statements by Killigrew about his diplomatic services that are not included in *Lansdowne 106*. My opinion is that the memoir in Howard's *Letters* is a copy of an original document which has been lost or destroyed. Apparently Killigrew wrote a memoir of his services for Elizabeth since the last year of Mary's reign in 1573 by commandment of his brother-in-law, Lord Burghley, in support for a request that Elizabeth grant him the manor of Lanrake in Cornwall. Subsequently, Burghley who obviously was helping Killigrew to obtain the grant, probably used the memoir to have a briefer summary of Killigrew's services drawn up in a formal petition. This

Both accounts are extremely interesting in that they reveal that Killigrew was acting under the partial direction of his future sovereign. As in the case of Sir William Cecil, Sir Nicholas Throckmorton and Thomas Randolph, all of whom were to become distinguished servants of Elizabeth, Killigrew's labours on her behalf began in the reign of Mary. For her own preservation Elizabeth took no part in conspiracy during her sister's lifetime. After her accession, however, she did not forget those who had done loyal and hard service for their country and herself in her own time of peril. She gave a very different reception to a traitor like Henry Dudley.[1]

Nothing is known concerning Killigrew's mission in 1558 except his later statement that he had been sent to discover the intentions of the French against his country.[2] After the fall of Calais early in January, reports reached the ears of Mary and her Council concerning an impending invasion from France. A large fleet under the command of the Lord Admiral Clinton patrolled the English and French coasts in anticipation of an attack.[3] Killigrew's task was probably to search out the truth of these reports. Following the completion of his assignment he returned to Randolph at Strasbourg who then forwarded the advertisements his friend had brought to the Lord Admiral in England.[4]

Killigrew was still living in Germany at the time of Mary's death. Shortly thereafter a messenger arrived from Sir Nicholas Throckmorton with word that the new Queen wished to employ him on a diplomatic mission. Killigrew hurried home

---

petition, I believe, is the document contained in *Lansdowne 106*. It is not only briefer but is written in the third person. Conyers Read, *Mr Secretary Cecil and Queen Elizabeth*, London, 1955, p. 116, footnote 30.

[1] Dudley was probably regarded with particular distrust by Elizabeth and her councillors just after her accession because of his intrigues to deliver Calais to the French. Harbisor, pp. 308–9.

[2] Howard, p. 184.

[3] *C.S.P. Spanish, 1554–8*, pp. 352, 361, 388–90, 398–9.

[4] Howard, p. 184.

and there received two commissions from his government, one to the Protestant princes of Germany, the other to France "about the matter of Calais." [1]

When Killigrew returned to England in the autumn of 1558 he was only about thirty years of age, but he already had some years of government and diplomatic service in the reign of Edward VI behind him. Thereafter he had spent nearly five years in exile as a conspirator, diplomatic agent, and soldier. This had been a scaring experience, but it had afforded an invaluable schooling for his career in Elizabeth's reign. As he journeyed homeward he had reason to feel confidence and elation at the opportunities which awaited him. The Protestant restoration under Elizabeth, which he and his fellow conspirators had sought vainly to achieve by revolution, had at last been attained without bloodshed by her peaceful accession. To the Queen Killigrew was already known as a loyal servant. To Cecil, Throckmorton, and Robert Dudley who shared her counsels he was known as a seasoned man of affairs.

If he had ever felt the fire and impetuosity of youth they were well damped down by the hard life he had led in recent years and were only to rise up again occasionally under the stimulus of his religious and patriotic ardor. Killigrew's experience in exile had strengthened in him qualities of common sense and resourcefulness as well as a strong desire for personal security. Such a man would prove most useful to the young Queen provided that she could restrain his Protestant zeal.

[1] B. M. Lansdowne MSS. 106, f. 31. Howard, p. 184.

CHAPTER II

THE QUEEN'S SECRET AGENT IN GERMANY AND FRANCE, 1558-9

THE circumstances relating to Killigrew's Germany embassy are significant. Sir Nicholas Throckmorton, who had gone into exile after the Dudley conspiracy, and had been in touch with both Killigrew and Thomas Randolph at that time, received a pardon in May, 1557.[1] He was a distant relation of the Princess Elizabeth, and he soon entered on terms of friendship with her that were sufficiently close for him to feel able to assume the rôle of a personal advisor.[2] In an undated letter, probably written on 17th November, 1558, the day of Mary's death, he presented Elizabeth with a series of recommendations for the policies and personnel of the new government.[3]

One of Throckmorton's suggestions was that "your Highness do not discover to any of the old (Catholic, conservative) members of the Council, but to a chosen few others that Mr Wrothe, Dr Cope, and Henry Knollys shall treat with any princes Protestant other than the King of Bohemia..."[4] The fact that his recommendation was immediately put into effect suggests that men of this cast of mind exerted considerable influence in the counsels of the Queen at the outset of her reign. Those whom he suggested as suitable for the German enterprise were all present or former Protestant exiles, and the man Elizabeth actually chose to carry it out was his friend, Henry Killigrew.

[1] Garrett, pp. 306-7. Randolph to Throckmorton December 6, 1558. S.P. 70/1 f. 22. P.R.O. Patent Rolls C. 66/915, m.l.

[2] Article on Sir Nicholas Throckmorton, *D.N.B.* vol. 19, pp. 810-14.

[3] J. E. Neale "Advice to the Queen," *The English Historical Review*, vol. 65, pp. 91-7.

[4] *Ibid.*, p. 95.

The Queen's action in opening negotiations with Protestant Germany, however, was not determined by religious considerations but by the harsh realities of England's situation at the time of her accession. Exhausted by a disastrous and costly war and threatened by invasion from France, the country was in desperate need of diplomatic and military support. Hostilities had been suspended the previous summer and treaty negotiations begun at Cercamp, but it was by no means certain that England's ally, Spain, would continue to stand by her until a settlement was reached for the restoration of Calais.[1] If Spain should suddenly abandon them and make a separate peace with France the English would find themselves alone in a war which they lacked the resources to continue. Under the threat of isolation Elizabeth took up the policy that Henry VIII pursued in similar circumstances of making diplomatic overtures to the Protestant powers of Germany.

Like considerations impelled the Lutheran princes towards friendship with England. Since the Peace of Augsburg they had become increasingly conscious of their own weakness and disunity in the face of a growing strength among their enemies. These apprehensions were intensified by the renewal of demands for the convening of the Council of Trent which had been prorogued since 1552.[2]

At the same time peace negotiations began between France and Spain. Cessation of hostilities between these two powers, and the clamour for an ecumenical council were a conjunction of events too ominous for German Lutherans to ignore. Few members of that faith could forget that the Peace of Crépy had been followed by the Council of Trent, and that less than two

[1] See the letter of Sir Nicholas Wotton, English ambassador at Brussels, concerning rumours that Philip II intended to make peace with France without first ensuring that England received satisfaction in respect to Calais. Wotton to Cecil 9th January, 1559. B. M. Cotton MSS. Calba C. 1. f. 4.

[2] A. W. Ward, G. W. Prothero, Stanley Leathes eds., *The Cambridge Modern History*, vol. 2, *The Reformation*, Cambridge 1907, pp. 672, 674.

years later Charles V was able to deliver a shattering blow to the Schmalkaldic league at the Battle of Mühlburg.

As the Catholic powers of Europe seemed about to embark on a religious and political counter-offensive there appeared among German Lutherans a greater awareness of the need for Protestant unity. This awareness was most strongly marked in those principalities of southern and western Germany which lay exposed to attack from their Catholic neighbours. Two of the foremost champions of political and religious confederation were Otto Henry, Elector of the Palatinate and Duke Christopher of Württemberg. They were interested not only in promoting unity among their fellow Lutherans, but also in reaching limited agreements with Protestant countries outside the Empire.[1]

Because of his sojourn in western Germany Killigrew may have been able to appraise his government of the favourable climate of opinion in these two principalities, for it was with their rulers that he was directed to make contact.

Killigrew, according to David Lloyd, was Elizabeth's first ambassador, a statement that appears to be supported by contemporary evidence.[2] Certainly his negotiations in Germany in the autumn and winter of 1558-9 are the earliest of which there is record in her reign.[3]

[1] In December, 1558, after receiving word of Elizabeth's accession, Duke Christopher wrote to the Elector Palatine that the Queen and her ministers should be persuaded to adopt the Augsburg Confession in return for support from the Protestant princes against Spain and France. Victor Ernst, *Briefwechsel des Herzog von Wirtemberg im Auftrag der Kommission für Landesgeschichte*, vol. 4, 1556-1559, Stuttgart, 1907, pp. 373-7. (hereafter: Ernst).

[2] Lloyd, p. 587.

[3] Sir Thomas Challoner, ambassador to the Emperor Ferdinand at Brussels, and Henry, Lord Cobham, emissary to Philip II at Brussels, are the earliest of the Queen's envoys for whom written instructions have survived. Neither Challoner or Cobham, however, had actually begun their negotiations before the middle of December, 1558. Killigrew's instructions, if they were drawn up in written form, appear to have been destroyed, but it is certain that he was already in Germany actively engaged in his negotiations at Heidelberg as early as the first week of December. In a letter to Throck-

Travelling with exceptional speed over roads rendered almost impassible by the severity of an early winter he reached Heidelberg before the middle of December.[1] There he consulted with the councillors of the Elector Palatine and then went on to Stuttgart in the following month.[2] Since the English government was simultaneously endeavouring to strengthen its ties with the Catholic rulers of Spain and the Empire Killigrew had to conduct his diplomacy with the Protestant princes in strict secrecy.[3]

During the negotiations at Heidelberg he was assisted by an Italian ecclesiastic named Paolo Vergerio. Before embracing the Lutheran faith Vergerio had been an important figure in the Catholic world; chaplain to Pope Paul III, Papal nuncio, and finally Archbishop of Capo D'Istria. Now, however, he was merely councillor of the Duke of Württemburg, an ageing, senile man whose greatness survived only in the inflated world of his own imagination.[4]

Vergerio was an enthusiastic exponent of schemes of Prot-

---

morton of December 6th, Thomas Randolph wrote "I have not lately seen but many times heard from Mr Harry who leads his life most in the Palsgraves' (Elector Palatine's) court. P.R.O. S.P. 70/1 f. 22. On 14th, December, 1558, Paolo Vergerio, councillor to the Duke of Würtemberg, in a letter to Queen Elizabeth, mentions Killigrew's presence in Heidelberg. P.R.O. S.P. 70/1 f. 32.

[1] Sir Thomas Challoner, ambassador to the Emperor, who was then travelling to Augsburg, complained of the frozen condition of the roads. Challoner to Cecil 20th December, 1558, S.P. 70/1 f. 40.

[2] Ernst, no. 511.

[3] Vergerio informed Killigrew on 1st February, 1559, that Duke Christopher had told him that he realized the necessity of moving quietly in negotiations with the English government in order not to "give rise to disturbances." P.R.O. S.P. 70/1 f. 127.

[4] The best full life of Vergerio is: Christian Sixt, *Paulus Vergerius, Päpstlicher Nuntius Katholischer Bischof und Vorkampher des Evangelicus Eine Reformation Geschichtliche Monographie*, Braunschweig, 1855. The Anglo-Lutheran negotiations in which Killigrew and Vergerio took part are treated in E. von Kausler and T. Schott, *Briefwechsel Zwischen Christoph, Herzog von Würtemberg und Petrus Paulus Vergerius in Bibliothek des Litterarischen Vereins* in Stuttgart, vol. 122, Tubingen, 1872, pp 30–2.

estant confederation, but he was also excited by the hope that his services for the English government would be rewarded with the grant of some diplomatic or eccesiastical preferment for himself and his hungry relations.[1] This credulous, rather pathetic old man proved a willing agent for the furtherance of Killigrew's commission. He and his superiors in London, the Queen and her Secretary of State, William Cecil, took Vergerio's measure exactly. They regarded him as a fool whose folly could be exploited to serve their own aims.

This attitude was reflected in a letter, almost ludicrous in the grossness of its flattery, which Killigrew wrote to Vergerio in January, 1559, addressing him reverently as "my illustrious master" and urging him to continue his heroic efforts to inspire a Protestant crusade against their Catholic foes.

"It is not necessary, Master Paul," he wrote, "for me to persuade you more fully and to commend this cause which I have placed in your hands, seeing that you, who have deserved the good and pleasant things of this world, in order that you might—increase the glory of Christ and of his Church, cannot wish for a better opportunity of entering into the open field and unfurling your banners against the Anti-Christ and his practices, especially at that time when he himself hoped to be able to defeat—the most illustrious princes of Germany." [2]

One can well imagine the delight with which Vergerio read this letter, but it would have been even more interesting to have seen the expression on Killigrew's face as he wrote it. Both Elizabeth and Cecil wrote in a similar vein to the old Italian, but their real opinion of him is expressed in Cecil's letter to Christopher Mundt, the Queen's resident agent in Germany, two years later where he remarked that he never

[1] See Vergerio's letter to Elizabeth of 14th December, 1558 in which he expresses his desire "to take a share in restoring the true religion" in England. P.R.O. S.P. 70/1 f. 32. See also his letter to Elizabeth of 30th January, 1559, in regard to securing diplomatic employment for his nephew, Ludovico, in England. Kausler and Schott, p. 192.

[2] Kausler and Schott, p. 189.

saw much weight in Vergerio and did not wish him to come to England.[1]

Happily unaware of the contempt with which he was regarded and glowing with zeal over the rewards, both spiritual and material, that might accrue to himself for his work on behalf of an Anglo-German league, Vergerio promised Killigrew to communicate the proposals of the English government to the Duke of Württemberg and to urge him to convey them to the other Protestant princes whose representatives were then convening at the Diet of Augsburg.[2]

At Stuttgart, in January, 1559, Killigrew and Vergerio again conferred on the English proposals for alliance with the Lutheran states.[3] Apparently either the English ambassador exceeded the commission given him by the Queen or its terms were misunderstood by the Duke's councillor. According to his own statement he was only empowered to conclude "a defensive league for religion."[4] Yet the letters which Vergerio wrote to Elizabeth and Killigrew the following month reveal that both he and his master believed the English plan to envisage a full offensive-defensive alliance.

Vergerio informed the Queen that, in Christopher's opinion, an alliance of this kind would not be acceptable to the other princes and would tend to bring with them "great suspicions and some hinderances."[5] To Killigrew he declared: "If the Queen will be contented with friendship in which these princes will feel bound to assist her with their counsels and their help the Duke believes she can obtain the alliance, but not an offensive and defensive league pertaining to matters that had no reference to religion."[6]

However, Vergerio had one important reservation to make.

[1] P.R.O. S.P. 70/35 f. 713.
[2] Vergerio to Killigrew, 1st February, 1559, P.R.O. S.P. 70/2 f. 128.
[3] *Ibid.*
[4] Howard, p. 184.
[5] Kausler and Schott, p. 207.
[6] P.R.O. S.P. 70/1 f. 128.

The achievement of this league, he said, was contingent upon England's acceptance of the Augsburg Confession. Suspicions had already arisen among the princes because Elizabeth had summoned the Calvinist theologian, Peter Martyr, to England. The Duke's councillor may have been just perceptive enough to suspect that a desire to gain the good will of a group of relatively insignificant German princes would not of itself exercise a decisive influence on English policy, for he added another consideration which was likely to attract careful scrutiny from the Queen.

He wrote: "the Emperor and the King of Spain say ... that since England is not to have the religion of the Pope they do not care about it so long as no other doctrine than the Augsburg Confession is introduced. If any other is adopted these two persons will be the Queen's chief enemies; they will help the Pope and the King of France against her ..." If, on the other hand, she adopted the Augsburg Confession "the Emperor and the King of Spain will stand shoulder to shoulder with her." [1]

Neither Elizabeth nor her ministers were prepared to sacrifice the independence of their religious policy in order to conciliate Lutheran Germany. Even had they been willing to do so Protestant opinion in the country would have bitterly opposed concessions in this direction.[2] The Queen was equally uninterested in a full offensive and defensive alliance.[3] Killigrew's apparent indiscretion in allowing a misunderstanding

---

[1] *Ibid.*

[2] The hostility of many English Protestants to dealings with the Lutheran princes is indicated in the letter Catherine, Duchess of Suffolk, wrote to Cecil on 5th March, 1559. "Christ's plain coat," she declared, "is better than all the jags of Germany. This I say, for it is also said here that certain 'Duchers' would commend us to the Augsburg Confession—but Christ—who has left his Gospel, him, a rule sufficient and only to be followed." P.R.O. S.P. 12/3 f. 9.

[3] On 2nd March, 1559, Cecil informed Vergerio "that it was never in her Majesty's mind to bind your prince to the cause by any means—." Kausler and Schott, pp. 193-4.

to arise on this point perhaps served as useful lesson to the young sovereign. She afterwards learned to keep a tight reign on the 'hot-gospellers' who served as her emissaries in foreign lands.

Yet Killigrew's mission was not without some constructive results. He had established friendly contacts with the princes, and supplied information from which future policy towards them could be formulated. Schemes for religious confederation were destined to fail in Elizabeth's reign, as they had in her father's time, because of divergence of political interest and religious doctrine between the respective parties. More successful were English efforts to tap the plentiful supply of mercenaries which German princes offered to the highest bidder. Killigrew's negotiations at Heidelberg opened the way for later moves in this direction by his government.[1]

One of the objects of his diplomacy in Germany was probably to enlist military assistance in case war should break out again with France.[2] For military purposes the relations he had established with the Palatinate were to prove extremely useful. Frederick III, who succeeded Otto Henry in 1559, became a keen exponent of Protestant confederation, and Elizabeth sometimes found it expedient to support his visionary plans.[3] But it was in the mercenary troops of his son, John Casimir, that she found a better weapon to counter the threats of her enemies.

Early in February, 1559, following his departure from

[1] See the letter of Vitus Polantus, councillor to the Elector Palatine, to Killigrew on 15th February, 1559, in which he suggested that Elizabeth pension one of the brothers of the new Elector, Frederick III, who "would levy and head the troops of Germany." B. M. Cotton MSS. Galba BXI, f. 193.

[2] This can be inferred from Christopher's offer that the defensive league which he contemplated would enable the Queen to apply for 10,000 or 15,000 men, horse or foot if she were molested. Vergerio to Killigrew, 1st February, 1559, P.R.O. S.P. 70/2 f. 127.

[3] Vitus Polantus, Otto Henry's councillor, announced the death of his master and the accession of the new Elector on 15th February, 1559. B. M. Cotton MSS. Galba B. XI f. 193.

Germany, Killigrew proceeded to execute his second commission concerning Calais. Again he was involved in secret negotiations, this time in connection with private discussions which were in progress between the English and French governments with respect to the conclusion of peace and the future status of Calais. The peace negotiations begun the previous summer had been terminated by the death of Mary. A truce was then declared; Elizabeth, her ally, Philip of Spain, and Henry II of France agreed to send representatives to a new conference at Cateau-Cambrésis in February, 1559.

Killigrew's mission was concerned with secret diplomatic exchanges between the governments of France and England prior to and during this formal conference. The exact nature of his task is difficult to determine. In his memoir he says that he was directed to get in touch with his old friend, the Vidame of Chartres, now governor of Calais, "to deal with him and see what might be done ... so that Calais might have been rendered."[1] It was probably intended that he should exploit his friendship with the Vidame in order to secure a softening of French determination not to restore Calais. The dispute between England and France on this issue was now the principal obstacle to the conclusion of peace.

Shortly after Elizabeth's accession, during the truce which preceded the resumption of public negotiations at Cateau-Cambrésis, Henry II sent Lord Grey, who had been taken prisoner during the fighting at Calais the previous year, to England. Grey's mission on behalf of the French government, was to explore the possibility of a private settlement of the outstanding differences between the two countries.[2] With some

[1] Howard, p. 184.

[2] The consideration of Lord Grey's message with a purpose for answer thereof. P.R.O. S.P. 70/1 f. 51. Patrick Forbes, *A full view of the public transactions in the reign of queen Elizabeth or a particular account of all the memorable affairs of that Queen transmitted unto us in a series of letters and other papers of state written by herself and her principal ministers and by the foreign princes themselves with which she had negotiations. Published from original and authentic manuscripts in the Paper Office, Cottonian Library and other public and*

reluctance Elizabeth took up these overtures, and a correspondence was begun between herself and the French King. One of
the chief intermediaries between the two rulers was François
de Vendôme, Vidame of Chartres, a cousin and trusted servant
of Henry II, who was on friendly terms with important
members of the English government.[1]

In her letters Elizabeth tried to induce the King to restore
Calais. There was strong public pressure on her government
to secure the return of this prized relic of England's past
glories, but equally strong pressure in France prevented Henry
from surrendering his conquest. The King, however, was too
shrewd to overlook an opportunity of driving a wedge
between Elizabeth and her ally, the King of Spain. If Philip
discovered that she was seeking an agreement with the French
behind his back there was a possibility that he might be
persuaded to conclude a separate peace with Henry.[2]

In view of England's present weakness this would be a disastrous turn of events, but the very awareness of her country's
weakness made it impossible for the Queen to neglect any
opportunity which negotiation might offer. Moreover she and
her ministers doubtless realized that self-interest made it certain
that Philip would not leave his ally to the mercy of the French.
Henry II was supporting the claims of his daughter-in-law,
Mary Stuart, to the English throne. If he prosecuted these
claims by a successful invasion of England the Spanish King
would find himself faced with a hostile chain of territory lying
directly across his communications with the Netherlands.

After a month of private exchanges with Elizabeth Henry

private repositories at home and abroad, London, vol. 1, 1740-1, p. 4. (hereafter:
Forbes). Lord Grey to the Duke of Guise, 28th December, 1558. P.R.O.
S.P. 70/1 f. 51. The Queen to Dr Wotton, 30th December, 1558. P.R.O.
S.P. 70/1 f. 56.

[1] See the Vidame of Chartres' letter to the Earl of Pembroke, 3rd
January, 1559. P.R.O. S.P. 70/1 f. 21.

[2] An interesting discussion of Anglo-French negotiations prior to and
during the conference at Cateau-Cambrésis is contained in Milton Waldman,
King, Queen, Jack, Philip of Spain courts Elizabeth, London, 1931, pp. 176 ff.

proposed that a secret conference be held between represent-atives of the two governments. This conference was to meet at Boulogne without Spanish participation, and was to be entirely independent of the formal peace negotiations at Cateau-Cambrésis. On the evening of 8th February, 1559, he sent the Vidame of Chartres to Cateau-Cambrésis where discussions were about to begin between the representatives of England, Spain, and France. The Vidame was directed to inform the King's minister, the Constable of France, of the plan for a secret conference at Boulogne.[1]

Killigrew arrived in France at about the same time that the Vidame of Chartres departed from the royal residence at St Fiacre bearing Henry's message. He encountered the French envoy between Calais and Paris and, finding that his friend was enroute to Cateau-Cambrésis, he accompanied him there. The Vidame apparently beguiled him with glib assurances concerning England's chances of recovering Calais by independent negotiation with the French government.

Killigrew relates in his memoir that, while changing horses at a post-house on the way to Cateau-Cambrésis, he met Sir Robert Stafford, the Marian exile and conspirator, who was then returning to England. He employed Stafford to convey an important message to the English government. "The effect of my speech to him," he said, "was that I had learned that the French with handling would rather make peace with us and deliver Calais than to render to King Philip so much as was desired." [2]

[1] P.R.O. S.P. 70/2 f. 151.
[2] Howard, p. 184. For Stafford's career as an exile see Garrett, pp. 294–5. Stafford arrived in London about 11th February and requested a personal interview with Cecil. Stafford to Cecil 12th February, 1559, S.P. 12/2 no. 24. Evidently, he did not succeed in rehabilitating himself with the government immediately, for in March he again wrote to Cecil asking him to intercede with the Queen on his behalf. P.R.O. S.P. 12/2 f. 17. Nevertheless, he seems to have gotten a hearing at court. Elizabeth's cousin and commissioner at Cateau-Cambrésis wrote to her that he had heard of Stafford's presence in England, adding angrily: "If he be sent to practise anything with your

It is doubtful whether Killigrew showed good judgement in using such a man as his messenger. Stafford was an irresponsible and quarrelsome individual of much the same type as Henry Dudley. Like Dudley he was suspected of treasonable dealings with the French during his exile. At any rate he seems to have gotten a hearing at court, and the communication he brought from Killigrew probably caused the Queen and her ministers to prolong their diplomatic intrigue with the French government.[1]

Whatever hopes Killigrew may have entertained of a more conciliatory attitude on the part of the French government should have been dispelled when he reached Cateau-Cambrésis. Henry II's commissioners told the Queen's representatives at the peace conference that they had been instructed to refuse even to discuss the retrocession of Calais. If the English insisted on pressing the point they threatened to break off negotiations immediately.[2]

Killigrew recalls in his memoir that the French King's chief representative, the Constable Montmorency, became highly annoyed when he learned that the Vidame had brought him to Cateau-Cambrésis, and that on the Constable's orders he was placed under confinement. He, nevertheless, found an opportunity to speak with John Somers, secretary of the English commissioner, Dr Nicholas Wotton, and directed him to urge the Queen's commissioners "to stick hard for Calais, for I was assured by good intelligence that ... we should have it rendered to us ."[3] Apparently Killigrew still clung to the illusion which

---

Highness touching the peace—mine opinion is that it is evil trusting to a traitor." Howard to the Queen. 2nd March, 1559. P.R.O. S.P. 70/3 f. 170.

[1] The hopes encouraged by Stafford's communication, sent by Killigrew, may be reflected in Elizabeth's letter to her commissioners at Cateau-Cambrésis on 28th February, 1559. "These present instructions," she wrote, "are based upon some arguments that our enemy is not so stiff, but will be content to hear of peace." P.R.O. S.P. 70/2 f. 151.

[2] The English commissioners to the Queen, 14th February, 1559. P.R.O. S.P. 70/2 f. 146.

[3] Howard, p. 184. Contemporary records give no indication of Killigrew's presence at Cateau-Cambrésis.

had been planted in his mind by the Vidame of Chartres. Perhaps the Constable discovered his purpose to encourage the English commissioners not to yield on the matter of Calais.

This discovery would have been sufficient to explain Montmorency's anger, and it must have aroused his suspicions concerning Elizabeth's intentions in her private negotiations with his sovereign. He sent a message to Henry II advising him not to go ahead with plans for a conference at Boulogne until he had heard from him again. He believed that it would be wise to discover what proposals the English commissioners offered in the discussions at Cateau-Cambrésis before final action was taken on this matter.[1] Montmorency evidently wished to find out whether they intended to maintain a common front with their Spanish colleagues and to be intransigent on the question of Calais. As a result of his recommendation the King decided to delay further negotiations with the Queen concerning a secret conference until the attitude of her representatives was known.[2]

The Constable's suspicions seemed fully justified by the behaviour of Lord William Howard and the other English commissioners. They announced their refusal to agree to any terms which did not provide for the restoration of Calais. Howard, an honest blockhead in diplomatic matters, was especially belligerent. He gave open demonstration of friendship for the Spaniards and of his confidence that they would fulfil their pledge not to make peace unless England obtained satisfaction in respect of Calais. When the French ministers mentioned the exchanges between Elizabeth and Henry, Lord William was said to have dismissed the whole affair as "smoke," and added that Elizabeth had entrusted her real instructions to him.[3]

When the King learned of this state of affairs he promptly

[1] Baschet Transcripts, (P.R.O. 31/3, bundle 24, f. 37).

[2] P.R.O. S.P. 70/2 f. 151.

[3] P.R.O. S.P. 70/2 f. 150. English commissioners to the Queen. 14th February, 1559. P.R.O. S.P. 70/2 f. 146.

broke off his private negotiations with the Queen, complaining that his friendly intentions had been greatly hindered by Howard's manner of dealing.[1] Because of the apparent obstinacy of both parties to the dispute war now appeared inevitable. In fact, however, the three nations were exhausted by their recent struggle. Subject only to France's determination not to surrender Calais, they were unanimous in their aversion to a renewal of war. When Elizabeth's commissioners informed her of the impasse which had now been reached she told them that unless they received unequivocal support from the Spanish commissioners, rather than allow the conference to be broken off, they were to make peace on the best terms they could get.[2]

The English representatives learned that their country could expect assistance from Spain only if its military forces could assume a major share of the ensuing operations.[3] Realizing the weakness of England's fighting strength they were left with no choice. They finally achieved a temporary solution of the problem of Calais according to which the city was to remain in French hands for a period of eight years. At the end of this time it would be restored to England with payment of a suitable recompense.

England and France reached an agreement on this formula on 12th March, and the peace was formally concluded three weeks later.[4] Up to the very last moment, however, Elizabeth strove to get better terms by personal negotiation with the French King. Killigrew, who had at last obtained his release

[1] Guido Cavalcante's report of his mission into France P.R.O. S.P. 70/2 f. 151. Henry II to Elizabeth P.R.O. S.P. 70/2 f. 151. Forbes, vol. 1, p. 65.

[2] The Queen to the English commissioners 19th February, 1559. P.R.O. S.P. 70/2 f. 149. Forbes, vol. 1, p. 59.

[3] English commissioners to the Queen. P.R.O. S.P. 70/3 f. 169. 2nd March, 1559.

[4] P.R.O. S.P. 70/3 f. 188. Jean Dumont, *Corps Universel Diplomatique du Droit des Genes; contenant un recueil des Traitez d'alliances, de Paix etc. faits en Europe depuis le Règne de Charlemagne jusqu' à présent etc.*, vol. 5, The Hague, 1725, p. 28 (hereafter: Dumont).

from the Constable's surveillance, brought Henry's final answer
to the Queen's overtures on his return to England late in March.
When he departed from Calais he carried a letter from the
Vidame of Chartres to Elizabeth which declared the King's
opinion that "all she wishes she is more likely to secure by a
conference between them two selves than by the mediation
of the King of Spain." But concerning the only thing which
would have made a betrayal of Spain worthwhile, the restoration of Calais, the Vidame said: "weighty reasons ... will
prevent the King from consenting thereunto unless they appear
to him to be more conclusive than at this present time they
do." [1] To this predictable conclusion had come the Queen's
first essay in personal diplomacy.

In his memoir Killigrew expresses the conviction that "if the
matter had been well handled" England could have secured the
restoration of Calais as a result of the negotiations with France
in the winter and spring of 1558–9.[2] Since he does not explain
his reasons for this statement, his views can only be surmised.
He would certainly have been too discreet to blame the Queen
or her chief councillors for their failure. His criticism was
probably directed against Wotton, Thirlby, and Howard,
Elizabeth's representatives at Cateau-Cambrésis.

She showed violent dissatisfaction with their proceedings on
one occasion, and it was afterwards said that she attributed to
Thomas Thirlby, Bishop of Ely, responsibility for the loss of
Calais.[3] No reason was given for her attribution of special
blame to Thirlby, but the general source of Elizabeth's discontent with her commissioners was her belief that their
excessive deference to the Spanish deputies had aroused Henry's

---

[1] Instructions given by the Duke of Vendôme to Henry Killigrew to be
by him communicated to the Queen, 25th March, 1559. B. M. Caligula
E.V., f. 67. Forbes, vol. 1, p. 67. Vendôme states that he has detained
Killigrew by order of the King since 14th February. *Ibid.*

[2] Howard, p. 184.

[3] J. Strype ed., *The life and acts of John Whitgift, D.D., the third and last
Archbishop of Canterbury in the reign of Queen Elizabeth*, vol. 1, Oxford,
1822, p. 436.

distrust and frustrated her efforts to reach a more favourable settlement with him by means of private negotiation.[1]

Killigrew probably shared this view and believed that firmness combined with greater willingness on the part of the English commissioners to deal independently with the French would have induced Henry to restore Calais. There is, however, no evidence that he would have granted better terms in private negotiation than in the formal conference although, to serve his own ends, he sought to instil this belief in the Queen's mind. Probably Elizabeth and her ministers never really entertained much hope of recovering Calais through negotiation. Their apparent earnestness in the matter may simply have reflected an awareness of the need to placate the injured national pride of their countrymen concerning the loss of the city.

The Peace of Cateau-Cambrésis was an event of decisive importance in Killigrew's career and for the age in which he lived. He and other forward Protestants of his type became convinced that the religious strife which engulfed Europe in the years that followed was the direct result of a secret agreement between France and Spain, the chief Catholic signatories of the treaty, to exterminate the Protestant religion.

Killigrew's entire outlook on matters of national policy during the reign of Elizabeth was conditioned by this belief in an international Catholic conspiracy directed against England and other Protestant powers. To a considerable extent it explains his eagerness as a diplomatic agent to encourage internal discontent against Catholic governments. During the years immediately following the Peace of Cateau-Cambrésis his activities in France made him a perfect example of what one historian has called an "ambassador of ill-will," a Protestant

---

[1] The Queen's irritation with her peace commissioners was violently expressed when she learned that they had listened without protest when the French questioned the validity of her title to the throne, and that they themselves had presumed to debate the matter with them. She was also annoyed by the fact that they had dealt with the French representatives only in the presence of or through the mediation of their Spanish colleagues. 7th March, 1559, P.R.O. S.P. 70/2 f. 178.

prototype of Spanish envoys like Bishop Quadra and Guerau Despés who abused their diplomatic immunity by intriguing with Catholics and other disaffected elements in England.[1] Killigrew's conviction of the irreconcilable nature of the religious struggle also explains the way in which he constantly emphasized, and indeed exaggerated, the hostile designs of the Catholic rulers in order to win the support of his government for the Protestant cause in Scotland and Europe.

Many years later he wrote a brief survey of England's foreign relations during the early years of Elizabeth's reign.[2] First he singled out a clause which he believed to be included in the Treaty of Cateau-Cambrésis. It provided, he said, for an agreement between the rulers of France and Spain to "not only root out the true professors of the reformed religion within their own domains, but also in so far as they might, from other countries where the Bishop of Rome's authority was not absolutely confessed and obeyed which was confirmed by the sequel of their actions following..."

He then described the steps taken by the two Catholic powers to stamp out Protestantism at home and abroad, and of the measures employed by those of the "reformed religion" with English assistance "to provide for their defence against so murderous a resolution..."[3] Killigrew's account is of interest, not only because he himself played a part in several of the events which he depicts, but because his narrative expresses so well the ultra-Protestant outlook.

His statement that the treaty of April, 1559, contained an article calling for joint action by Spain and France to suppress Protestantism is false. The one provision pertaining to the subject of religion merely stated that Philip and Henry had agreed to use all their power for the convocation of a General Council to bring about "the reformation and reduction of the entire Christian Church into one true union and concord."[4]

---

[1] Garrett Matlingly, *Renaissance diplomacy*, London, 1955, Chapter 21.
[2] Hatfield MSS., vol. 25, f. 70.
[3] *Ibid.*   [4] Du Mont, vol. 5, p. 35.

Nevertheless, large numbers of Protestants in England and in Europe were convinced that a pact for their destruction had been made at Cateau-Cambrésis.[1] From this conviction the militant Protestants in English governing circles concluded that the survival of their nation and religion required active assistance to the Protestant factions in Scotland and Europe. Although this policy was based in part on a factual error the belief in a possible Catholic crusade against those of the Protestant faith was not entirely without foundation. After the conclusion of peace in 1559 the governments of France and Spain seriously discussed means by which the rising threat of the "sect" could be crushed.

Attempts to achieve this aim by joint military action in France and the Netherlands were never successful, but it was by no means evident at the outset of Elizabeth's reign that they would not succeed. There is a considerable measure of truth in the view which Killigrew expressed thirty years later—that the extinction of the Protestant religion in the dominions of Spain and France would have been followed by its destruction in England and in the rest of Europe. He was probably also right in believing that the timely intervention of English military and financial aid prevented the achievement of this result.

The Queen did not entirely reject the theory of Catholic conspiracy held by the ultra-Protestants in her Council and diplomatic service. Elizabeth, however, was essentially a politique who judged matters from a secular, nationalist point of view. She believed that territorial and dynastic considerations were of greater importance than religion in the determination of national policy. Despite the increasing bitterness of the

---

[1] On 4th January, 1560, Killigrew and Jones, chargé d'affaires at the French court, assert as a fact the existence of such an agreement concluded by France and Spain at Cateau-Cambrésis. (P.R.O. S.P. 70/10 f. 233). Forbes, vol. 1, p. 297. This is the earliest reference I have been able to discover concerning the supposed secret agreement between France and Spain to exterminate Protestantism in the treaty of Cateau-Cambrésis.

religious struggle during the course of her reign she generally relied on the probability that conflicts of interest would prevent France and Spain from combining against her, and time proved the correctness of this belief.

But time was also to demonstrate the validity of that conception of foreign policy supported by Protestant zealots like Killigrew and Walsingham. During the last eighteen years of Elizabeth's reign the threat of Spanish hegemony in Europe and particularly in the Netherlands caused her at last to commit her country's strength to the scales of war.

CHAPTER III

FRANCE AND SCOTLAND, 1559-60

IN May, 1559, Killigrew returned to France as secretary to Sir Nicholas Throckmorton, Elizabeth's first resident ambassador at the French court.[1] The two men knew one another well, and their friendship was strengthened by a community of outlook on politics and religion. Both were militant Protestants who advocated an aggressive policy on behalf of their co-religionists in Scotland and Europe. Their recent experiences as exiles had filled them with a burning desire to strike a blow against the French for the humiliations which had been inflicted upon themselves and their countrymen during those years.

Throckmorton was one of the most remarkable personalities of his time. Highly intelligent, confident, good looking, a brilliant talker, he had every quality to attract the favour of Elizabeth and her court—except discretion. His diplomatic correspondence fairly bubbles over with life. The character of the writer is stamped on every page—his humour, his indiscretion, his interest in people. For ten years he was an intimate advisor to the Queen. Yet, for all his great gifts, she never made him a member of her Council. The fact was that Elizabeth never wholly trusted him—he was too rash, too outspoken, too inclined to drive others onto courses which he favoured.

Despite apparent similarities in background and view point, it would be hard to imagine two men so strikingly different in temperament as Killigrew and Throckmorton. Killigrew was cautious and discreet—Throckmorton, a bold, fiery tempered enthusiast. In a fit of rage he drew a dagger on his fellow diplomat, Sir Thomas Smith. Though endowed with a Machiavellian skill at intrigue—a French historian has called

[1] Forbes, vol. 1, p. 90. Lansdowne MSS. 106 f. 31. Howard, p. 186.

him "le grand agitateur de l'époque"—he was also something of a romantic.[1] In spite of his ardent Protestantism and his loyalty to his own sovereign, personal sympathy led him later to espouse the claims of Mary Stuart to the succession to the English throne. He carried his support for her to such lengths that he finally earned Elizabeth's lasting disfavour and thereby contrived the ruin of his own career.

Throckmorton possessed another attractive trait not common among statesmen of his time. He showed open reluctance to assist in or condone certain public acts which affronted his private conscience, and one of these was political assassination.

Killigrew, on the other hand,—as his subsequent behaviour was to prove—felt not the slightest qualms about murder as an instrument of public policy, nor the least unwillingness to act as his government's agent when that method was chosen. He was, in fact, much less likely to allow emotion or ethical considerations to guide his actions. Unlike Throckmorton, personal contact with the young Queen of Scotland never caused him to surrender to the spell of her charm. Even though she helped to secure his release from captivity in France in 1563, Killigrew showed neither friendship nor gratitude in return after her imprisonment in England. He then regarded Mary as an enemy of his country who merited quick and ruthless destruction. Hard, single-minded devotion to the interests of the state was a desirable quality in a servant of the Tudor monarchy, and this trait he possessed to a marked degree.

Killigrew and Throckmorton also differed greatly in their abilities. Killigrew was never called upon to act as an important advisor in matters of high policy. It is doubtful whether he even aspired to such a rôle. His views were listened to with respect, but he was valued by his government primarily as an able craftsman in the art of diplomacy who could skilfully mani-

[1] La Ferrière Percy, Hector De La, *Le XVI siècle et les Valois d'après les documents inedits du British Museum et du Record Office*, Paris, 1879, p. 31. For Throckmorton's life and career see A. L. Rowse, *Raleigh and the Throckmortons*, London 1962, Chaps I-III.

pulate a specific situation to the advantage of his government.

Unlike as they were in temperament and ability the two
men worked in complete harmony during their sojourn together at the French court. Indeed the personalities of Killigrew
and Throckmorton were so complementary as to make theirs
an ideal diplomatic partnership, for the qualities of each
supplied the defects of the other. Perhaps at this time, as on
later occasions, Killigrew's discretion helped to restrain his
friend's headlong impetuousity. At any rate he proved an
invaluable assistant to Throckmorton who employed him for
the transmission of vital messages to the Queen and strongly
recommended him to her favour for his "good and painful
service." [1]

Six weeks after their arrival in France Henry II was fatally
injured by a lance thrust in the eye during a tournament in
Paris. His death ten days later created a situation fraught with
dangerous possibilities for England. The seriousness with which
the two English diplomats viewed this event is indicated by the
speed Killigrew used in reporting it to his government. On
July 10th, the day of the King's death, he set out at once from
Paris. Despite attempts of the French government to debar
anyone from getting out of the country with this news, he
crossed the Channel and arrived just 48 hours later at Greenwich Palace to inform the Queen—an amazing feat in sixteenth
–century conditions of travel.

Elizabeth herself showed appreciation of this fact by commenting on Killigrew's "great speed" and noting the exact
time of his arrival—3 :00 in the afternoon on July 12th.[2] With
some complacency he recalled many years later: "I brought
home the news of the French King's death with that speed that

[1] In July, 1559, Throckmorton informed the Queen that Killigrew had
"done your Highness divers and sundry ways so good and painful service
as he had deserved to be well rewarded." Throckmorton to the Queen,
10th July, 1559. P.R.O. S.P. 70/5 f. 472.
[2] P.R.O. S.P. 70/5 f. 487.

I think will not be forgotten: notwithstanding that stay was made of the posts that none should pass, inasmuch that five days after my arrival it was doubted that I had brought uncertain advertisements." [1]

Killigrew's urgency arose from his realization of the changes in French policy that were bound to result from the King's death. His successor, Francis II, was a sickly nonentity fifteen years of age, but as Killigrew and Throckmorton foresaw, his accession entailed a transfer of power to Francis Duke of Guise and his brother, the Cardinal of Lorraine, who were leaders of the extreme Catholic anti-English party in France. Their niece, Mary Stuart, was the King's wife, and Francis II was completely dominated by Mary and her two uncles.

The Guises were determined to stamp out Protestantism both in France and in Scotland where the reins of government were held by their sister, the Queen Regent Mary of Guise. When in the spring of 1559, the Scottish Calvinists rebelled against the Regent's attempt to impose Catholic uniformity upon them the Guises made preparations to send troops to her aid. Killigrew and Throckmorton believed that once French arms had reduced the Scots to submission the Guises intended to prosecute the claims of their niece, Mary Stuart, to the English throne by force.

Whether this belief was correct or not it is impossible to say with certainty. But there can be no doubt that the successful consolidation of French power in Scotland would constitute a potent source of danger to England's security. From the spring of 1559 onward the aim of English policy was to undermine the French position in Scotland, to prevent military aid from reaching the Queen Regent, and to secure the expulsion of French troops from Scottish soil. Killigrew and Throckmorton made it their business to encourage strong measures for the realization of these objectives by arousing the Queen and her councillors to a full awareness of their peril.

The aggressive plans of the Guises, however, were severely

[1] Howard, *Letters*, p. 184.

impeded by the spread of unrest within France, as well as by financial and economic difficulties that were the result of the recent wars.[1] Religious discontent aroused by the oppressive measures of the government to crush the growing Protestant minority was combined with political and social opposition to the rule of the Guises and to the centralizing power of the French state.

In these internal divisions Elizabeth and her advisors saw an opportunity to weaken the power which threatened them. The aim of the French rulers to dominate Scotland could be thwarted if their energies were absorbed by insurrection in their own dominions. The English government therefore gave secret encouragement and aid to the dissident factions in both France and Scotland. What was required were skilled espionage agents who could harness the forces of discontent to the aims of their government.

Killigrew and Throckmorton were ideally suited for this task. Both were well grounded in the arts of conspiracy and subversion during Mary's reign. With the added satisfaction of paying off old scores against the French they set eagerly to work kindling the flames of rebellion in the house of their enemy.

Under the direction of his government and of Throckmorton, Killigrew became one of the most active agents of intrigue in France. In July, 1559, he was employed to assist the Earl of Arran to escape to Scotland where he became one of the leaders of the Calvinist party.[2] The following month

---

[1] In December, 1559, Killigrew and Jones, chargé d'affaires at the French court, reported that "the government was 18,000,000 crowns in debt, the country poor, the noblemen and gentlemen not recovered since the last wars, having much to do for the ordering of religion." Killigrew and Jones to the Council 14th December, 1559. P.R.O. S.P. 70/9 f. 174. Forbes, vol. 1, p. 277.

[2] On returning to France after he had brought home news of the death of Henry II, Killigrew was directed by Elizabeth "to devise the most secret and speedy way to convey the Earl of Arran—either into this realm or to his father (the Duke of Châtelherault)." "Memorial of things committed

Killigrew went to Vendôme to open communication between Elizabeth and Anthony, King of Navarre, whom the French Protestants hoped would assume the leadership of their movement.[1] When Throckmorton departed to England temporarily in the autumn of 1559 to urge the Queen and her ministers to give a greater measure of assistance to the Scottish rebels Killigrew acted as chargé d'affaires at the French court.[2] There he continued to keep close contact with opposition elements in the country while sending home detailed reports to his government concerning the fleet which sailed for Scotland under the command of the Marquis d'Elbeuf in January, 1560 to help the Regent crush her rebellious subjects.[3] The storm that blew this fleet to destruction was almost as providential for England as the one which destroyed the Spanish Armada thirty years later.

Killigrew, Throckmorton and other English agents were

---

to Killigrew's charge," P.R.O. S.P. 70/5 ff. 489–90. Arran had already escaped from France to Geneva. The task of actually bringing him to England fell to the charge of Thomas Randolph and Richard Tremayne. Throckmorton to the Queen B. M. Cotton MSS. Caligula V. f. 79. Forbes, vol. 1, pp. 172–3. The young nobleman reached England by the end of August and joined his father early the following month. C.S.P. Spanish, 1558–67, pp. 81, 90, 92.

[1] Throckmorton to the Queen 15th August, 1559, P.R.O. S.P. 70/6 f. 605. Anthony of Navarre, however, proved to be a spineless creature whose later behaviour entirely justified Killigrew's estimate of him as a turncoat who was easily controlled by the House of Guise. Hatfield MSS. vol. 25, f. 70.

[2] Killigrew was appointed chargé d'affaires on October 11, 1559. Acting with him in this capacity was Robert Jones, another of Throckmorton's secretaries. The Queen to Throckmorton P.R.O. S.P. 70/8 ff. 18–19. Forbes, vol. 1, p. 201–2.

[3] For the reports of Killigrew and Jones on D'Elbeuf's fleet: P.R.O. S.P. 70/8 f. 24; S.P. 70/10 f. 232. Forbes, vol. 1, pp. 254–303, passim. On 6th January, 1560, Killigrew and Jones wrote that sure agents must be sent to France to keep in contact with their co-religionists. The nature of Killigrew's and Jones's activities in that country may be inferred by the fact that they were kept under constant watch by the French government. P.R.O. S.P. 70/10 f. 231–2.

deeply involved in the intrigues with the French Protestant faction which led to the Tumult of Amboise in March, 1560. The extent of Killigrew's personal connection with the Huguenots is shown by the fact that when he returned to London at the end of February he was able to give his government the first news of the intended revolt—information which had been transmitted to him by one of the French conspirators.[1]

Still more important, the effectiveness with which he and Throckmorton had dramatized the danger threatening from France played an important part in moving Elizabeth and her councillors to the aid of the Scottish Calvinists. On the very day of Killigrew's departure from France the Queen concluded a pact with the Calvinist party for the preservation of their freedom and liberties against French oppression.[2] In March, 1560, an English army under the command of Lord Grey was ready to march north to join forces with the Calvinist troops encamped before the French fortress of Leith.

Killigrew was now given another opportunity to further the aim to which he had devoted himself with unremitting zeal for nearly a year—that of destroying France's foothold in Scotland. At the end of March the English government appointed him to accompany the French ambassador, Jean de Monluc, Bishop of Valence, to Edinburgh. Monluc's purpose was to delay the entry of the Queen's army into Scotland until a plan for a joint Franco-Spanish military expedition to suppress the Calvinist rebels could be put into effect.[3] The Huguenot outbreak at

---

[1] Howard, p. 186. The rôle of the English government in fomenting the upheaval at Amboise is discussed by A. Dureng, "La Complicité de L'Angleterre au Complot d'Amboise." *Revue Historique Moderne et Contemporaine*, vol. 6, Paris, 1904–5, pp. 249–56.

[2] T. Rymer, *The Foedera, Conventiones, Literae et cujuscunque generis Acta Publica inter Reges Angliae et alios quovis Imperatores, Reges, Pontifices, Principes, vel Communitates ab Anno 1101 ad Nostra usque Tempora Habitata aut Tractata—Accurante*, vol. 15, 3rd editio, 1728, p. 569. (hereafter: Rymer). P.R.O. State Papers Scotland S.P. 52/2 f. 62. (hereafter: P.R.O. S.P. 52).

[3] The Cardinal of Lorraine and the Duke of Guise to the Queen Dowager, 12th March, 1560. P.R.O. S.P. 52/2 f. 82.

Amboise, and the destruction of a major portion of D'Elbeuf's fleet at sea temporarily incapacitated the French government from further military enterprise. It therefore was compelled to fall back on negotiation as the only available means of preserving the Queen Regent's authority in Scotland.

Killigrew and Throckmorton warned their government that the French overtures were designed merely to win time until they could assemble new forces.[1] Under strong pressure from Spanish envoys in London and reluctant to give open assistance to rebels in arms against their lawful sovereign, Elizabeth decided to try the path of negotiation.[2] She acceded to Monluc's demand that he be allowed to go to Scotland to work for a peaceful settlement between Mary of Guise and the Calvinist faction. The Duke of Norfolk, who commanded the troops at Berwick, was ordered to give him a safe conduct to visit the Queen Regent at Edinburgh. At the same time, Elizabeth directed Norfolk to order Lord Grey to enter Scotland, adding that force should not be used until other means had been tried first.[3]

Ostensibly, Killigrew was acting as a representative of the English government to facilitate the Bishop of Valence's negotiations in Scotland. In actuality, his function was that of a spy to ferret out the real intentions of the French envoy, and, if necessary, frustrate them. If Monluc revealed any other purpose than the one he avowed—to make peace between the Regent and her adversaries with provision for withdrawal of a major portion of the French troops from Scotland—he was to be

[1] See the letters from Throckmorton to members of the English government brought home by Killigrew on his departure from France dated 27th February, 1560. P.R.O. S.P. 70/11 ff. 350-2. Forbes, vol. 1, pp. 334 ff.

[2] *Calendar of State Papers, Spanish, 1558-57*, pp. 139, 140, 143 ff.

[3] Samuel Haynes and Murdin, William, ed., *A Collection of state papers relating to the reigns of king Henry VIII, king Edward VI, queen Mary, queen Elizabeth from the year 1547 to 1571 transcribed from original letters and other authentic manuscripts never before published left by William Cecil, Lord Burghley, now remaining at Hatfield House in the Library of the Right Honorable, the present Earl of Salisbury*, vol. 1, London, 1840, p. 274. (hereafter: Haynes).

brought back to London at once.[1] Killigrew carried out his duties to the letter and probably with more zeal than the Queen intended. His selection for this task indicates the government's estimate of him as a quick witted and perceptive man, for Monluc had the reputation of being a diplomat of great skill and experience.[2] The ardent Protestant and the aged, querulous Catholic Bishop were obviously an ill-assorted pair and their association was not to prove a happy one.

They set out for Edinburgh at the beginning of April but did not reach Berwick until the evening of the 6th. Killigrew, Cecil, and the Duke of Norfolk were apparently cooperating in a plan to delay Monluc's journey.[3] Their aim was to allow the Anglo-Scottish army time to bring pressure on the Queen Regent to yield to the demands of her opponents. By this means there would also be a fuller opportunity to sound out the Bishop concerning his intentions.

He did nothing to arouse Killigrew's suspicions until the last day of their journey. Near Alnwick they met four French soldiers who had been captured by the Calvinist leader, Kirkaldy of Grange. Monluc tried to speak with his countrymen out of Killigrew's hearing, but the latter was not so easily hoodwinked. By pretending to lose control of his horse he got close enough to overhear them discussing the condition of the French garrison and fortifications of Leith. When the

[1] These instructions can be inferred not only from Killigrew's behaviour towards the Bishop of Valence, but by Elizabeth's orders to Norfolk on 30th March, 1560, in which she said the Monluc should be allowed to visit the Queen Regent unless he should give contrary occasion by demonstration of any outward act of malice towards this realm. *Ibid.*

[2] Throckmorton told Elizabeth that Monluc was "wise and sober and often employed in embassades and other services" 9th March, 1560. P.R.O. S.P. 70/12 f. 393. Forbes, vol. I, p. 356. He described the French envoy to Cecil as "a man of great experience and cunning practise." Throckmorton to Cecil 2nd March, 1560. Forbes, vol. I, p. 352.

[3] Such a plan is suggested by Killigrew's comment to Cecil on 7th April, concerning his trip to Berwick with Monluc. "I could not linger his journey any longer, he said, without evident cause of suspicion." P.R.O. S.P. 52/3 f. 9.

Bishop realized that Killigrew was eavesdropping he quietly warned his companions. One of them, as Killigrew reported, quickly "framed his answer thereafter" and said that Leith"was nothing strong." [1] The English army soon learned to its misfortune the strength of the French position at Leith.

When the two men arrived at Berwick they were received by Thomas Howard, Duke of Norfolk. Norfolk was a young man of considerable personal charm and not devoid of military ability, but subsequent events were to prove his utter want of capacity in any other sphere. Despite his treasonable complicity in Catholic intrigues in later years, at this time he was as enthusiastic a supporter of the Scottish Protestants as Killigrew himself.

Together they made life difficult for the choleric old gentleman who had been committed to their charge. When Monluc expressed the wish to depart immediately for Edinburgh Norfolk refused. He said that he lacked the power to guarantee his safety beyond the Scottish border, and that it would be necessary to obtain a safe conduct from the Lords of the Congregation.[2]

One would have thought that the Duke had no thought closer to his heart than the welfare of the French envoy, but Monluc was not impressed by this apparent concern for his safety. He demanded permission to make the journey on his own. Norfolk again refused, but it was finally agreed that the Bishop could send one of his servants to the Duke of Châtelherault, leader of the rebel faction, with a request for a safe conduct.[3]

Seven days later the servant returned with a flat refusal of his request unless he could show that he had sufficient authority

[1] *Ibid.*

[2] Realizing the animosity with which the Scots regarded the Bishop, Norfolk informed Cecil that he felt unable himself to guarantee his safety if he should venture beyond the Border without permission granted by the Duke of Châtelherault. Norfolk to Cecil 7th April, 1560. P.R.O. S.P. 52/3 f. 10.

[3] *Ibid.*

to agree to the withdrawal of all French troops from Scotland.[1] Angrily, the Bishop now declared his intention to return immediately to London. The situation had begun to get out of hand, for both Killigrew and the Duke of Norfolk knew that the Queen wished to reach a peaceful settlement by Monluc's mediation if possible. Should the Bishop throw up his mission under circumstances which allowed him to attribute its failure to the English government, Elizabeth's claim to be acting in the interest of peace would be gravely compromised. Norfolk therefore became more conciliatory, and agreed that the message was unreasonable. Asking Monluc to be patient, he directed Killigrew to go to Scotland to persuade the Lords of the Congregation to grant the safe conduct.[2]

Killigrew himself was almost convinced that Monluc might be a means to obtaining an agreement that was consistent with the interests of his country and its ally. While awaiting the return of the Bishop's servant he had a private talk with the French envoy. He bluntly informed him that unless he told him frankly what terms he was prepared to offer the Scots he would do nothing further to help his negotiations forward. In reply the Bishop said that he would be willing to see the rebels pardoned for their past actions against the Regent, and all French troops withdrawn from Scotland except a few to guard Dunbar and Inchkeith. Moreover, he would agree to have the Regent call a Parliament, and if the Protestants held a majority therein, to have Protestantism established as the state religion in Scotland.

Killigrew realized that these were important concessions and might afford the basis for an equitable settlement. In transmitting Monluc's proposals to Cecil he felt constrained to admit: "... if the difference is to be ended by treaty no man can do it better for the Queen's honour or the Scot's safety." But a fixed distrust of the French caused him to add: "In my

[1] Châtelherault to the Queen, to the Bishop of Valence. 13th April, 1560. P.R.O. S.P. 52/3 f. 26.
[2] Killigrew to Cecil 24th April, 1560. P.R.O. S.P. 70/3 f. 27.

opinion the French ... have deserved to be more quickly used that the Queen's Majesty hath done hitherto. God forbid that it (the dispute in Scotland) should end by appointment, for the Queen's Majesty should lose all her charges besides the dishonour and danger of the state." [1]

In his mission to Scotland on Monluc's behalf Killigrew was faced with a difficult task. The rebel leaders were extremely reluctant to deal with the Bishop of Valence, for they feared that he intended to use negotiations as a mask for trickery and delay. Moreover, they were becoming increasingly concerned over the attitude of their ally. The Queen, they feared, would drive them to a "disadvantageous appointment." [2] Even the English military and civilian officials in Scotland were becoming lukewarm in their support and showed irritation over the failure of the Calvinists to provide their agreed contributions of men and equipment. [3]

Nevertheless, Killigrew succeeded in persuading the Scots to accept Monluc's mediation. He probably pointed out that their resistance on this matter would alienate Elizabeth and further endanger the alliance with England. Speaking as a friend who was as convinced as they of the futility of negotiating with the French, his words doubtless carried weight with the Scottish Lords. [4]

On 19th April the English diplomat returned to Berwick with a safe conduct of eight days' duration. [5] The rebel leaders, however, stipulated that the Bishop would only be allowed to see the Regent if he could first show them that he possessed full authority to negotiate. The French envoy declared angrily that

[1] *Ibid.*

[2] Maitland to Killigrew 10th April, 1560. *Ibid* (enclosed with Killigrew's letter to Cecil of 14th April.).

[3] See Norfolk's letters to the Privy Council of 10th and 26th April, and to Cecil of 26th April. P.R.O. S.P. 52/3 f. 19. 44.

[4] Maitland informed Cecil that the Bishop was allowed to go to Scotland "to satisfy the Queen rather than any good we look for." Maitland to Cecil 17th April, 1560. P.R.O. S.P. 52/3 f. 31.

[5] Norfolk to Cecil 19th April, 1560. P.R.O. S.P. 52/3 f. 34.

this condition was unacceptable, and he again announced his intention to return to London. He only changed his mind when Norfolk gave an explicit promise that Lord Grey would have him conveyed to the Regent without seeing the Scottish leaders.[1]

The next day Killigrew and the Bishop of Valence set out for Edinburgh. When they reached Haddington, according to Killigrew's memoir, they were suddenly set upon by James Hepburn, Earl of Bothwell and some of his followers. He added: "The Bishop of Valence should have been taken from me … so I was constrained to use all the shifts that could be for the sudden." [2]

Killigrew did not mention this episode in his despatches at the time, nor is it referred to in any contemporary source. Why Bothwell, an adherent of the Queen Regent, should attempt to seize a representative of the French government who was coming to negotiate in her interest is not immediately obvious. Perhaps he intended to take the Bishop under his protection because violence had been threatened against him by some of the rebel faction. It is also possible that he was acting secretly under orders from the Regent to delay Monluc's journey since she also wished to prolong negotiations, hoping for the arrival of reinforcements from France. On the other hand, Bothwell—whom Throckmorton called "this glorious, rash and hazardous young man"—with his Border ruffians may simply have been looking for a victim to plunder.

Perhaps this incident explains the sudden fit of nerves which the old Frenchman suffered at Haddington. He told Killigrew that he would go no further without a larger escort and despatched a servant to Lord Grey demanding protection. Grey

[1] The Bishop of Valence's account of his negotiations in Scotland is contained in A. Teulet, *Papiers D'Etat Pièces et Documents Inédits Peu Connu À L'Histoire De L'Écosse Au XVI Siècle Des Bibliothèques et Des Archives De France. Pour Le Bannatyne Club D'Edinbourg*, tome Première, Paris, (Hereafter: Teulet). Teulet, vol. I, p. 574.

[2] Howard, p. 186.

immediately sent 100 horsemen under Sir Henry Percy for this purpose. As Killigrew and his companion neared the English encampment they were met by an additional 600 men who conveyed them into the presence of Lord Grey. In accordance with Norfolk's promise, the Bishop was permitted to go directly to Mary of Guise at Edinburgh Castle accompanied by Killigrew and Thomas Randolph, Elizabeth's agent in Scotland. After a brief talk with the Regent Monluc went to the Scottish camp and negotiations for peace began.[1]

As the conference opened all three parties were in a state of tension and anxiety. Welcome news had arrived that the English government intended to throw its full weight behind the Calvinist party, but the Scottish leaders realized that prolonged negotiations with the French were making some of the nobility withhold support from their cause out of doubt as to the ultimate outcome of the struggle.[2]

Ardent champions of the Protestant party in Scotland shared these anxieties. While the peace discussions were in progress Killigrew and Randolph conferred with the Earl of Huntly, the most powerful member of the uncommitted nobility, in order to win his support to the rebel side. He made them large promises, but it was clear that his loyalty belonged only to the winning side.[3]

If the problems of the English and their allies were difficult those of the Bishop of Valence proved insoluble. For nearly six days he strove to secure an agreement between the Regent and her antagonists. In Maitland of Lethington, however, he found an opponent worthy of his mettle. Throughout the negotiations this astute politician kept in close touch with his friend, William Cecil, the Queen's Principal Secretary of State, and therefore possessed an accurate picture of the prevailing current of opinion at Elizabeth's court. As English support became more firm he and his fellow negotiators naturally grew more

[1] Teulet, vol. 1, p. 574.
[2] Maitland to Cecil 17th April, 1560. P.R.O. S.P. 52/3 f. 31.
[3] Randolph to Norfolk 25th April, 1560. P.R.O. S.P. 52/3 f. 43.

obdurate in their attitude. They were determined to accept no settlement which did not provide for demolition of the fortifications at Leith and the withdrawal from Scotland of all French forces.

Monluc might still have obtained some measure of success had it not been for the inflexibility of Mary of Guise. She submitted a series of demands to the Lords of the Congregation, the most important of which were that the rebels must submit to her authority and dissolve their alliance with England. In addition, she forbade the Bishop of Valence to alter these terms in the slightest degree. To the Calvinists this was simply a demand for unconditional surrender, and nothing the Bishop could do was now sufficient to prevent a collapse of the negotiations.[1]

Monluc himself seems to have been prepared to make large concessions in order to reach an agreement with the rebels. He was doubtless aware that the French troops at the Regent's disposal, though well trained and efficient, were not numerous enough to withstand indefinitely the Anglo-Scottish force opposing them. Nor was there any immediate likelihood of help from France. The only sensible line of action was to make terms which would leave the Regent with some degree of authority and military power to await a future day when new armies could be summoned to her deliverance from abroad.

In this intention, however, the Bishop of Valence was thwarted by the iron resolve of Mary of Guise.[2] Mortally ill, with scarcely a month to live, this courageous woman refused

[1] Monluc's account of the negotiations is contained in Teulet, vol. 1, pp. 578–95. For English and Scottish accounts see: Grey to Norfolk 25th April, 1560. P.R.O. S.P. 52/3 f. 42. *Ibid.*, 27th April, 1560. P.R.O. S.P. 52/3 f. 49. Maitland to Cecil 26th April, 1560. P.R.O. S.P. 52/3 f. 45. *Ibid* 28th April, 1560. P.R.O. S.P. 52/3 f. 51.

[2] Perhaps Mary was deluded by assurances from her brothers in France that military assistance would soon be sent to her. The Cardinal of Lorraine and Duke of Guise to the Queen Regent, 12th March, 1560. P.R.O. S.P. 52/2 f. 82.

to yield one jot of the authority committed to her by God. Her attitude ended all hope of a peaceful settlement.

Killigrew and other Englishmen in Scotland chose to throw blame for failure of the negotiations on Monluc. After the termination of the conference he was forbidden further communication with the Scots, and the following day Killigrew came to escort him back to London. According to Monluc's report, Killigrew refused to secure an escort for him on the return journey.[1] Now that the French envoy had served their turn the English apparently showed no further concern for his safety.

As the two men set out from the English encampment they were both in an anxious frame of mind, for they knew that the Anglo-Scottish army was about to deliver an assault upon Leith. Again Killigrew deliberately delayed the journey. Monluc's unconcealed rage at the failure of his mission and at his alleged mistreatment by the English in Scotland made it certain that he would bring his complaints to the attention of Elizabeth and of the Spanish ambassadors in London. Better to keep the Frenchman where he could not stir up trouble until, as Killigrew doubtless hoped, the sound of his invective would be drowned out by the glad tidings of victory at Leith.

The journey was a trying one. During a pause at Darlington on the 5th of May, Killigrew sent to Cecil a graphic description of his companion's state of mind. The Bishop bewailed his failure to secure peace and, over Killigrew's protests, put the blame on Elizabeth and her ministers. The letter continued: "I have never seen him quiet or merry, but a man the most wayward and full of extreme passion that ever I saw." With

[1] Teulet, vol. i, p. 595. See Killigrew's brief account of Monluc's embassy to the Scots in his letter of 29th May, 1560. Forbes, vol. i, pp. 592-3. He hotly refutes the charges levelled against himself and other English representatives in Scotland by the French ambassador while accusing him of various acts of treachery. It is impossible to discover the truth from these conflicting accounts, but there was doubtless some basis to the accusations of both parties.

weary exasperation he added: "Would to God I were once well delivered of him." [1]

Killigrew and the Bishop of Valence arrived in London on the evening of 11th May. That same night word came that the attack on Leith four days earlier had ended in failure.[2] This disaster had a predictable effect on the Queen's mind. She felt no love for the Scottish Calvinists, and she entertained grave doubts as to the wisdom of assisting rebels against their lawful sovereign. Elizabeth therefore turned her spleen against those who had urged this policy upon her, and her anger was further inflamed by Monluc's report. He complained that the English officials in Scotland were to blame for the failure of his negotiations, and he was vehement concerning the mistreatment he had suffered—apparently with particular reference to Killigrew's behavior towards him.[3] For the moment, at any rate, Monluc's account was quite successful in arousing the Queen's wrath against Killigrew and others of her servants who had been dealing in Scottish affairs.

The tense atmosphere at court following the setback at Leith is reflected in Killigrew's letters to Throckmorton who still held his post at the French court. Two days after his return to London Killigrew sent his friend a summary of recent events in Scotland and at home. Concerning the Bishop of Valence he wrote: "It seemed to some that her Highness did bear too much with his relating...," and that the effect of the defeat was to make the Queen "renew the opinion of Cassandra." As to his own favour with Elizabeth he wryly commented: "It is as you left it save the Bishop of Valence has made it somewhat worse..."[4]

The tide of events continued, however, to run in England's favour. Internal disorder and financial weakness made it impossible for the French to capitalize on their success. At the end of May a French ambassador arrived in London with directions to assist in negotiations for peace in Scotland.

[1] P.R.O. S.P. 52/3 f. 70.   [2] Forbes, vol. 1, pp. 454-5.
[3] Ibid. C.S.P. Spanish 1558-67, p. 155.   [4] Forbes, vol. 1, p. 457.

During the last week of May Killigrew and others of the pro-Scottish faction at court still had many anxieties weighing on their minds. Their leader, Sir William Cecil, was appointed as member of a commission to negotiate peace terms in Scotland. His supporters feared that their country might forfeit at the conference table the strong position it had achieved in Scotland. They were also concerned lest his absence from court should rebound to the benefit of those who opposed his policies. Nevertheless, if any success could be gained from negotiation they believed that he was the man best qualified to achieve it.

Killigrew wrote to Throckmorton on 28th May, the day before Cecil departed for Scotland: "Upon the return of Monsieur Valence, the coming of Randan (the new French ambassador) and our loss at Leith, the Queen's Majesty hath been so desirous of an end in this matter, as it was thought, for divers respects by the Council, that the Secretary should make the same who, for his country's sake, hath been contented to take the matter in hand. The worst hath been cast of his absence from hence and at length judged for the best. If he brings home peace I must think it for the best."

Perhaps still smarting under Elizabeth's displeasure, he added: "I know of none that love their country better. I would the Queen's Majesty could love it so well." [1]

Cecil fully justified the hopes of Killigrew and his other friends. In the negotiations which culminated in the Treaty of Edinburgh he achieved most of the aims for which they had striven during the past year and a half. It was agreed that French troops should be withdrawn from Scotland. The Queen of France was no longer to claim the arms and title of the English crown; the liberty of the Protestant religion was recognized by France, and effective control of the government transferred into native hands. [2]

For his contribution to this triumph Killigrew won the praise of Englishmen and Scotsmen alike. Probably as a result of his

[1] *Ibid.*, p. 501.   [2] Rymer, vol. XV, p. 593.

services in Scotland he was appointed Teller of the Exchequer in June, 1561, an office which he held for nearly forty years thereafter.[1] The devoted efforts he had made on behalf of the Calvinist party brought him the respect and good will of its leaders.[2]

In relation to his future career the associations which he established in Scotland at this time were particularly important. Killigrew seems to have gotten on friendly terms with Maitland of Lethington, for example, who was one of the most brilliant and enigmatic men of the age. Maitland's friendship proved to be of great value to Killigrew when he was taken prisoner in France in 1562. For some time Maitland continued to be a leading figure in the Anglophile Calvinist party. Finally, however, he switched his alliegance to the anti-English faction that maintained the cause of Mary Stuart. In that rôle he and Killigrew became opponents in a conflict which culminated in Maitland's tragic death.

In light of the complex struggle in which his country had been engaged, Killigrew's account of it thirty five years later has an entertaining simplicity. He first lists the various reasons which induced Elizabeth to enter into alliance with the Scots: "the mission of the Marquis d'Elbeuf by the Queen of Scots to be a viceroy in Scotland with a mission too full of jealousy for her Majesty to endure, frustrated by his being driven back by contrary winds... Also the despatch thither of Mons. de Martigues with a band of old soldiers which moved the Scots to call upon her Majesty..." He concludes with the pious statement that Elizabeth "being moved in pity and through the greatness of the injuries offered, yielded thereunto and by God's grace and happy success therein." [3]

[1] P.R.O. C. 66/970, Part 8, m. 13.
[2] On 15th April, 1560, Randolph wrote from the Duke of Châtelherault's house at Holyrood. "Your letter written on Good Friday deserves my best thanks. I read it in the hearing of those who commended your zeal to the cause and praised your wit." P.R.O. S.P. 52/3 f. 4.
[3] Hatfield MSS. vol. 25 f. 75.

CHAPTER IV

"THE CHRISTIAN SOLDIER,"
MILITARY AND DIPLOMATIC CAREER,
1560–1567

IN the autumn of 1560 Killigrew was living at court, a witness to the stir created by the Queen's relationship with young Robert Dudley. Her affection for this dashing, handsome, ambitious adventurer had been a matter of public comment for over a year, but in the summer of 1560, it seemed to have reached the point of infatuation. According to rumour only the existence of Dudley's neglected wife, Amy Robsart, prevented his marriage with Elizabeth. Her sudden death under suspicious circumstances at Cumnor Hall early in September afforded an opportunity which England's enemies were quick to seize.[1]

From France Sir Nicholas Throckmorton wrote home to his friends of the discreditable gossip that was being circulated at his sovereign's expense. With characteristic vehemence he bewailed his lot to the Marquis of Northampton. "I wish," he wrote, "I were either dead or hence that I might not hear the dishonourable and naughty reports that are made here of the Queen..." He added that the comments about her at the French court were such that "every hair of my head stareth at and my ears glow to hear..." Some let not to say: "What religion is this that a subject shall kill his wife, and the Prince not only bear withal but marry with him?"[2] Throckmorton's letters at this time make clear his bitter opposition to Elizabeth's marriage with her favourite, an attitude that was shared by Cecil and most of the Council.[3]

[1] *C.S.P. Spanish, 1558–1567*, p. 112.
[2] P.R.O. S.P. 70/19 f. 358.
[3] Philip Yorke, 2nd Earl of Hardwicke ed., *Miscellaneous state papers from*

Killigrew now faced the danger of getting himself involved in the controversy over Dudley whom he had known for some years past, and whose power and influence in the government were to have a decisive effect on his own career. The two men had certainly known one another since the end of Henry VIII's reign when Killigrew became a servant in the Dudley household. Although there is no evidence that Robert's assistance played any part in his advancement at the outset of Elizabeth's reign—at that time his principal benefactor seems to have been Throckmorton—from 1560 onwards he increasingly looked to Dudley as his foremost patron. Dudley's favour not only procured his appointment to several important diplomatic posts, but he relied upon Dudley's great personal influence with the Queen to sway her policies in the direction he favoured. In the present situation it therefore behooved Killigrew to step very carefully if he valued his future prospects.

In the midst of the furore which followed Amy Robsart's death, he corresponded frequently with Throckmorton. Learning of the latter's violent reaction to the rumours concerning the tragedy at Cumnor Hall and of the Queen's association with Dudley he was at particular pains to assure his friend that Lord Robert was innocent of his wife's death. On 10th October he wrote to him the following words underlined for emphasis: "I cannot imagine what rumours they be you hear there (in France), as you write so strange, unless such as were here on the death of my Lady Dudley; for that she brake her neck down a pair of stairs, which I protest to you was done only by the hand of God to my knowledge." [1]

1501 to 1726 in two volumes, vol. 1, London, 1778, p. 121 (hereafter: Hardwicke).

[1] P.R.O. S.P. 70/19 f. 360. An English doctor, who has recently examined the evidence uncovered at the time of Amy Robsart's death, concluded that her death resulted from a spontaneous fracture of the spine caused by her fall down a staircase. He believed that she was suffering from cancer of the breast which tends to produce a softening of the spine. He concluded that Amy's death was a result of an accident, not suicide or murder. Ian Aird, "The death of Amy Robsart," E.H.R., vol. 71, pp. 69–79.

Five days later he sent another letter to Throckmorton in which he mentioned the presence or imminent arrival at court of the ambassadors of several foreign suitors for the Queen's hand and offered his own views on the heated issue of her marriage. "Touching the Queen's marriage," he said, "Englishmen would be glad to find an English husband for her; therefore they were sorry to hear of Sweden's coming, likewise of the Duke of Holstein... whose ambassador is here presently..., but of all strangers at present they fear the Earl of Arran because the Lords of Scotland are coming to this court to treat of marriage." With a dry humour that sometimes emerges in his correspondence Killigrew concluded: "They have every week a new husband for the Queen. When all is done I think every man has cause to hope. For my part I cannot tell what to say, but only that I am an Englishman by affection and a stranger by reason that I speak in the feminine gender." [1]

A letter to Throckmorton of 17th October gives a clearer indication of Killigrew's hope that Elizabeth would marry one of her own subjects. "All such as be not with us" (in support of an English marriage), he wrote, "are taken as enemies. All such as love their own country ought also to prefer their own nation before strangers." [2] Perhaps for fear of alienating his hot-tempered friend, whose opinions on this subject he probably knew by this time, he did not mention Dudley's name. Nevertheless, as Dudley was the only English candidate then in the field, Killigrew's comments suggest that he belonged to that faction at court which favoured Dudley's suit for the Queen's hand.

A month later, however, the Cornishman's views appear to have undergone a marked change. At the end of November Throckmorton sent over to England his secretary, Robert Jones, to expostulate with Elizabeth on the folly of her reported intention to marry Dudley. Jones's persuasive efforts were without success for Elizabeth answered him with a coy dexter-

[1] P.R.O. S.P. 70/19 f. 366.
[2] *Ibid.*, f. 373.

ity that defied argument. He informed Throckmorton that on the evening before his interview with the Queen at Greenwich he spoke with Killigrew on the subject of her possible marriage with Dudley. At the end of their conversation, Jones reported, Killigrew had said to him "with a sad look I think that my Lord Robert shall run away with the hare and have the Queen..." [1]

This statement may have indicated a genuine change of attitude. Perhaps he had begun to share the doubts of most responsible men whether the nation's interest would be well served by Elizabeth's marriage with her favourite. More probably, however, it was an expression of opinion calculated to win Throckmorton's approval, to whom he knew it was certain to be reported.

Whatever his real view may have been one thing is certain: Killigrew did not intend to allow himself to become involved in a contest that was dividing the government into bitter factions. His position was a difficult one. As a new man of slender means he could not afford to antagonize either side. He was not likely to risk a severance of his connection with Robert Dudley and his family. On the other hand, he could not take a stand which would earn the enmity of powerful men like Cecil and Throckmorton, with whom he was also closely associated, and upon whom he was dependant for favour and advancement.

Moreover, he had gained a sufficient knowledge of the Queen's personality to realize that Throckmorton's high-pressure tactics would do nothing but harm and perhaps defeat the very purpose for which they were intended. The latter had written fiery letters of protest concerning Elizabeth's indiscretions with Dudley to most of his friends in the government. He may have expressed some annoyance to Killigrew because of his unwillingness to support his views on this subject. Throckmorton seldom hesitated to lecture his friends on their duty to their country and himself.

[1] Hardwicke, vol. 1, p. 175.

On 13th January, 1560, Killigrew wrote to him: "I would be loath that you should mistake me to whom I wish to show myself grateful." He did not neglect, however, to give his friend some excellent advice: "Some think that what you inveigh against serves to no purpose, and by so doing, you increase the displeasure of the Princes and such as be able to do most with her. This chiefly I wrote to the Earl of Bedford's cousin who was willed of the Council to let you know that you did but strive against the stream… In a few words whatsoever you do that tendeth to mislike or disallow of the great liking that some have of my L. (ord) R. (obert) is taken but practise of your own hand, rather of ill will than well meaning to the state."

On his own behalf Killigrew added: "I can say no more unto you, but if you write unto me let it be so as all men may see it, and yet I pray you write to avoid the suspicion that may else be conceived." [1] Sir Nicholas Throckmorton must have been a person worth knowing … a man of great wit and charm, but he also must have been extremely trying at times as a friend and associate.

For some time thereafter Killigrew continued his effort to lessen Throckmorton's hostility towards Dudley and to impress upon him the danger and futility of opposing the latter's suit for the Queen's hand. The task was no easy one. Jealous, sensitive, and highly strung Throckmorton was a man who required careful handling, and Killigrew was entirely conscious of the risk he ran of incurring his displeasure. But loyalty to an old friend and benefactor impelled him to urge a course of action which he knew to be in his own interest. Indeed, Killigrew's sense of obligation to Throckmorton for past favours was so great that he regarded him almost as a father.

In November, 1561, he wrote again to Throckmorton in eloquent terms of friendship and entreaty: "I do wish unto you as I would unto my own father, as God knoweth, who always

[1] P.R.O. S.P. 70/10 f. 560.

so rule you as the world may not find you to be an ill courtier in these days, nor so constant in those opinions (against Dudley's marriage to Elizabeth) wherein you cannot prevail but rather hurt yourself more and more with small pleasure of your friends. I would not have written this much unto your Lordship, but that I trust upon the little experience you have had of my poor good will you will be persuaded to take my humble meaning in good part, whereof I humbly beseech you as one that shall never be ungrateful whatever befall unto me besides." [1]

A few weeks later Killigrew sent another letter somewhat different in tone. "This afternoon," he reported, "Lord Robert and Lord Windsor, shooting a match in the park, the Queen's Majesty stole out upon them accompanied only by Kate Carey and two others whom she followed as maid and told Lord Robert openly that he was beholden unto her, for that she had passed the pikes for his sake." "It seems," he added, somewhat unnecessarily, "his favour began but now." [2]

In writing this detailed account of Elizabeth's bold behavior towards Dudley was Killigrew being merely the dutiful correspondent? Certainly he must have realized how the excitable Throckmorton would react to it—what apprehensions it would arouse in his mind. There seems more than a slight possibility that he was enjoying a quiet laugh at Sir Nicholas's expense, taking an impish delight in stirring up his feverish imagination, and perhaps in depriving him of a night's sleep! If there was concealed malice in this letter one can hardly blame Killigrew. After all, Throckmorton had caused him a good deal of anxiety. His letters to Killigrew have not survived, which is not surprising, since their indiscretions must have prompted him to destroy them at once. It is also likely that he tried to pressure Henry into taking his side against Dudley.

Whatever the truth of these matters, Killigrew's counsels of moderation produced the desired effect, for Throckmorton

[1] B.M., Additional MSS., 3583 f. 285.
[2] P.R.O. S.P. 70/32 f. 527.

soon availed himself of Henry's assistance in effecting a reconciliation with Dudley.[1] Although his efforts were not immediately successful, ultimately they achieved their object. In the spring of 1562, when Dudley and Throckmorton joined forces to urge English intervention on behalf of the Huguenots, a permanent bond of friendship was cemented between the two men. Doubtless Killigrew regarded his work in bringing Dudley and Throckmorton together, not only as a benefit to the state, but as a contribution to his own peace of mind. His success in this task shows that his skill as a conciliator was displayed as effectively in domestic matters as in affairs of foreign diplomacy.

Killigrew obtained his next important diplomatic assignment in the autumn of 1562 following the outbreak of civil war in France. At this moment the position of the Huguenot party was desperate. The Queen Mother Catherine de Medici had cast her lot with the Guises and authorized an invitation to Spain for military assistance against her son's heretical subjects. Havre, Dieppe, Rouen and other important cities in western France had revolted to the Protestant side, but the Huguenot forces under the Prince of Condé were bottled up within the walls of Orléans while the Catholics, heavily reinforced by mercenaries from Switzerland and Germany, were scoring one victory after another. The Huguenot leaders realized that unless foreign aid was obtained immediately the armies of Guise and the King of Navarre would soon be able to march against the coastal cities of Normandy in overwhelming force.

To forestall this disastrous eventuality a group of Huguenot emissaries came secretly to Elizabeth's court in July to request assistance in both money and troops.[2] The opportunity for

[1] See Killigrew's letter to Throckmorton of 5th November, 1561, which was obviously written in reply to a request for advice from Throckmorton concerning the wisdom of his writing or sending a present to Dudley. Killigrew, evidently judging that Dudley was not yet in the mood to accept a peace offering from Throckmorton, advised his friend not to send it. P.R.O. S.P. 70/22 f. 491.

[2] *C.S.P. Spanish, 1558–1568*, pp. 255–6.

which the English government had been waiting had now arrived. During the past several months the Queen and her councillors had been considering plans to induce the Huguenots to turn over Havre and Dieppe in return for military aid as a means of compelling France to restore Calais. Throckmorton strongly urged various projects to secure this objective on his government, and he especially recommended his friend, Henry Killigrew as a fit instrument for the execution of one of them.[1]

Even before the coming of the Huguenot embassy preparations were under way for the despatch of a considerable fleet under the command of Sir William Woodhouse to make a demonstration on behalf of the French Protestants in Normandy. Although the fleet was not allowed to engage in any military enterprise, the intentions of the government were clearly indicated by a detailed plan which Cecil drew up for the occupation and garrisoning of Havre.[2]

One of the principal members of the Huguenot embassy was Jules de Ferrieres, Vidame of Chartres, governor of Havre, a cousin of the man with whom Killigrew had dealt at Catcau-Cambrésis. On the 23rd of July he departed again for Havre accompanied, as the Spanish ambassador reported, by the Queen's servant, Killigrew. Killigrew returned to London on the 29th and left for Havre the following day carrying 3000 crowns for the revictualling of the city.[3]

Killigrew's mission to France in August, 1562, had objects more important than the mere transmission of money to the garrison at Havre. Before despatching a large force to Normandy the government wanted to have a careful assessment made of the risks and opportunities of such an enterprise. It was

[1] P.R.O. S.P. 70/37 f. 49.
[2] Instructions given to Sir William Woodhouse, 4th August, 1562. Haynes, pp. 394–5. The Queen to Clinton: 30th July, 1562. P.R.O. S.P. 70/40 f. 294. Memoranda by Cecil: P.R.O. S.P. 12/23 f. P.R.O. S.P. 12/24 no. 21.
[3] C.S.P. Spanish, 1551–1567, pp. 255–6.

necessary to learn the present strength of the fortifications and garrisons at Dieppe and Havre. Of even greater moment was the morale of the troops and population in these cities and their attitude concerning the admission of English troops. The reports of Cecil's agents on this point a month earlier had not been encouraging, but the recent reverses suffered by the Huguenots appeared to have produced a change.[1]

Such were the questions for which Killigrew had been sent to Normandy to find answers. In his plan for the occupation of Havre Cecil mentioned the advisability of sending "a skilful man-of-war to Newhaven to see the strength thereof."[2] Killigrew's previous military experience made him well qualified for such a task, and his earlier contacts with Huguenot rebels were probably an additional reason for his selection.

He arrived at Dieppe on the evening of 4th August and wrote to Dudley on the following day that he had found the town well fortified and provisioned, but that the garrison, numbering only 400 men, was insufficient for its defence. A few weeks before, the citizens and soldiers of Dieppe had been unwilling to permit the entry of English troops, but now, their primary concern was whether the Queen would send ships and men in time to help them resist siege by greatly superior forces.[3]

"I am now out of doubt," he informed Dudley, "of the scruple your Lordship had lest the ships came the men would be refused." The Captain of Dieppe had admitted to him that his present garrison could not withstand a siege without reinforcements and had little hope of securing them unless they were provided by the English. The Huguenots, Killigrew wrote, desired at least a thousand men, but if 3000 came they would not be refused, and this number would be sufficient to warrant all Normandy from Dieppe to Rouen.[4]

---

[1] Reports of Edward Horsey and Armigail Waade; P.R.O. S.P. 70/38 ff. 132, 141, 144–5, 159, 168, 178.   [2] P.R.O. S.P. 70/24 f. 21.

[3] P.R.O. S.P. 70/40 f. 315. On 25th June, 1562, Waade wrote to Cecil that Dieppe and Newhaven would hear of no aid. P.R.O. S.P. 70/38 f. 71.

[4] P.R.O. S.P. 70/40 f. 315.

Killigrew's comments reveal a keen awareness of the strategic importance of these towns, both to England and to the Protestant cause in France. Dieppe and especially Havre, on the estuary of the Seine, were vital ports of supply for Paris. By controlling them as well as Rouen the rebels could reduce the capital to the verge of starvation. Killigrew would certainly have endorsed Napoleon's remark that "Paris, Rouen and Havre are but one city, of which the main street is the Seine." To Dudley he observed: "These towns (Dieppe and Havre) are the chief keys to France, without which neither Paris nor Rouen would be able to live; and for matters of the sea I believe they are able to encounter half of France. Besides, on the other part of Normandy there is Caen so by the aid of 5000 or 6000 men the Queen could command all Normandy, and the country could victual them so that a sufficient number came in time to provide for the same, which must be 3000.[1]

On the following day, 5th August, Killigrew went to Havre. When he first arrived efforts were made to keep his presence a secret. Neither Elizabeth nor the Huguenot leaders were yet willing to make an open avowal of their negotiations for an English occupation of Dieppe and Havre.

Writing to Cecil on the 10th of August Killigrew set forth a careful survey of the commercial and military capabilities of the town and of the state of mind of its Protestant occupants. Neither its garrison nor its supplies were sufficient to endure a long siege.

The troops numbered only 600, and not all of these were considered dependable. Due to a lack of men the garrison was unable to obtain provisions because the Catholic army under the Duke D'Aumale had captured most of the nearby towns. Moreover, the food supply was further diminished by the arrival of destitute refugees from these towns (Pont Audemar, Honfleur, and Harfleur).[2]

On the 5th and 6th of August Killigrew conferred with the Vidame of Chartres and other Huguenots in Havre. He found

[1] *Ibid.*   [2] P.R.O. S.P. 70/40 f. 338.

the Vidame in a terrible state of anxiety. He realized that with the forces at his disposal he lacked the means to endure a full scale siege, and a large Catholic army was expected in the near future. Since Condé and Coligny were unable to send help from Orleans, England was almost his only hope. Yet, by calling in the troops of his country's ancient enemy he risked the hatred of every patriotic Frenchman. Moreover, in his negotiations with the English government the Vidame apparently believed that he had already committed himself so far in the matter of delivering Havre in return for English assistance that he could not now turn back.

Killigrew understood and sympathized with the Frenchman's unhappy position. To Dudley, he wrote: "Your Lordship has need to make haste to aid this man; for I would not be in his case for all France who has gone so far forward that he cannot draw back again." He was, nevertheless, determined to exploit his predicament to the utmost. As one who possessed an intimate knowledge of the negotiations at Cateau-Cambrésis, Killigrew knew how great a risk the Queen ran by intervening on behalf of the rebels. According to the terms of the Treaty of Cateau-Cambrésis France was obligated to return Calais at the end of eight years, but only if England had not committed acts of hostility in the meantime. Therefore, Elizabeth could not be expected to aid the Huguenots unless she received guarantees, such as the occupation of Havre and Dieppe would provide, to ensure her rights to Calais.

In conversations with the Vidame and other Huguenot leaders he learned that they were desperately casting about for an alternative to English aid under these harsh conditions. They began to discuss the possibility of waiting for the German troops which were being brought into France by Coligny's brother, D'Andelot. "This aid of the Alamains," Killigrew wrote, "put them in hope of liberty without endangering any strong place." He, therefore, pointed out to the Huguenot leaders the weakness of their position, and the certainty of their destruction unless they received immediate aid. He asked them to consider the relative power of the Queen of England and the German princes and reminded them that in choosing assistance they must obtain the favour of one who is able to sustain a long war.

He also impressed upon his listeners the greatness of Elizabeth's sacrifice in identifying herself with their cause—"that if the Queen succoured them, how much they were bound to God considering that thereby she lost her interest in Calais and entered into war with France, Scotland, and Spain." For these reasons, he said, they should make such offers as might induce her to take so great a matter in hand. Finally, he assured them that unless they used matters frankly, it would not only make Elizabeth afraid to meddle but also undo them.[1] As Killigrew spoke the smooth veneer of the professional diplomat dropped away, and an aspect of his personality emerged which later caused Robert Dudley to say in surprised admiration: "Harry Killigrew is a quicker and stouter fellow than I took him for. He can deal roughly enough when it pleaseth him."[2] He grimly warned the Vidame of Chartres that he would not set a man on land without assurance of Newhaven, and that unless the Vidame and his friends resolved thereupon it would be the means to lose the Queen forever.[3]

Killigrew's frank assessment of their situation compelled a glum endorsement from the Huguenots, but they replied only that when they saw the ships, they would say more. Nevertheless, he was sure that the greatness of their peril would force the Huguenots to consent to the occupation of Havre and Dieppe. Concerning the Vidame Killigrew declared to Dudley: "I leave you to judge what case this man is in... We may, therefore, the more assuredly deal with him and believe that for aid and succour he would do anything ... which he did not let to say unto me."[4]

[1] *Ibid.*

[2] J. Bruce ed., *Correspondence of Robert Dudley, Earl of Leicester, during his governorship in the Low Countries* (Camden Society publication), London, 1844, p. 375. (hereafter: Bruce).   [3] P.R.O. S.P. 70/40 f. 338.   [4] *Ibid.*

On the following day (7th August) he heard rumours of a conspiracy in Havre against the Vidame which had probably been organized by an anti-English faction in the town, and of an imminent attack by the Catholic forces without. The Vidame told him that his presence did more harm than good and urged him to return to Dieppe to hasten the English ships and to ask the Captain of Dieppe to send reinforcements to him.

Killigrew departed from Havre the same afternoon in a fishing boat. During the journey a storm arose of such violence that he almost despaired of his life. To save themselves he and the other passengers were compelled to throw overboard the mast and all their baggage. They reached Dieppe on the 9th, but the storm had still not abated, and boat and passengers nearly perished at the entrance to the harbour. Writing to Cecil the following day, with the memory of his harrowing experience still fresh in his mind, Killigrew said: "I was never in danger before the like to be compared." [1]

He spent four days in Dieppe in consultation with the Protestant leaders. Here also he eloquently besought the Huguenots to realize their complete dependence on his sovereign for aid, and the necessity of making her some good offer in return. Apparently they believed that Sir William Woodhouse's fleet was to bring troops for their relief, and Killigrew encouraged this belief in order to induce them to yield to the demands of his government.[2]

The English ships appeared off the Normandy coast about the 15th of August. Woodhouse held conferences with the garrison commanders at Dieppe and Havre, but in accordance with his instructions he put no troops ashore or took any warlike action on behalf of the Huguenots. But the ground work for the occupation of these towns had been laid, and Killigrew returned to England with the fleet to await the conclusion of negotiations to this end in London.[3]

At the end of August an agreement was reached between the Huguenot commissioners and the English government by

[1] *Ibid.*   [2] *Ibid.*   [3] *Ibid.*, f. 368.

which the Queen was to send 6000 men to garrison Havre and to aid in the defence of Rouen and Dieppe. The agreement further stipulated that she would advance one million crowns as a loan to Condé. Havre was to remain in English hands until the restitution of Calais.[1] The following month preparations were under way for the despatch of an army to Normandy, and before the end of September a fleet was ready to sail from Portsmouth.

Then word came suddenly that the Prince of Condé had forbidden the entry of English troops into Havre without his express permission.[2] This action was prompted by Elizabeth's refusal to abide by the treaty she had signed. Because of the violent reaction in France to news of the Anglo-Huguenot alliance and of the intended occupation of Havre the Queen drew back. She refused to allow her soldiers to go to the aid of Rouen, which was now under siege, or even to advance beyond Havre and Dieppe. The Huguenot leaders had expected that when the English army arrived in Normandy it would give them active assistance in the field. Naturally they regarded Elizabeth's decision as an outright betrayal, an attempt to use the alliance with them simply as a means of appropriating French territory.[3]

The position of the Protestants at Havre was so critical, however, that it was almost certain that they would ignore Condé's orders and admit the English forces upon their arrival. Nevertheless, the English government was determined to remove all doubts on the matter or, as Cecil expressed it, "to obtain a probability to receive us if we would enter." [4]

The accomplishment of this important task was entrusted to Killigrew. At the end of September, just as the fleet was preparing to set sail for Havre, he made another secret journey over

[1] P.R.O. S.P. 70/40 f. 403.
[2] Cecil to Challoner 11th October, 1562. B. M. Cotton MSS. Vespasian VCII, f. 224-6.
[3] Forbes, vol. 2, pp. 64-5.
[4] B. M. Cotton MSS., Vespasian VCII, f. 224.

to that city to learn the attitude of its Huguenot defenders towards their English allies and obtain the 'probability' that the army would be allowed to land.

As an enthusiastic supporter of his fellow Protestants in France, Killigrew was eager to take part in the Normandy enterprise. Early in August he had requested Dudley for some type of military assignment "in this cause that toucheth your service and my country so near," and he reminded him of his past experience as a soldier.[1]

Killigrew's Protestant zeal was excited by the opportunities which lay at hand, and he hoped that an opening would be found for his capacities in war as well as diplomacy. On his departure from England at the end of September he took with him five light horsemen whose wages and equipment were paid out of his own pocket.[2] Killigrew's hopes were not disappointed, for he soon found his soldierly talents put to a stern test.

On arriving at Havre he discovered that the garrison was desperate for English aid. Word of the proposed landings in Normandy had caused the Catholic leaders to divert their forces from Orleans in order to meet the new threat from the west. Armies under Guise, the King of Navarre, and the Constable Montmorency were now battering at the walls of Rouen, and the Protestants at Havre and Dieppe knew that its capture would be followed by attacks upon themselves. They were, therefore, only waiting for the arrival of the English before sending troops to its aid.[3]

A delay in the arrival of the fleet, however, was having an ill effect on the morale of the soldiers in Havre. Although their commander had refused great offers from the Queen-mother if he would refuse entry to English troops, Killigrew could not vouch for the constancy of the garrison if the fleet did not soon make an appearance. He warned Cecil: "All my policy cannot

[1] P.R.O. S.P. 70/40 f. 315.
[2] B. M. Lansdowne MSS. 106 f. 31.
[3] P.R.O. S.P. 70/42 f. 541.

assure the people here because they do not hear from you nor from Portsmouth since I came hither." [1] To Sir Adrian Poynings, commander of the English forces, he wrote: "Tell your soldiers that unless they make speed the French will eat their victuals." [2]

In anticipation of the coming of the army Killigrew kept himself occupied with a variety of activities. He informed Cecil—perhaps with a certain humourous resignation—that he had now become a kind of factotum; a purveyor of lodgings for the soldiers, a stower of victuals, even a sheep keeper.[3] Such were the humble tasks which could fall to the lot of a diplomat in the Queen's service!

On 8th October, 1562, at 3 o'clock in the afternoon the English fleet carrying the first contingent of 1500 men dropped anchor in the roadstead of Havre and was joyfully received by the garrison and inhabitants of the town.[4] The successful entry of Poynings was due in part to Killigrew's diplomacy, and the measure of his enthusiasm over this achievement is reflected in a letter he wrote to Cecil on the same day. It breathes the very spirit of militant Protestantism and suggests the writer's impatience with Elizabeth's niggardly and dilatory policy towards her Huguenot allies.

"Besides," he said, "The Queen's Majesty is bound in honour, a penny spent now will save three. You have a good and true foundation to work upon. God prosper you as he has begun, and inspire her Majesty to build up the temple of Jeruselum. Her fame is great, and if her good will be to her power ... no doubt it lieth within her hand to banish idolatry out of this realm." He concluded: "You will think me over holy for a soldier; indeed, I received the communion this day amongst a great number of Christian soldiers who be of that opinion." [5]

---

[1] *Ibid.*
[2] *Ibid.*, f. 543.
[3] Forbes, vol. 2, p. 83.
[4] *Ibid.*, vol. 2, p. 88.
[5] P.R.O. S.P. 70/42 f. 571.

Prior to the arrival of the English forces Killigrew had promised the governor of Havre that he would take part in the expedition which the latter intended to send to the relief of Rouen.[1] The Cornishman now found an opportunity to redeem his promise. Although Poynings had no authority to use his troops in such an enterprise he finally gave way to the appeals of his allies and agreed to send 200 men. The total force consisted of about 400 soldiers; half were English under the command of Thomas Leighton, and half were French commanded by Killigrew.[2]

Leighton was a Worcestershire gentleman, a professional soldier who later held the governorship of the Isle of Guernsey. Like Killigrew he became a staunch Puritan and a follower of Robert Dudley. Also like Killigrew he served Elizabeth throughout a long career in both a diplomatic and military capacity.[3] Another officer on the expedition to Rouen was the pirate, Henry Strangeways, who had sailed with Thomas and Peter Killigrew during Edward VI's reign.[4]

[1] *Ibid.*, f. 541.

[2] *Ibid.*, ff. 582–3.

[3] John E. Neale, *Elizabethan House of Commons*, London, 1949, p. 295.

[4] Service in the English navy under Mary afforded Strangeways a brief flirtation with respectability, but he was an engaging rogue who could never stay out of trouble for long. Soon after Elizabeth's accession the Privy Council sent letters to the port authorities at Southampton requiring them to detain him and a companion named Wilsford who, it had been reported, were planning to sail from England with the intention of seizing an island of the King of Spain. With calm effrontry the two men presented themselves to the Privy Council at Westminster. They virtuously declared that they only intended to go to the seas as merchants. Oddly enough, their word was accepted, and they were allowed to proceed on their voyage. The councillors soon discovered their mistake, for Strangeways promptly crossed over to Normandy where he resumed his piratical operations against English shipping. Within a few months, however, he was captured and thrown into prison. But the Queen's government found itself unable to dispense with the services of a skilled seaman, and his ability in this respect was doubtless the reason for his selection for the Normandy expedition of 1562. Harbison, p. 316 footnote 44. *Acts of the Privy Council, 1558–1570*, pp. 9, 97. P.R.O. S.P. 70/5 ff. 425, 435. P.R.O. S.P. 70/7 f. 691.

On 8th October the Anglo-Huguenot relief force set out from Havre.[1] Its journey was one of extreme danger since Rouen lay over fifty miles to the east, and most of the intervening countryside was in the hands of the enemy. For this reason the soldiers travelled up the Seine in boats. No doubt because of his expertness as a navigator Strangeways was put in charge of directing the vessels up the river.[2]

Their progress was unimpeded until they reached Caudebec eighteen miles west of Rouen. Here half the river had been staked so that the boats were compelled to pass close to the shore beside the town, and the occupants suddenly found themselves set upon by enemy troops. From the shore a deadly hail of gun shot poured upon the ships killing and wounding a large number of their passengers.

According to the report of an English soldier who had taken part in the enterprise, the first boat, which was occupied by his countrymen, managed to get away and the next one, in which were Killigrew and a number of Huguenot soldiers, also escaped.

Three other vessels, however, were not so lucky. They were being towed by Frenchmen under the direction of Strangeways. Floundering helplessly in the water, the French became panic-stricken under fire and cut the ropes, leaving the ships to drift into shore where they became stuck in the sand and their occupants captured by the enemy. Strangeways was badly wounded in the battle at Caudebec, and though rescued by a small boat, he died on the way to Rouen.

Among those captured were a number of Englishmen, eleven of whom were hanged from a tree by order of the Constable Montmorency. This incident was a grim fortaste of the treatment that was to be meted out to Englishmen who fell into the hands of the Catholic forces.[3]

[1] P.R.O. S.P. 70/42 f. 596.
[2] P.R.O. S.P. 70/43 f. 731.
[3] *Ibid.* The expedition in which Leighton and Killigrew took part was apparently only the first of three that attempted to reach Rouen. According

When Killigrew, Leighton, and the other survivors reached Rouen they found its defenders in desperate straits. Shortly before their arrival Mount St Catherine, the principal defensive bastion to the southeast of the town, fell to the besieging army.[1] From its summit the enemy sent cannon fire directly into the ranks of the besieged. Outnumbered, exhausted, and despairing of succour, the garrison was on the verge of surrender. The arrival of the Anglo-Huguenot force, however, gave them new heart and enabled the town to fight on. Leighton's troops played an especially gallant rôle in its defence. A witness to the battle later said that only the English had pikes, and that they showed themselves at one section of the walls after another in order to make the besiegers believe that there were armed men in every part of the town.[2]

But the odds were too great. On the 26th of October two assaults were repelled during the morning; in the second the enemy succeeded in entering Rouen but were driven out again by Leighton's men. A third assault delivered in the afternoon burst through a large breach in the walls and swept triumphantly into the town. English troops, who had defiantly planted their ensigns in the breach, were in the very forefront of the defence and bore the full fury of the attacking army. Many were cut down where they stood fighting valiantly to the last. Eighty wounded survivors, however, had their throats cut and their bodies stripped and cast into the river, for Guise

to the Venetian ambassador in Paris, the troops were divided into three groups; the one which succeeded in getting through to Rouen was the vanguard. The other two were either destroyed or turned back by hostile forces. *Calendar of State Papers, Venetian, 1558–70*, pp. 345–6. Sir Thomas Smith, the newly arrived English ambassador in France, said that the number of English in Rouen was 600, but an English soldier, who was in town during the siege, reported that there were only 200, and this figure is confirmed by Killigrew's memoir. Howard, p. 187. "News sent out of France by Sir Thomas Smith," P.R.O. S.P. 70/46 f. 662. Forbes, vol. 2, pp. 165–8.

[1] P.R.O. S.P. 70/42 f. 603.
[2] P.R.O. S.P. 70/43 f. 731.

had given order that all the English taken "should pass the sword." [1]

Killigrew had been shot in the foot by an arquebus during the first assault, and when Rouen fell on the same day, he was lying in a lodging within the town with a Huguenot officer who had both legs blown off. This was a moment of fear and mortal danger for Killigrew. Rouen was now filled with drunken riotous soldiers of the victorious army who threw themselves wholeheartedly into an orgy of looting, murder, burning and rape—the usual aftermath of a successful siege in sixteenth-century warfare. They were especially eager to find any Englishmen whose throats had not already been cut.

Disabled by his wound Killigrew could neither defend himself nor attempt to escape, and he was soon discovered by Captain Causin, a gentleman of the horse to the Duke de Longueville. Probably only the fact that Killigrew was an officer and a man of some station kept his captor from despatching him on the spot. No doubt another consideration entered his mind—a person of Killigrew's standing might be able to raise a substantial ransom to obtain his release. At any rate, Causin had him removed from his lodgings and placed in the Castle of Rouen—the place where Joan of Arc had been imprisoned before her execution in 1431.[2] There he found himself in the company of Thomas Leighton who had also been taken prisoner when the town fell. They were almost the only Englishmen who received reasonable treatment as prisoners of war. Of the other survivors, about twenty in number, nearly all were condemned to serve as galley slaves.[3]

But Killigrew's peril had not yet passed. Early in November his younger brother, William, came over from England with instructions from Cecil to learn of his condition. William discovered from a Frenchman who had escaped from Rouen that soon after his capture, Henry had been sent for by the

[1] *Ibid.*
[2] P.R.O. S.P. 70/44 f. 780.
[3] *Ibid.*, f. 766.

Queen Mother, Catherine de Medici, who had been present at the siege. Thereupon he was taken to her on horseback still suffering great agony from his wound. For a time, in fact, it seemed likely that his leg would have to be amputated—an operation which, in the primitive state of surgury, would probably have resulted in his death.[1]

When Killigrew arrived at the court the Duke of Guise declared his intention of having him put to death, saying that he was one of those who had deserted his country unknown to his Queen.[2] Probably there was a deliberate irony in Guise's words, for it was generally believed in France that the English-men in Rouen had been sent on Elizabeth's order. By the standards of his time Guise was not an inhumane man, but he and most his countrymen—Protestants as well as Catholics— regarded the English as interlopers who were taking advantage of the dissensions in France by seizing its territory. Moreover, Elizabeth had publicly disavowed any warlike intentions against France, and the English attempt to relieve Rouen had been made without her official sanction. From the French point of view, therefore, those who had taken part in this enterprise had no claim to protection under the laws of war.

Killigrew only escaped the fate of most other Englishmen because of the intervention of D'Anville, son of the Constable Montmorency. D'Anville's action appears to have been the result of his friendship for Lord Robert Dudley, Killigrew's patron and protector.[3] The same motive doubtless explains his kindness to Thomas Leighton.

Killigrew's brush with death had been so close that for a short time it was believed in England that he had been killed, and there was something almost ghoulish in the way certain English officials—including his friend, Robert Dudley—began to bid for his profitable office in the Exchequer until the fact of Killigrew's survival had been established.[4]

[1] *Ibid.*, f. 780. P.R.O. S.P. 70/48 f. 84.
[2] *Ibid.*, ff. 780, 798.
[3] *Ibid.*, f. 780.   [4] Forbes, vol. 2, pp. 143, 155.

Following D'Anville's intervention he was transferred to the Castle of Merlou in Picardy where he remained in D'Anville's charge until the following spring. During this period he was well treated and allowed communication with his friends in England, though the Constable at first wished to see him hanged.[1]

This brutal old warrior would have taken great pleasure in seeing Killigrew dangling from a gibbet. He must have remembered him as a friend and agent of that troublemaker, Sir Peter Carew, in Queen Mary's reign, and as the man sent by the English government in February, 1559, to create difficulties for himself and other members of the French delegation at Cateau-Cambrésis. Probably only the fact that Killigrew was in the custody and under the protection of his son, D'Anville, prevented the Constable from satisfying his wish.

A letter which Killigrew wrote to Cecil during his captivity in Picardy reveals a man who is fully aware of his good fortune merely to be alive. Although he describes himself as a "poor lame soldier" he wastes little time in bewailing his present plight or past suffering. Indeed he claims that the strictness of his confinement during the first weeks of imprisonment, though it then seemed rigorous, proved beneficial to his recovery in the long run. The enforced inactivity assisted the restoration of his strength and the healing of his wound. He also expressed appreciation for the kindness with which he had been treated by D'Anville to whom he owed his life.

There was another matter of greater personal concern that was now weighing on his mind. How would the Queen and her councillors receive him when he was permitted to return to England? Would Elizabeth bear ill-will towards him because he had taken part in an enterprise which she had forbidden, and still worse, which had failed? Of course, in so far as the English were responsible for the fall of Rouen, a heavy share of the blame rested upon the Queen herself. But Killigrew naturally ignored that point, and in order to justify his own

[1] P.R.O. S.P. 70/48 f. 84.

conduct, he felt obliged to find some other more convenient object of censure.

Excusing his failure to write before he said: "If my silence hath bred any scruple in any of those I owe duty unto, I require humbly that that they will suspend their judgement until I may answer by mouth or by writing. I mean touching my journey to Rouen and the service done there. Although the town was not saved thereby, I trust it shall appear that if more lives had been spent more honour and commodity would have followed. If they of Dieppe had kept their countenance, by themselves' own confession the Prince (of Condé) had won Paris..."[1]

In criticizing the defenders of Dieppe for the capture of Rouen and for the failure of Condé's campaign Killigrew was not only blaming the Huguenot garrison, but also by implication Edward Ormsby and the 600 English troops under his command who had been sent to Dieppe at the same time that Poynings had occupied Havre. He evidently believed that if those at Dieppe had come to the relief of Rouen in support of the 400 brought by himself and Thomas Leighton, the town might have been saved. However, in view of the size of the besieging army, it seems unlikely that a few hundred more soldiers could have turned the scales.

On the other hand, it is true that some of the English at Dieppe behaved badly. Throckmorton reported that while England had won much honour at Rouen, those at Dieppe were not so well spoken of, and Ormsby himself admitted that a large number later deserted and sold their weapons and armour in ale houses and villages.[2] But he and his men were in an extremely dangerous position. Many of the French soldiers and civilians in Dieppe wanted to save their own skins by making terms with the government, and they regarded their English allies with barely concealed hostility. In the event of an attack Ormsby believed that his troops had more to fear

[1] P.R.O. S.P. 70/46 f. 981.
[2] Forbes, vol. 2, p. 192. P.R.O. S.P. 70/45 f. 867.

from their backs than from the enemy. Moreover, not long after their arrival in the town, the citizens of Dieppe opened negotiations for peace with the French government.[1]

Under these circumstances he felt that his first duty was to keep his slender forces intact. When Briquemault, one of the Huguenot officers, asked him to have some of his men join with part of the garrison in an expedition to relieve Rouen, he refused until he knew the outcome of the negotiations then in progress. Two hundred French soldiers were despatched from Dieppe, but their attempt to reach Rouen ended in failure, and the majority were killed or captured. As soon as the gallant Briquemault received word of this disaster, he lost not a moment's time. Waiting only for the first favourable wind he boarded a ship and set sail for England.

Ormsby had this to say about his late and unlamented comrade-in-arms: "We thank God we be rid of him as one whom few or none could have any good opinion, both for that he was so timorous and likewise so overthrown with every blast of evil news as his face and looks could not but inform his fear, by which means the common people were brought into great fear and muttering." [2] A week after Brique-mault's departure, at the end of October, the citizens of Dieppe made peace with the enemy on favourable terms. They had not the stomach to risk the terrible fate that had overtaken their fellow Protestants in Rouen a few days before. Under the terms of the treaty the English contingent commanded by Ormsby was compelled to withdraw to Havre.[3]

Whatever the true measure of blame that may be justly allotted to the English at Dieppe, it was less than honourable for Killigrew to protect himself by impugning the courage of his own countrymen. This, however, is a small example of the lengths to which even a normally upright man was prepared to go in order to keep himself in the Queen's favour. But he need not have worried. Throckmorton had already sent to her

---

[1] P.R.O. S.P. 70/43 f. 673.
[2] *Ibid.*   [3] *Ibid.*, f. 726.

a report of his valiant conduct at Rouen.[1] Moreover she herself was prepared to accept a portion of the blame for the capture of the town. When Dudley, by way of breaking the news of its fall, suggested that prompter and more forthright action might have prevented the disaster, Elizabeth startled him by a remarkable display of remorse. She confessed her sorrow that she had not behaved more frankly and sent aid while there was still time. As to Poynings, who had despatched the ill-fated relief force without her consent, she said that she only blamed him for sending so few men. His blame, she added, would have been as much for 200 as for 1000.[2] Very likely this rare mood of self-reproach can be attributed in part to the fact that she was at that moment recovering from a virulent attack of smallpox which had nearly taken her life.

Killigrew's well-wishers in Scotland and France as well as England worked hard to secure his freedom. A few weeks after his capture at Rouen his brother, William, informed Cecil that the governor of Havre had a prisoner by the name of Pecquillon, the son of Mary Stuart's Master of the Household, whom he was willing to exchange for him.[3] This plan fell through because Killigrew was not considered a man of sufficient rank to be traded for the son of a high officer in the household of the Queen of Scotland.[4]

Members of the Protestant party in that country, however, had not forgotten his service to their cause, and it was through their exertions that his release was finally obtained. When Maitland of Lethington visited France in the spring of 1563 he brought a letter which he had secured from Mary to D'Anville requesting his freedom.[5] At the same time William Killigrew arrived at the French court with a letter from Lord Robert Dudley to the Prince of Condé asking his assistance in obtaining Henry's liberation from captivity. Finally Killigrew was

[1] *Ibid.*, f. 716.
[2] Forbes, vol. 2, p. 155.
[3] P.R.O. S.P. 70/44 f. 780.
[4] P.R.O. S.P. 52/8 f. 16.   [5] *Ibid.*

allowed to depart for England at the end of May, but not before he had paid a considerable sum in ransom and had given an explicit promise not to return to France until the end of the war.[1]

Killigrew never forgot the part he played in England's unsuccessful gamble for the recovery of Calais. Ten years later, at the end of the memoir of his services to Elizabeth, he wrote: "I had almost forgotten that which I had most cause to remember, for it yet doth stick by me; I mean the dangerous and painful travels I endured about the service of Newhaven (Havre), both before it was ours and after, whither I made many a voyage, and at length put Mr Poynings in possession conveying with 200 Englishmen under the conduct of Mr Leighton, 200 Frenchmen to the aid of Rouen by which means Newhaven was preserved..."

With soldierly pride and a consciousness of services well and bravely performed he concluded: "Although the sequel of that journey (the failure to recover Calais and the loss of Havre in July, 1563) were not so happy, yet I trust my person and services not to be misliked. At the least I am sure the French doth think me worthy of some remembrance who ever since have thought more of me than there was cause." [2]

During the five years following his return from France Killigrew's diplomatic activities were concentrated primarily in Scotland.[3] In the spring of 1566 he was sent to Edinburgh to

---

[1] Pepys MSS. Preserved at Magdalene College, Cambridge, vol. 1, f. 75. P.R.O. S.P. 70/56 f. 666. In a letter written to Sir Thomas Challoner shortly after his return from France, Killigrew says that it was only through the Laird of Lethington that he gained his freedom. P.R.O. S.P. 70/58 f. 792. In his memoir Killigrew stated that to obtain his release he had to pay a ransom of "200 and 4." Howard, p. 187. The denomination of this sum is not given, but it was probably either English pounds or French crowns. Whether in pounds or crowns a ransom of this amount must have been a heavy burden for a man of Killigrew's modest means.

[2] Ibid.

[3] In the spring of 1564 Killigrew accompanied Lord Henry Hunsdon to Lyons for the ratification of the Treaty of Troyes. Pepys MSS. vol. 2, f. 525.

protest to Mary against the secret aid given to Elizabeth's rebellious subjects in Ireland.[1]

At the moment of his departure on this mission, Scotland was passing through one of its periodic crises. David Rizzio, Mary's Italian favourite, had just been brutally murdered in her presence by a band of conspirators of whom her own husband Darnley was a principal member. Heavy with child and reeling under the shock of this terrible episode, Mary nevertheless managed, with an amazing show of courage and resourcefulness, to regain control of the government. She won over her weakling husband, and escaping with him by night from Edinburgh, placed herself at the head of an army and drove her enemies out of the country. Having betrayed his former associates in order to regain his wife's favour, Darnley succeeded only in winning her hatred when they in turn revealed that he had been a prime mover in Rizzio's murder. It now remained for him to await the vengeance which his betrayals had earned.

While Killigrew was travelling through Berwick into Scotland he heard that Mary had given birth to a son. Shortly after his arrival in Edinburgh he was taken to see the child. Killigrew was the first Englishman to set eyes upon the future King of England and Scotland. With his usual meticulous attention to detail he reported that he had seen James "as good as naked, that his head, feet and hands were well proportioned, and that he seemed "like to prove a goodly prince." [2] These observations on James's physical normality immediately after birth are ironic in view of the deformity which he afterwards showed. In later life James's weak legs, his awkward shambling gait, aroused the pity and laughter of his contemporaries.

Killigrew's dealings with Mary and her councillors left him with a reasonably favourable impression concerning the prospects of continued amity between his country and Scotland. He saw no evidence that active measures were being taken on

[1] See Killigrew's instructions: P.R.O. S.P. 52/12 f. 72.
[2] *Ibid.*, f. 76.

behalf of Catholic malcontents in England or that assistance
was to be given to the Irish rebel, Shane O'Neil.[1]

Nevertheless the keen eyes of the English diplomat detected
signs of trouble beneath the surface tranquillity at the Scottish
court. Although Mary had effected an outward reconciliation
with Darnley and his family since the assasination of Rizzio,
Killigrew observed: "Methinks—there is small account made
of them." Even more significant was his comment on the Earl
of Bothwell. "It is thought," he said, "that his credit with the
Queen is greater than all the rest together."[2] But even the most
prophetic observer could hardly have forseen that in less than
a year's time Mary would cast her fortune and reputation to the
winds and marry her husband's chief assasin.

Killigrew returned to Scotland in March, 1567, three weeks
after the murder of Darnley. He carried a letter from his
sovereign which eloquently entreated Mary to clear herself of
the suspicions arising from her husband's death by taking
prompt action against his murderers.[3] That one of the primary
objects of his mission was to discover the extent of the Scottish
Queen's complicity in the crime is indicated by the detailed
report he made of her appearance and reactions during his
interview with her at Holyrood. His letter to Cecil was brief,
factual, and wholly devoid of emotion. How much more
vividly Throckmorton might have described such an episode.
Yet the professional detachment of Killigrew's account cannot
hide the fact that his meeting with Mary on this occasion was
one of the most dramatic confrontations of the period.

Because the windows were half-closed, he wrote, the room
was so dark he was unable to see Mary's face. By her words,
however, she seemed grief-stricken and expressed her gratitude
at Elizabeth's kind letter.[4] The English diplomat informed Mary
of the general belief that Bothwell was one of the murderers of

[1] *Ibid.*, f. 90.
[2] *Ibid.*, f. 76.
[3] P.R.O. S.P. 52/13 f. 17.
[4] *Ibid.*, f. 19.

Darnley and secured from her a promise that he would be put on trial.[1]

Fifteen years later, in an account of his embassies to the Scottish Queen, Killigrew described Mary's conduct after Darnley's death in terms that reflect fairly accurately the judgement of historians. He recalled that when he was sent to Scotland in March, 1567, he "had no other instructions than from her Majesty's own mouth, but they were so loving and kind that her natural mother, I think, if she had then been alive could have shown no more sorrow for her estate nor care to preserve her honour than her Majesty did; which, if she had followed in effect as she had promised to have done, I believe verily that she had not fallen into the great calamity that since befell her in neglecting so wise and princely counsel, for had she dealt bona fide in bringing the Earl of Bothwell to his trial, who was the suspected murderer of her husband, which was her advice she should do to any whomsoever in Scotland, the sequel had not, in all likelihood, happened to her that has done since…" [2]

The most important event in Killigrew's personal life during these years was his marriage to Catherine Cooke in November, 1565.[3] Catherine was the daughter of the distinguished scholar and statesman, Sir Anthony Cooke, whom Killigrew may have known at the court of Edward VI and later when they were exiles in Germany during Mary's reign. This marriage increased Henry's stature both as a courtier and diplomat by bringing him into alliance with several of the chief families of the Elizabethan governing class.[4] Of Catherine's three elder sisters, Mildred was married to Sir William Cecil, the Queen's leading

[1] P.R.O. S.P. 59/12 f. 851.

[2] P.R.O. S.P. 53/12 f. 85.

[3] *Notes and Queries*, vol. 11, p. 17.

[4] In December, 1571, when he was ambassador at the French court, Killigrew wrote to Cecil: "I have put the Queen Mother in good hope of my sovereign's good affection which she seemeth to believe, the rather at my mouth, seeing I was allianced, as she said, with them that knew best her mind." P.R.O. S.P. 70/12 f. 1384.

minister; Anne was married to Sir Nicholas Bacon, the Lord Keeper; and Elizabeth: first to the ambassador, Sir Thomas Hoby, Killigrew's travelling companion in Italy in 1549, second to John, Lord Russell, the son of Francis Russell, second Earl of Bedford.

Like her sisters Catherine received an excellent education in the best Renaissance Humanist tradition. She was said to be proficient in Latin, Greek, and Hebrew.[1] In addition she could turn a clever hand at poetry when the mood was upon her. Like her sisters also Catherine was a woman of forceful character and strong Puritan convictions. Among her acquaintances were noted scholars and men of learning. They included the Cambridge Puritan reformer, Edward Dering, the Scottish Presbyterian leader, Andrew Melville, and the historian, William Camden.[2]

Henry and Catherine were a devoted couple whose ties of

[1] George Ballard, *Memoirs of several ladies of Great Britain who have been celebrated for their writings or skill in the learned languages and sciences*, Oxford, 1772, p. 202. In his will dated 1st June, 1576, Sir Anthony Cooke left two volumes from his library to Catherine, one in Latin and one in Greek. Somerset House, Prerogative Court of Canterbury, 1 Bolein. (hereafter: PCC.)

[2] See Dering's letters to Catherine in Edward Dering, *M. Dering's works. More at large than ever hath been here-to-fore printed in any one volume*, (containing a sermon preached at the tower of London, XXVII godly and comfortable letters, a brief and necessary catechism, and godly and private prayers), 4 parts, James Roberts for Paule Linley and John Flasket, London, 1597, pp. 36-8. Catherine's friendship with prominent English, Scottish, and French Calvinist clergymen was noted by John Stow in his *Survey of London*. He stated that in the church of St Thomas the Apostle there was a "very fine', neat and well contrived monument, but without any date, in which verses were inscribed to Catherine by three Puritan divines; the Scotsman, Andrew Melville, the English Presbyterian, William Charke, and Robert Formanus, pastor of the French reformed church in London. John Stow *A survey of London and Westminster containing the original antiquity, modern estate and government of these cities written at first in the year MDXCVIII*, vol. 3, London, 1720, pp. c 3-5, 7-8. See also: Camden's epitaph to Catherine Killigrew in which he praises her knowledge of Greek and Latin. B.M., Additional MSS., 36, 294, f. 43b.

affection were strengthened by the intensity of their Protestant beliefs and by their common academic attainments. There is no doubt that Catherine gave considerable assistance to Killigrew's career, for she was prompt to enlist on her husband's behalf the favour of her sister, Mildred, and of her brother-in-law, Sir William Cecil.[1]

Killigrew showed constant concern for Catherine's welfare. Out of his slender resources he purchased from the crown a life annuity of £100 for her.[2] The hazards of the diplomatic profession caused Henry to fear that his life might suddenly be cut short and his wife and family left in poverty, and he made every effort to protect her against such a contingency. In March, 1569, as he was about to set out on a long trip to Heidelberg through country filled with bands of pillaging mercenary soldiers, Killigrew wrote rather pathetically to his friend, Robert Dudley, now Earl of Leicester: "I pray your good Lordship to be kind unto my poor wife if God call me in this journey." [3] Four years later, when requesting Cecil's assistance in securing the manor of Lanrake from the crown, he earnestly entreated him: "I beg your Lordship to have pity on me and the state of my poor wife and children in my extreme need." [4]

Catherine showed an equal degree of concern for her husband's safety and well being. On learning in January, 1573, that Killigrew's duties as ambassador in Scotland were likely to involve him in military operations against Edinburgh Castle she confided her fears to Cecil. When he received word of Catherine's anxieties from Cecil, Killigrew wrote to him: "I have written my wife to quiet her, most humbly thanking

[1] In November, 1582, shortly before her death, Catherine wrote to Cecil: "I have understood very lately from Mr Killigrew how it hath pleased your Lordship to—condescend to my bold and humble suit of granting to my husband the preferment of the piece of the third part of the lands lately grown unto her Majesty at his suit—." P.R.O. S.P. 12/155 f. 97.

[2] P.R.O. C. 66/1048, part 4, m. 9.

[3] Pepys MSS., vol. 2, f. 227.

[4] P.R.O. S.P. 52/25 f. 4.

your Lordship for us both and for your goodness to us." [1]

With her strong character and wide learning Catherine was doubtless a formidable personality. Possibly she also possessed the less attractive Puritan traits of severity and prudery—the Spanish ambassador, Feria, called her sister, Mildred Cecil, "an intolerable blue stocking." [2] But Catherine had too a feminine gentleness and humour that is revealed in a poem she sent to Mildred upon receiving the unwelcome news that Henry was about to be sent abroad. She wrote: "If Mildred, by thy care, he be sent back whom I request. A sister good thou art to me, yea better, yea the best. But if with stays—thou keepest him still or sendest where seas may part. Then unto me a sister ill, yea worse, yea none thou art. If to Cornwall he shall please, I peace to thee fortell. But Cecil, if he to seas, I war denounce Farewell."[3]

Unfortunately there is no record as to when this wifely petition was made or what success it had. Perhaps it was written in the autumn of 1571 when Catherine was expecting a child and her husband was about to be sent to France on a diplomatic mission. In January, 1572, Killigrew wrote from the French court at Blois an urgent appeal to Cecil for his recall because, as he said, "My wife draweth near her time and therefore hath great need of me..." [4]

It is a tribute to Killigrew's astuteness as a courtier that he was able to maintain during a long career his close friendship with Robert Dudley, Earl of Leicester, without sacrificing the intimacy he had established with the Cecil family through his marriage to Catherine Cooke. Initially, Cecil opposed their marriage, and this opposition seems to have engendered ill feeling between himself and Killigrew. In April, 1564, Sir

[1] P.R.O. S.P. 52/24 f. 17.
[2] C.S.P. Spanish, 1558–1567, p. 18.
[3] Thomas Fuller, *The history of the worthies of England endeavored by Thomas Fuller, first printed in 1662. A new edition with a few explanatory notes by John Nichols in two volumes,* vol. 1, 1811, p. 348.
[4] P.R.O. S.P. 70/122 f. 48.

William noted in his diary: "Easter Day H. Killigrew wrote to me an invective for my misliking of his marriage with my sister, Cooke." [1] It is unfortunate that this letter has perished since it would afford a refreshing contrast to the courtly discretion which fills most of Henry's letters to Elizabeth's chief councillor.

The reason for Cecil's hostility to Killigrow's marriage at this time is unknown, but one would suspect that it was due to the latter's well known liking for the Earl of Leicester. A sharp division between Leicester and Cecil had existed since the time when Leicester's marriage to Elizabeth had first been mooted. Thereafter they differed frequently on matters of public policy, especially as Cecil grew more nationalist and conservative in the 1570s and as Leicester rose to the leadership of the Protestant faction in the Council.

On this vital question of national policy Killigrew's support was firmly behind Leicester, but Cecil also opposed Leicester's influence because he feared that the Queen's favourite would use his power and patronage to advance his personal friends at court. In April, 1566, Cecil drew up a list of reasons designed to prove the inadvisability of Leicester's marriage to Elizabeth. One of the reasons given was that Leicester "shall study nothing but to entice his own particular friends to win to offices, to lands and to offend others." He then set down a list of eighteen such friends, and Killigrew was named as one of them.[2] Whatever disagreements existed between Killigrew and Cecil on this score they do not appear to have lasted. For the greater part of Elizabeth's reign Killigrew looked to Cecil for friendship and favour, and events proved that his confidence was not misplaced.

[1] Haynes, vol. 2, p. 755.
[2] Haynes, p. 44.

CHAPTER V

MISSION TO THE PALATINATE, 1569

I N the winter of 1568–9 Killigrew and his wife paid a visit to their land in Cornwall. The day after their homecoming a courier arrived suddenly with a message from the Queen summoning him back to court.[1] On his return he learned that upon recommendation of his friend, the Earl of Leicester, Elizabeth had appointed him ambassador to the Protestant princes of Germany.[2] Her instructions directed him to Heidelberg where he had opened negotiations for an Anglo-German league ten years before. The purpose of the mission was to discuss proposals which had been put before the English government by a Dr John Junius on behalf of Frederick III, Elector of the Palatinate.[3]

The Elector's envoy made two requests: first, that Elizabeth join his master and other Protestant princes of the Empire in an alliance for the defence of their religion, and second that she either loan or extend credit for the sum of 100,000 crowns to enable Frederick's son, John Casimir, to lead an army into France and the Netherlands in support of the Protestant factions in those countries.[4] Although the Queen was not disposed to

[1] Howard, p. 186.

[2] In a letter to the Earl of Leicester on 6th April, 1569, Killigrew reminds his friend that he was the cause of his being sent on the mission to Germany. Pepys MSS. vol. 2, f. 257.

[3] The negotiations between England and the Protestant princes in 1569 are treated in Moritz Ritter, *Deutsche Geschichte im Zeitalter der Gegenreformation und des Dreiszigjährigen Krieges*, (1555–1569) *im Bibliothek Deutscher Geschichte herausgeben von jh. v. Zweidineck-Suedenhoff*, Stuttgart, 1889, pp. 419 ff. (hereafter: Ritter). Friedrich von Bezold ed. *Briefe Des Pfalzgrafen Johann Casimir mit verwandten Schriftstücken*, Brunswick, vol. 1, pp. 48 ff.

[4] Killigrew's instructions, 26th January, 1569. B.M., Cotton MSS., Galba B. XI, f. 309. Junius to Elizabeth (n.d.) B.M. Cotton MSS., Galba B. XI, f. 309.

close with these offers immediately she acceded to his petition that an English ambassador be sent back to Heidelberg with him for their further consideration. When Junius departed for Germany in February, 1569, Killigrew was selected to accompany him.

Killigrew's mission to the Palatinate took place at a moment when his government faced the worst domestic and foreign crisis since the opening of Elizabeth's reign. At home a dangerous coalition of discontented Catholics, conservative nobles, and opportunist politicians was taking form. One of the aims of this group was the overthrow of the Queen's chief minister, William Cecil. Its fundamental intention was to bring about the destruction of that governmental and social structure which Elizabeth and Cecil had successfully worked for during the past ten years—a strong, centralized Protestant monarchy that drew primary support from the gentry and middle classes.

The conspirators, moreover, looked for assistance from Spain and France, and they were actively assisted in their plans by foreign Catholic agents. For the realization of their plan to reestablish Catholicism in England many supporters of the old religion centered their hopes on Mary Stuart who was now held in custody by Elizabeth since her flight from Scotland the previous year.

Abroad Protestantism was also on the defensive and threatened with extermination. In France the Third Religious War had broken out. Catholic armies, with the assistance of troops sent by the Duke of Alva, made ready to crush their Huguenot opponents. In the Netherlands Spanish control was complete. William the Silent's army had been driven headlong out of Brabant and its leader, a discredited and penniless refugee, forced to flee in disguise to escape death at the hands of his unpaid mercenaries.[1]

For her own part Elizabeth would not willingly spend a

[1] Cecily Veronica Wedgwood, *William of Nassau, Prince of Orange, 1533–1584*, London, 1956, pp. 110–111. (hereafter: Wedgwood, William of Nassau).

single farthing or the life of a single English soldier in the
interest of the French and Dutch Calvinists. But she realized
that a complete victory by the Catholic party in France would
result in the ascendancy of the Guise faction which had not
renounced its intention of enforcing the claims of Mary Stuart
to the English throne by armed conquest.

On the other hand, if the Duke of Alva was allowed to
consolidate his power in the Netherlands there was a great
likelihood that the Low Countries would eventually become a
base from which an invasion army could be launched against
England. At this very moment Despés, the Spanish ambassador
in London, was making every effort to foment a revolution
on behalf of the Scottish Queen and to win the support of
Philip and Alva for his designs.[1]

These dangers caused Elizabeth to revive the policy of inciting discord in the dominions of her Catholic neighbours.
Her government sent money, munitions, and ordinance to the
besieged Huguenot garrison at La Rochelle. Similar assistance
was also sent to the Netherlands while ships of the Dutch Sea
Beggars obtained arms and supplies in English ports. In the
meantime agents of the Prince of Condé, of William of Orange
and other German princes such as the Elector Palatine and
Wolfgang, Duke of Zweibrücken (sometimes called Biponts),
were present at Elizabeth's court urging her to lend financial
support to military action from Germany in the cause of the
French and Dutch Protestants.[2]

Like their English co-religionists German Protestants feared
that the Catholic powers were about to embark on a crusade
for their destruction. They believed that the French would soon
send an army over the western borders of the Empire while

---

[1] C.S.P. Spanish (1568–1579), p. 83 ff.

[2] Bertrand De Salignac De La Mothe Fénélon, Ambassador De France en
Angleterre De 1568 à 1575, Correspondence Diplomatique, Publié Pour La
Première Fois sur les Manuscrits conservés aux Archives du Royaume, Tome
Premier Années 1568 et 1569, (A. Teulet, ed), Paris et Londres, 1838, pp. 45–6.
(hereafter: Fénélon).

Alva would either send supporting forces to their assistance or, when he had secured his position in the Netherlands, attack them directly from his vantage point in the Low Countries.[1]

Of the leading Protestant princes in the Empire only the Calvinist Elector, Frederick of the Palatinate, was prepared to take effective political and military measures in order to meet this threat. This intelligent and enlightened prince possessed a crusading religious zeal that was entirely lacking in most Lutheran statesmen. He firmly believed in the existence of a concerted plan on the part of the Papacy and other Catholic powers to destroy Protestantism, and that survival necessitated the creation of a universal alliance among all those professing the reformed faith.

Within the Empire he stood forth as the leading advocate of 'German liberties', and as an opponent to the authority of the Hapsburgs. Unlike many of the Lutheran princes he placed no trust in the Emperor or in the institutions of the Empire as guarantors of peace in Germany. The Imperial constitution, he regarded as a mere facade behind which the Catholics plotted the destruction of their enemies. Throughout 1568 and 1569 the Elector Palatine patiently sought to win the Lutheran princes to an alliance for the preservation of the Protestant religion and to overcome their reluctance to confederation with England.[2]

Frederick was not content to limit his policy to defensive ends alone. During the Second Religious War he had provided the financial backing which enabled his son, John Casimir "the knight errant of the Protestant cause," to bring an army of mercenaries to the support of the Huguenots. In the autumn of

---

[1] According to Fénélon, the envoys of the German princes told Elizabeth and her councillors that they had two reasons for allying themselves with the Protestant rulers of Germany—first, because of their common religion and second, because of their mutual need to drive the Spaniards from the Low Countries. The German ambassadors pointed out that once the Spanish had established control in this area they would be in a position to molest both England and the Protestants of Lower Germany. *Ibid.*

[2] Ritter, pp. 413-4.

1569 he loaned money for a new army to be raised by the Duke of Zweibrücken. A few months later, when Killigrew and Junius were on their way to Heidelberg, this mercenary freebooter, a fanatical Lutheran, was marching with a force of 17,000 men into France to do battle in the cause of French Calvinism. In his espousal of alliances with Protestant powers outside Germany Frederick laid the foundation of future Palatinate policy which half a century later drew Germany into the vortex of a great international conflict.[1]

Elizabeth possessed none of the Elector's evangelist enthusiasm and she distrusted the practicability of some of his far reaching plans. Nevertheless, she believed that the schemes of Frederick and his son might be usefully employed to further her interests. The presence of Casimir's army in France was a decisive factor in gaining for the Huguenot party favourable terms at the Peace of Longjumeau.[2] It now seemed possible that his forces might again have some effect in weakening the power of the extremist faction in the French government. Moreover, one of the aims of Casimir's proposed enterprise, doubtless included to engage the self interest of the Queen and her advisors, was the recovery of Calais for England.[3]

In the Anglo-German negotiations of 1569 commercial motivations played as important a rôle as those of politics or religion. Two months before Killigrew set out on his mission the growing hostility between England and the Spanish government in the Netherlands reached a climax when Alva closed Antwerp to English trade.[4] Now compelled to establish a new outlet for its commodities the Merchant Adventurers turned its attention to north Germany. In February, 1569, preparations were under way to send a great fleet of

---

[1] *Ibid.*, Bezold, vol. 1, p. 49.
[2] Ritter, p. 416.
[3] B.M., Cotton MSS., Galba B. IX, f. 295.
[4] Richard Ehrenberg, *Hamburg und England im Zeitalter der Königin Elizabeth*, Jena, 1896, pp. 102, 107 ff. John William Burgon, *The life and times of Sir Thomas Gresham*, London, 1839, vol. 2, pp. 317 ff.

twenty-eight ships laden with cloth and wool to Hamburg.[1]

The English government directed Killigrew, before proceeding further on his mission, to inform the merchants and city authorities of Hamburg concerning the fleet that was soon to set sail for their port and to prepare the way for its arrival by cementing good relations between his country and the merchants of the city. He was also to ascertain the probability of an attempt on the part of the Spanish government to intercept the fleet on its way to Germany.[2] A considerable portion of the commercial wealth of London had been invested in this enterprise, and the enemies of England knew that the destruction of the ships would be a blow of major importance.[3] Such a setback to its vital export trade in wool and cloth might compel the Queen to make humiliating terms with the Spanish King rather than face economic ruin.

The Hamburg venture also had an important bearing on the political negotiations in Germany. By agreement with the London merchants the government planned to use the money realized from the sale of the cloth for its loans to Zweibrücken and Casimir.[4] Elizabeth also intended that the proposed Anglo-

[1] Fénélon, vol. 1, p. 200.

[2] There is no mention in Killigrew's instructions of such directions governing his dealings in Hamburg, but his subsequent conduct in that city indicates that they must have been transmitted to him verbally by the Queen or members of her Council.

[3] Fénélon estimated the value of the cargo to be between 400,000 and 700,000 crowns. Fénélon, vol. 1, p. 200. Ehrenberg said that even if the envoys of France and Spain greatly exaggerated in their reports that half or even the entire fortune of the London merchants was sunk in the enterprise, the destruction of the fleet would have been a heavy loss for England, in addition to the disastrous effect on public morale. Ehrenberg, p. 108. See also the urgent appeals of Despés to Alva and Philip to take measures for the interception of the fleet. On the 27th of February, 1569, he wrote to Alva: "—to take this fleet is to take all England—" C.S.P. Spanish, 1568–1579, pp. 135–6.

[4] On 30th April, 1569, Fénélon reported that there was a plan in Hamburg to put a large sum of money in the hands of Killigrew from the sale of wool and cloth. A few weeks later he said that these funds were to be used

German league should be employed as a weapon of economic retaliation against Spain. Killigrew was ordered to make as an essential condition of the alliance that the Kings of Denmark and Sweden, as well as the Duke of Holstein and the powers bordering on the Baltic coast should be included.[1] Though the intention is not explicitly stated in his instructions, it seems probable that the Queen wished to secure an agreement among the Baltic powers to exclude Spanish trade from this area.

Killigrew and Dr Junius set sail from Harwich on 18th February, 1569.[2] During their voyage to Hamburg the two diplomats got first hand experience of the perils of the north German trade route. To make matters worse the winter of 1569 was one of the coldest of the sixteenth century.[3] Shortly after midnight on their first day at sea, they were struck by a violent northerly gale and almost driven onto the coast of Holland. The ship was driven so close to shore that at the point of greatest danger, the leadsman sounded a depth of just five fathoms. Destruction was only averted by the sudden veering of the wind, an event which Killigrew characteristically attributed to the intervention of divine providence. To Cecil he wrote: "God, I trust, favoureth the service whereunto I am appointed, did by a larger wind deliver us from thence..." They reached Heligoland a few days later and were informed by the inhabitants that they ought to thank God that they had come to this island rather than to have attempted to reach the Elbe directly, for the river was more completely frozen than at any time within living memory.[4]

The Cornishman and his companion then chartered a small

---

to raise troops to fight against the Duke of Alva. The French ambassador also reported a great effort by the Protestants in London to raise 200,000 talers in Germany for Zweibrücken's army. Fénélon, vol. 1, pp. 368, 387.

[1] B.M. Cotton MSS., Galba B. XI, f. 296.

[2] B.M. Cotton MSS., Nero B. IX, f. 106. Pepys MSS., fol. 2. f. 227.

[3] This information was given to me by Dr D. Justin Schove who is making a study of the history of climates.

[4] B.M. Cotton MSS. Nero B. IX. f. 106.

craft and set out for the mainland. With great difficulty and personal danger they had to cut their way through the ice in order to reach the opposite shore. Stopping briefly at the town of Ritzebüttel near the mouth of the Elbe, they crossed over the ice clogged river and pushed on toward Hamburg. The weary travellers reached their destination at last on 6th March.[1]

Killigrew received a warm welcome from the city authorities who offered him every possible assistance on his journey.[2] Concerning the reception of the wool fleet he informed Cecil: "Our merchants here do report that the lorde of this town be glad of the coming of our ships and will be ready to pleasure our nation in that they may conveniently." He added that he found no evidence that Alva was making plans to stop English traffic with Germany. In Hamburg and the surrounding country he discovered a general attitude of friendship towards his nation and was certain that the Queen could raise a loyal force of mercenaries in this region.[3]

Having successfully laid the diplomatic foundation for England's commercial venture in Germany, the English ambassador departed for Heidelberg, on the 12th of March, a journey of over 400 miles.[4] Travel was difficult at any time at this period, but especially so in the winter of 1569 when the countryside was swarming with mercenary soldiers.[5] Killigrew and his companion, Dr Junius, were twice nearly waylaid by bands of looting *reiters* (German mercenaries). Near Luneburg

---

[1] *Ibid.*

[2] *Ibid.*

[3] B. M. Cotton MSS., Nero B. IX, f. 111. English merchants had been settled in Hamburg since the conclusion of a commercial treaty between the Merchant Adventurers and the city in April, 1568. Ehrenberg, p. 109.

[4] P.R.O. S.P. 70/106 f. 182.

[5] On 11th March, 1569, Killigrew informed Cecil that "this discharge and cassing of soldiers and horsemen doth fill these parts with so many needy persons as the ways be very dangerous, and of necessity do force Mr Junius and me to spend the longer time on our journey ..." B. M. Cotton MSS., Nero B.IX, f. 111.

they had a narrow escape from cavalrymen in the pay of the Duke of Alva. On their way to Brunswick, passing through country so densely wooded that it reminded Killigrew of the wildest part of Windsor forest, they had a close brush with some disbanded troops of the Prince of Orange. Fortunately the Protestant rulers of the cities along their route—Luneburg, Brunswick, Cassel, and Frankfort—provided them with escorts for their further journey. After many delays the two ambassadors arrived at Heidelberg on the last day of March.[1]

The English envoy spent his first night at the house of Junius, and when the Elector learned of his arrival a generous allotment of wine was sent from the court.[2] Early the following morning, having provided himself with a fair horse and a white footcloth, he went to the Elector's residence in the company of Junius and several gentlemen from the court.[3] On the steps of the palace he was formally received by Frederick and John Casimir. After delivering commendations and letters from his sovereign he delivered a brief address summarizing the two proposals which Junius had brought to England and asked whether it concurred with their intentions. The Elector and his son signified that Killigrew's statement was in general conformity to their meaning. They then retired to a chamber within the palace for a private conference with Dr Junius, and, a short time later, Duke Casimir reappeared. He informed the English ambassador that several days would be required before a complete exposition of their views could be made. In the meantime, he begged Killigrew to avail himself of the hospitality of the court.[4]

In fact, nearly two weeks elapsed before he received the promised statement. Killigrew did not possess authority to conclude any agreement with the Elector Palatine or the other German princes. According to the precise and detailed instruc-

[1] P.R.O. S.P. 70/106 f. 182. Pepys MSS., vol. 2, f. 257.
[2] Hatfield MSS., vol. 4, f. 122.
[3] P.R.O. S.P. 70/106 f. 182.
[4] *Ibid.*

tions which the Queen had given him he was first to make a thorough assessment of Frederick's proposals and his capacity to put them into effect. Only then was he to indicate the conditions that would be necessary to win Elizabeth's assent.[1]

When these preliminaries were completed he had to transmit the full details of his negotiations to London and await the final decision of his government. Killigrew found the limitations placed upon his freedom of action extremely frustrating, but they indicate the doubts which the Queen entertained concerning the capabilities of the German princes.[2]

While waiting for the Elector's reply the Cornishman had a most pleasant sojourn at his court. "I cannot learn," he wrote to Cecil, "that any ambassador has been so much honoured as the Queens' Majesty's at this court."[3] He certainly felt the highest regard for Frederick whose Calvinist piety and advocacy of the Protestant cause were in complete accord with his own outlook. For companionship he had the Elector's two sons, John Casimir and Christopher. He probably found particular pleasure in the company of Duke Casimir, a bluff hearty young fellow, twenty six years of age who, as Killigrew informed Cecil, "for military affairs is accounted the flower of Germany."[4]

Angling, no doubt, for an offer of English money, the Duke told the Queen's ambassador that he had a force of 6,000 mercenaries in constant readiness for action.[5] Despite his loud professions of Calvinist zeal and eagerness to strike a blow on behalf of his afflicted Protestant brethren, Casimir was a typical German soldier of fortune—an irresponsible egoist whose reli-

---

[1] B. M. Cotton MSS., Galba IX, B.XI, ff. 297.

[2] Killigrew hoped that once he had laid the ground work for an agreement an ambassador would be sent over to Germany in his place with power to conclude a formal treaty. Killigrew to Leicester 11th May, 1569. Pepys MSS., vol. 2, f. 281.

[3] P.R.O. S.P. 70/106 f. 182.

[4] Bezold, vol. 1, p. 13.

[5] Pepys MSS., vol. 2, f. 257.

gious enthusiasm thinly concealed a ruthless greed for power and land. [1]

The pleasure of Killigrew's visit at the Elector's court was dampened by the receipt of unwelcome news. On the day he reached Heidelberg word came of the Huguenot defeat at Jarnac and the murder of Condé.[2] Soon afterwards a Huguenot agent named de Lambres came to him with the complaint that money, which was expected from England for the Duke of Zweibrücken, had not yet arrived.[3] The English diplomat knew that the Huguenots were in great need of support, and that lack of funds threatened to impede the progress of the mercenary force that was marching to their assistance. A mutiny might break out among Zweibrücken's unpaid soldiers, or the French government might succeed in its efforts to buy off the Duke, thereby causing him to desert his Huguenot allies.[4]

On the 10th of April Killigrew received the first detailed statement of the Elector's proposals.[5] After waiting a few more days to see whether he had anything further to say, Killigrew gave him a full exposition of Elizabeth's views. With respect to the question of an alliance between England and the Protestant princes he recalled the unhappy results of previous efforts by his sovereign to form a union for the defence of their

---

[1] Ritter, pp. 413–4.

[2] Hatfield MSS., vol. 4, f. 123.

[3] Pepys MSS., vol. 2, f. 257. The Huguenot leader, Cardinal Chatillion, who had recently fled to England, was endeavouring to secure a loan from its government for the assistance of Zweibrücken's army. For three months de Lambres had been waiting in Heidelberg for the arrival of the money which he planned to deliver to Zweibrucken. E. G. Atkinson, "The Cardinal Chatillion in England". Proceedings of the Huguenot Society in London, (1889–91), vol. 2, pp. 226–7. See also: Chatillion's letter to Frederick III of 10th June, 1569, excusing his failure to send the promised money. August Kluckhohn ed., *Briefe Freiderick der Frommen, Kurfursten von Pfalz mit verwandten Schriftstuüken gessamelt und bearbeitet*, vol. 2, first half, 1567–1572, Braunschweig, 1870, pp. 334–5. (hereafter: Kluckhohn, vol. 2.)

[4] On 16th May Killigrew wrote to Leicester that the French king "will leave nothing undone to agree with Biponts." Pepys MSS., vol. 2, f. 281.

[5] Hatfield Mss., vol. 4, ff. 129–30.

common religion. "As often," he said, "as her Majesty calls to mind how coldly ... many German princes had shown themselves in this cause, so often has she despaired of any good result so that, at my departure, she had not decided anything certain about the forms and conditions pertaining to it." Nevertheless, in Elizabeth's opinion, the proposed confederation ought to include such princes as Augustus of Saxony, the Duke of Zweibrücken, Württemberg, and Brunswick, the Landgrave of Hesse, and others of the most powerful Protestant rulers as well as those whose dominions lay on the Baltic sea-coast.

As to the matter of a subsidy for Casimir's army, the English ambassador asked the Elector to give the names of adequate and valid sureties or forms of bonds to insure repayment of the money after the termination of the war.[1] Frederick's reply on these points was by no means satisfactory from the view-point of the Queen's government, as Killigrew was quick to realize. There was no essential difference of opinion concerning the composition or nature of the confederation—it was to be a defensive union which would include the Baltic powers. However, realizing the difficulty of securing the adhesion of several of the Lutheran princes, the Elector declared himself ready to accept an alliance that would consist of only four or five of the leading rulers.[2]

Before a final decision could be reached concerning the details of the proposed union Frederick told the English ambassador that it would be necessary for him to take the matter up with Augustus of Saxony.[3] The Elector of Saxony was the most powerful and influential Lutheran prince in the Empire, and Frederick knew that without his concurrence the confederation was doomed to failure. Like most of his fellow Lutherans Augustus had hitherto been hostile to the idea of a Protestant alliance, particularly to any that included foreign powers.

[1] Killigrew gave the Elector a written transcript of his speech in Latin. B.M. Cotton MSS., B.XI, ff. 341–3.

[2] Kluckhohn, vol. 2, pp. 305–6.

[3] *Ibid.*, p. 306.

Since the summer of the preceding year Frederick had worked hard to gain the friendship of the Elector of Saxony. His efforts had been so successful that a treaty had been concluded for the marriage of Augustus's eldest daughter with the Elector Palatine's son, John Casimir.[1] Augustus even appeared favourable to an Anglo-German league.[2] Frederick now proposed to send Casimir and a councillor named Ehemius to Dresden to win the Elector's formal assent to the confederation. When this essential step had been achieved Casimir and Ehemius were to enlist Augustus's influence for the purpose of securing the support of the other princes.[3]

In the meantime, the Elector Palatine directed Killigrew to return to Hamburg and there await news of the outcome of the negotiations in Saxony.[4] From Hamburg he could more quickly communicate the results to his government. Another reason for cutting short the English ambassador's stay in Heidelberg was Frederick's fear that his presence might arouse suspicions among the other powers in the Empire. He knew that the Catholic states in Germany and in the rest of Europe were concerned over his dealings with England, especially as to information that subsidies from Elizabeth were to be used to send his son into France and the Netherlands at the head of a mercenary army. He was probably also aware that some of the other Protestant rulers were almost equally opposed to this military aspect of his plans. Unlike Casimir Frederick was not a warlike man. In the past he had kept his support for foreign military enterprises clothed in secrecy, for his country lacked the power and resources for war, and he had no wish to expose himself openly to the wrath of his enemies.[5]

The Elector's attitude was a wise one from his own point of

[1] Bezold, vol. 1, p. 55. Ritter, p. 419.
[2] Killigrew's notes from a letter of the Elector of Saxony to Frederick III. Hatfield MSS., vol. 4, ff. 129–30.
[3] Hatfield MSS., ff. 129–30.
[4] Ibid., f. 129. P.R.O. S.P. 70/107 f. 229.
[5] Bezold, vol. 1, pp. 50–1. Ritter, p. 417.

view, but it was unfortunate from that of the English ambassador. Killigrew knew that Frederick's methods would entail further delay at a time when the Protestant cause was in great danger. They might also alienate Elizabeth and make her suspect Frederick's sincerity and firm intentions. Equally unfortunate was the Elector's attitude concerning the subsidy. He gave no guarantees for the repayment of the loan to be advanced upon English credit, and Killigrew realized that this was an extremely damaging omission.[1]

Yet, he felt not the slightest doubt concerning Frederick's honest intent in the negotiations with his government. He told Cecil: "For aught I can see there is no prince that meaneth more plainly or more Godly than his Grace doth; wherefore if things fall out not so substantially as your honour looketh, the lack thereof is rather to be assigned to the weakness of his ministers or want of deep discourse than to any lack of sincerity in his Grace who desireth, by all possible means, to advance God's glory and relieve the poor afflicted of France and Flanders... whereof he spareth not himself, his children and his credit".[2]

The requested subsidy, Killigrew wrote, was to enable Casimir to raise an army and lead it to the support of Zweibrücken. He also reported that the sum which Frederick asked was less than a third of that named by his ambassador, Junius.[3] The English ambassador departed for Hamburg on the 18th April in the belief that he had secured offers which merited favourable consideration from his government.[4]

Soon after his arrival in that city early the following month he sent home a full account of his negotiations. Emphasizing the subsidy as the point most important to the success of his

[1] Killigrew informed Cecil on 23rd April that in regard to repayment of the loan there was "no assurance—but the common good that may grow to the common cause by levying a new army under Casimir who both has men and a good colour to lead them into France for want of a month's pay." P.R.O. S.P. 70/106 f. 207.

[2] P.R.O. S.P. 70/107 f. 229.

[3] Hatfield MSS., vol. 4, f. 130.

[4] P.R.O. S.P. 70/107 f. 229.

mission he said: "If her Majesty could forbear 20,000 pounds I think it would be well employed as also to serve great purpose for the surety of the Protestants in France. Duke Casimir will be ready to march by midsummer. To avoid suspicion Duke Casimir goeth to the Elector of Saxony to understand his inclination to the league. Upon his return he plans to march into such parts of France where he thinks good may be done. His purpose is not to return until liberty of religion be granted, the Duke of Alva and the Spaniards sent into Spain and Calais restored to England." If the Queen, he wrote, wished to disburse money for the furtherence of Casimir's enterprise she should have it sent by an agent appointed for that purpose.[1]

When he had despatched this message Killigrew settled down to await an answer from his government. His hopes for a favourable response were greatly enhanced by the arrival of letters from the Earl of Leicester. The Earl informed him that money would be sent with the cloth fleet for the support of Zweibrücken's army. Killigrew immediately transmitted this information to the Elector Palatine, to his councillor, Ehemius, and to Casimir.[2]

On the 24th of May the long awaited fleet arrived at Hamburg, as Killigrew said, "not a little welcome to them of this town."[3] Since early spring its sailing had been delayed by rumours of hostile preparations on the Dutch coast and by contrary winds. But the reports of Killigrew and other agents at last persuaded Elizabeth that there was no real danger from attack, and the merchant ships finally sailed from Harwich escorted by a squadron under the command of Admiral Winter.[4] Lacking explicit orders for action from his dilatory master, Alva could only look on in impotent rage as they

[1] *Ibid.*
[2] Kluckhohn, vol. 2, p. 320. Pepys MSS., vol. 2, ff. 281, 293. Haynes, pp. 515–6.
[3] Haynes, p. 515.
[4] Fénélon, vol. 1, pp. 227, 272, 300, 368, 387. Ehrenburg, p. 108.

travelled unmolested along the coast of Holland.[1] The safe passage of the fleet to Hamburg was a great moral and material triumph for England and a lost opportunity for Spain.

Under the inspiration of this happy event Killigrew penned these glowing words: "I think the Queen's Majesty be more feared this day of all countries what religion soever they be of, than ever any of her ... predecessors before her... I beseech God her Highness do hold fast, and then I doubt not to see in her days the ancient honor and fame of England restored to the glory of God."[2]

Killigrew's preparations in Hamburg bore good fruit, for the English fleet found eager buyers for its merchandise among the merchants of the city, and when the ships returned to England three months later they carried a cargo worth 100,000 pounds.[3] Despite the commercial success of the voyage the arrival of the fleet brought bitter disappointment to the English ambassador because neither money nor credit came with the ships for Zweibrücken's army. The assurances which he had sent to the Elector Palatine and others on this matter had been falsified, and he could now ask himself how much value the German princes would place in his word or that of his superiors in the future. Moreover, the fact that the money did not arrive raised doubts in his mind as to whether the English government intended to give serious backing to his negotiations.

Killigrew's letter to Leicester on the 26th of May reflects the mind of a disillusioned and bewildered man. He suspected that responsibility for withholding the money lay with Elizabeth, and he was unable to understand her failure to act. He believed that the Queen never had better means or opportunity to strike at England's enemies, than at the present time, and concerning

---

[1] Alva told Despés that without explicit orders from the King he could not make an overt act of aggression. Kervyn de Lettenhove, *Relations politiques de l'Angletterre sous le règne de Philippe II. Publiées par M. le baron Kervyn de Lettenhove, 1882–1900*, tome 5, pp. 58 ff., 375.

[2] Haynes, p. 516.

[3] Ehrenburg, p. 110.

her apparent hesitation to do so, he asked: "I wonder what should be the cause, for in France the Protestants were never stronger, and the princes (of Germany) never more inclined to aid them in Flanders, the Duke of Alva nothing strong nor has any ships at all in readiness ... to annoy you unless it be with countenance, which your Lordship knoweth is peculiar to the Spaniard though he were ready to yield the ghost, and if that amaze you what shall they think that did depend chiefly upon your proceedings and would gladly join with you to send both him and his unto Spain again? I must confess unto you that your honour's first letters did not a little consort me to write to the Count Palatine and others what hope I was in of your good answer..., but when Monsieur de Vezines arrived in the ships and brought neither money nor credit from the Cardinal (Chatillion) I was struck dumb. God knoweth how much more it may hinder the common cause than it hath done already. These Almayne princes cannot abide to be mocked nor their soldiers bear with it. It is sufficient to make them rebel against the Duke of Deuxponts and revolt to the King (of France)." [1]

Killigrew's view of the international situation was very different from that of his sovereign. At the time of his departure from England Elizabeth had seemed ready to bid defiance to the hostile forces arrayed against her. She had confiscated the treasure of the Spanish King, and she had given considerable assistance to the rebellious subjects of Charles IX. By the beginning of March, 1569, English provocations drove the French government to issue a warlike ultimatum through its ambassador in London.[2]

Then came news of the Huguenot defeat at Jarnac. With unrest stirring in her own country Elizabeth did not wish to risk open conflict with a victorious French monarchy supported, in all probability, by the King of Spain. Members of the pro-war faction in the government contended that the ancient jealousy between France and Spain would prevent them from

[1] Pepys MSS., vol. 2, f. 293.
[2] Fénélon, vol. 1, p. 219 ff.

uniting against England, but the Queen stood firm. Twice
during a meeting of the Council, Fénélon reported, she ex-
claimed vehemently: "I don't want war!" [1]

As a result of this decision Elizabeth naturally became more
reluctant to accept the danger of supporting the dissident forces
in France and the Netherlands. Moreover, in the spring of 1569,
such assistance seemed less urgent from her point of view.
Despite the setback at Jarnac and the death of Condé, the
Huguenot forces fought on under the far abler leadership of
Admiral Coligny. Inspite of the lack of English subsidies, Zweibrücken's reiters had not revolted. In May his army crossed the
Loire after hard fighting and joined forces with the Huguenots. [2]

The Queen did not desist from giving secret encouragement
to the Protestants, but she became more cautious and critical in
her attitude towards them. This attitude was reflected in her
dealings with the German princes. On 31st May she wrote to
Killigrew in response to his communications from Hamburg.
After praising the diligence and circumspection he had shown
in his negotiations she said: "We perceive that however the
Palsgrave is in our devotion earnestly bent to further the cause
of religion, yet he hath not satisfied us by his answer to you on
the great matters which were the principal cause of your
writings." As to the question of the subsidy for Casimir, her
only comment was that he would learn of her pleasure on this
matter from Cecil. [3]

Killigrew deplored the consequences of Elizabeth's failure to
intervence more decisively on behalf of her co-religionists. He
believed that the dangers threatening the Protestant cause had

[1] *Ibid.*, pp. 321–2.

[2] It is not clear whether the Duke ever received either money or credit
from Elizabeth. Ehrenburg says that assurances for repayment supplied by
the English government made it possible for a loan to be raised from
German merchants for the support of Zweibrücken's army. Ehrenburg,
p. 110. On the other hand, Cardinal Chatillion stated in September, 1569,
that Wolfgang had let his troops into France without receiving any money
for his soldiers. Kluckhohn vol. 2 p. 335.

[3] P.R.O. S.P. 70/107 f. 241.

not been lessened by recent events, and to confirm his fears he discovered that mercenaries were being levied for the Duke of Alva in the country around Hamburg. He warned Cecil and Leicester that England could only win German agreement to the league if money was provided for Casimir's army. Despite his earlier experience in 1558–9 he placed for too much trust in the capacity of the princes for common action.[1]

Since the middle of May he had been waiting for the conclusion of the Palatinate negotiations in Saxony. Although the councillor, Ehemius, had been in Dresden for over a month working on behalf of the Anglo-German league little had yet been accomplished. The Elector Augustus showed a cooperative spirit in the enterprise, but completion of the correspondence with the other princes involved much delay.[2] Finally, at the end of May Killigrew went to Magdeburg for a conference with Ehemius and then accompanied him to Dresden to take a hand in the negotiations.[3]

In an effort to speed matters up the English diplomat suggested to Frederick that, as a preliminary step to the formation of the confederation, he, the Elector of Saxony, the Elector of Brandenburg, and a few other of the leading princes should reach an understanding with the Queen of England.[4] Acting on this advice the Elector Palatine recommended that a joint letter be sent to Elizabeth signed by himself and the Electors of Saxony and Brandenburg expressive of their desire to make an alliance with her. This would prove to her the sincerity of their intentions, and the other rulers might then be expected to follow their example.[5] Frederick's proposal was rejected, however, because the Elector of Brandenburg was unwilling to act without first consulting the other Protestant princes. The Elector Palatine thereupon suggested the convening of an

[1] Haynes, p. 516. Pepys MSS., vol. 2, f. 293.
[2] Kluckhohn, vol. 2, p. 320 ff.
[3] P.R.O. S.P. 70/107 ff. 242.
[4] Kluckhohn, vol. 2, p. 329.
[5] *Ibid.*

assembly of the princes to decide upon a reply to the Queen's offer of alliance.[1] The acceptance of this recommendation proved to be the death blow of the Anglo-German league.

On the 8th September the question of the confederation with England was submitted to the consideration of a convention of Protestant Estates at Erfurt. Though strongly supported by the representatives of the Elector Palatine the league was rejected by the delegates of the other princes. In a letter to Elizabeth the princes gave as the reason for their decision the fact that they found in the Religious Peace a sufficient guarantee for their safety, and that they did not wish to give the Catholics any cause for distrust or counteralliance.[2] Behind the polite phrases lay the narrowly parochial outlook and the Imperial loyalties of the Lutheran rulers. Their hostility to alliance with England was strengthened by suspicion of its Calvinist and Zwinglian religious tendencies.[3] Events had therefore justified the doubts of Elizabeth, and falsified the optimism of her ambassador concerning the political capacities of the German princes.

Throughout the summer of 1569, Killigrew continued his efforts for the despatch of an army under Casimir into France. In London La Mothe Fénélon, the French ambassador, heard frequent reports that a sum of 40,000 pounds was to be placed in the hands of the English ambassador to pay Casimir's mercenaries. Although Fénélon later said that the full amount had been supplied, and that Killigrew himself was to accompany the army, Casimir's troops did not make their expected descent into France.[4] When Killigrew returned to London in September he was reported to have expressed complete satisfaction with the results of his negotiations.[5]

Fénélon quickly perceived the lack of substance behind these claims. Killigrew, he believed, had by no means achieved the

[1] *Ibid.*, pp. 350–1.
[2] Bezold, vol. 1, pp. 58–9. Ritter, pp. 423–5.
[3] Kluckhohn, vol. 1, p. 351 ff.
[4] Fénélon, vol. 2, pp. 13, 94, 109–10, 147–8, 196–8.
[5] *Ibid.*, p. 245–6.

success of which he boasted, nor did the Queen feel any real confidence in the support of the German princes.[1] Elizabeth was certainly ready to encourage belief in her close ties with them and to foster rumours of impending attacks by German armies to intimidate her enemies, but she had no intention of provoking retaliation from France or Spain or of squandering money in support of the high flown schemes of the Heidelberg princes.[2] Perhaps the only concrete result of Killigrew's negotiations was that he had found for his sovereign a willing servant in John Casimir. In return for English subsidies Casimir was later to wield a trusty sword in Elizabeth's cause on the battlefields of France and the Netherlands.

When Killigrew returned to England in September, 1569, the country hovered on the verge of revolution. Thomas Howard, Duke of Norfolk, had renounced the rôle of the Protestant patriot in which Killigrew had known him at the time of Monluc's embassy to Scotland. Norfolk never gave up his allegiance to the Protestant faith, but his political sympathies lay with the conservative nobility of the North. Through personal ambition he had allowed himself to be drawn into a conspiracy directed against the Protestant establishment and against the rule of the 'new men' of humbler origin which was embodied in the person of Sir William Cecil. This counter-revolutionary conspiracy, supported by the connivance of the Spanish and French ambassadors in London, sought a Catholic restoration through the marriage of Norfolk to Mary Stuart, and recognition of the Scottish Queen as Elizabeth's lawful successor.

During the spring and summer of 1569, while Killigrew was in Germany, the plans of the conspirators were gradually brought to completion. In September, however, Elizabeth suddenly called the Duke's hand by summoning him to court to answer for his actions. After a momentary hesitation Norfolk's nerve collapsed. Instead of joining forces with the

[1] *Ibid.*, p. 246.
[2] Fénélon, vol. 2, p. 336.

Northern Earls, who were only awaiting his signal to raise the standard of revolt, he tamely submitted to the Queen's command and was imprisoned in the Tower.

In connection with these events Killigrew's memoir contains an interesting comment. He says that he discovered "some part of the Duke of Norfolk's conspiracy." [1] No confirmation of his statement can be found in other sources, but it is not unlikely that he had a share in uncovering evidence concerning Norfolk's activities after the latter's imprisonment in October, 1569. Killigrew's role in this episode is a forecast of his diplomatic assignments in France and Scotland following the discovery of Norfolk's second conspiracy two years later.

[1] Howard, p. 186.

CHAPTER VI

"THE GREAT MATTER",
EMBASSIES TO FRANCE AND SCOTLAND,
OCTOBER 1571–NOVEMBER 1572

URING the "Years of Crisis," 1568–75, Killigrew moved forward to the front rank of the English diplomatic service.[1] About forty years of age at the end of the first eleven years of Elizabeth's reign, his advance in the Queen's service had been slow. Apart from the embassy to Heidelberg in 1569 he had held no diplomatic posts of great importance. By this time, however, he was widely regarded as a skilled and able hand at negotiation who was especially well qualified for service in France. In the autumn of 1567 Sir Nicholas Throckmorton suggested to Cecil that an envoy be sent to deal with the Huguenots. He wrote: "The aptest and ablest man I can think to take this journey at this time and to carry himself discreetly and sufficiently upon all events is Mr Henry Killigrew." [2]

Two years later Henry Norris gave him a strong recommendation for appointment as his successor to the resident ambassadorship at the French court.[3] Killigrew's opportunity did not come until October, 1571, when the Queen chose him to take the place of his good friend, Francis Walsingham, who had succeeded to Norris's post the previous year.[4] Walsingham was

---

[1] J. B. Black, *The reign of Elizabeth, 1858–1603, The Oxford History of England*, (G. N. Clark, ed.) Oxford, 1936, p. 87.

[2] P.R.O. S.P. 12/44 f. 23.

[3] P.R.O. S.P. 70/110 f. 565.

[4] On 20th October, 1571, Elizabeth wrote to Walsingham: "We have sent our trusty servant, Henry Killigrew—whom we know to be a faithful friend unto you." On the same day Burghley wrote to the ambassador: "You know my brother so well and love and trust him so entirely, as I think none could come more grateful to you." Sir Dudley Digges, *The*

temporarily incapacitated by illness, and Killigrew acted as chargé d'affaires until his recovery in February. The Cornishman then joined him and Sir Thomas Smith in the negotiations which resulted in the Treaty of Blois.[1]

As in the case of many English Protestants, the old animosity towards France had now been partially replaced in Killigrew's mind by hostility towards Spain.[2] A common fear of Spanish dominance in Europe brought a gradual rapprochement between England and France. The entente, as conceived by Walsingham and other supporters of the new policy, was to be strengthened by marriage between Elizabeth and a member of the House of Valois.

Support for an Anglo-French alignment greatly increased

---

compleat ambassador or two treaties of the intended marriage of queen Elizabeth of glorious memory comprised in letters of negotiations of Sir Francis Walsingham, her resident in France, together with the answers of the Lord Burghleigh, the Earl of Leicester, Sir Thomas Smith, and others. Wherein, as in a clear mirror, may be seen the faces of the two courts of France and England as they then stood and with many remarkable passages of state, not all mentioned in any history, London, 1655, pp. 145–6. D. Stählin suggests the possibility that Walsingham and Killigrew acted together in the plan to induce the Earl of Devon to join Dudley and the other English refugees in France in the spring of 1556. However, there is no evidence to support this hypothesis except the fact that Killigrew and Walsingham seem to have been in Italy at the time. Though Walsingham was a Marian exile there is nothing to indicate that he had any part in the activities of Killigrew and his associates. Dr Karl Stählin, *Sir Francis Walsingham und seine Zeit*, Vol. I, Heidelberg, 1908, p. 106 footnote 3. At any rate, they knew one another early in Elizabeth's reign. In April, 1560, Thomas Randolph asked Killigrew to commend him to Francis Walsingham. P.R.O. S.P. 52/3 f. 7.

[1] B. M. Lansdowne MSS., 106, f. 31. Howard, p. 185. Killigrew's part in the French negotiations of 1571–2 is treated in Conyers Read, *Mr. Secretary Walsingham*, Oxford University Press, 1925, vol. 1, pp. 167–82 passim. Martin Hume, *The courtships of Queen Elizabeth, a history of the various negotiations for her marriages*, London, 1904, pp. 144–7, 149–51. Stählin, pp. 414–57 passim.

[2] Killigrew's sentiments concerning the Spaniards are clearly indicated in his letters from Germany to Leicester and Cecil. Pepys MSS., vol. 2, f. 293. Haynes, p. 516.

after the discovery of the Ridolphi Conspiracy in September, 1571. The revelation of carefully laid plans by Spanish and other foreign Catholic agents for the overthrow of the government and the elevation of Mary Stuart to the throne made many Protestant Englishmen determined to end once and for all the threat presented by alliance with Spain's chief rival in Europe.

The Queen's diplomatic representatives in France—Killigrew, Walsingham, and Smith employed all the eloquence at their command to persuade Charles IX and his mother, Catherine de Medici, to abandon support of their Scottish relative. They put great emphasis on the newly discovered evidence of Mary's dealings with the King of Spain at the expense of France.[1] These revelations cooled the ardor with which Charles and his mother pleaded on Mary's behalf. Nevertheless, it seemed clear to Killigrew and his fellow diplomats that neither Catherine nor her son would entirely abandon the Scottish Queen as long as she lived. Elizabeth was plainly reluctant to deal harshly with her rival, and therefore there was always a chance that a future conspiracy on Mary's behalf would be successful. If, in the meantime, Charles and his mother had publicly deserted her cause Mary would never forgive them. Once she had secured the English throne with Philip's support Mary would become the firm ally of Spain and an assured enemy of France.

For this reason Killigrew added his voice to the swelling chorus which urged Elizabeth to put an end to the life that imperilled her own existence as well as that of her country. Probably because he realized the Queen's antipathy to the step he advocated, the words he used were vague, but their meaning was unmistakeable.

[1] In Killigrew's instructions he was directed to inform Charles IX and the Queen mother that Mary and her supporters "much misliked the friendship between our good brother, the King of France and us and especially gave charge that in seeking of foreign forces to win our realm none of the French King's should be made participant, wholly following the direction of the King of Spain." Digges, pp. 147–8,

On 8th February, 1572, he wrote from Blois: "I must crave pardon to utter unto your Majesty the judgement of some that have wondered at your wise and prudent government since you came to your crown and think your 'gests' shall be no less famous to posterity than any of your progenitors have been if you take profit of God's late miraculous saving of your Highness (the timely discovery of the Ridolphi Conspiracy), and thereafter do now assure yourself and your establishment against malicious enemies and underminers thereof which everyone sayeth may be so justly and easily compassed as unless you do the same it will call your former policy and act as in question."

"Now what your Majesty will do," he continued, "is earnestly looked for. I know by my own experience in your service here that the more you seek to assure yourself, the better your Highness succeeds in this court... So that you need not think whatever your Majesty did for your own preservation would be ill taken here. I must of duty say that if they saw you take the right way to assure yourself they would both honour and love you ten times the more. Nevertheless, while they see you take that course of policy they will use 'compramalis nisi forti in tempore futura,' but I hope and I say, as I did always that charity, in this case, ought to begin at yourself upon whose life so many thousands depend..." "And therefore," he concluded on a note of angry vehemence, "accursed be whosoever should persuade your Majesty to fear or forbear that which God alloweth you to do." [1]

This letter represents Killigrew's epistolary style at its best—clear, forthright and vigorous. In sending such advice, however, he could not have endeared himself with Elizabeth. One can well imagine the ironic laughter with which she read his letter. Sincere and well-intentioned as it was from Killigrew's point of view, she would regard his attempt to justify an act of violence by high-flown religious and moral sentiments as a typical piece of Puritan hypocrisy. Ready enough to deceive

[1] P.R.O. S.P. 70/122 f. 67.

others, the Queen probably told herself that she, at any rate, did not deceive herself. As one who was always nervously aware of his entire dependence on royal favour, it undoubtedly took some courage on Killigrew's part to write this letter.

Early in March, 1572, when negotiations for the Anglo-French league had reached their final stages, he returned to England.[1] Soon after his return to court he proceeded to broach with Elizabeth the question of her marriage with the Duke of Alençon, Charles IX's youngest brother. In this matter he was acting on the wishes of the French King and furthering a policy that was supported by his colleagues at Blois.[2] It seems paradoxical that zealous Protestants like Killigrew and Walsingham should favour the Queen's marriage to a Catholic prince, but their attitude can be explained by the importance which they attached to the alliance with France, and by their belief that it could be established on firm foundations through marriage. Moreover, Alençon was known for his close ties with the Protestant party of Admiral Coligny which was then dominant in the counsels of the French government.

Yet the topic of the Alençon marriage was one that required delicate handling. Alençon was an ugly, undersized youth, seventeen years of age. When Cecil, now Lord Burghley, first mentioned him to Elizabeth as a possible husband she flew into a rage.[3] Killigrew, nevertheless, was willing to accept the risk of another attempt. Posing now as a warm friend of France he assured Fénélon that he would make every effort to secure the consent of the Queen and her councillors to the marriage.[4] It is unfortunate that no record of Killigrew's conversation with his temperamental sovereign on this subject has survived. For his own sake, one hopes that he did not indulge his weakness for the kind of pious moralizing which he had employed in his letter of advice concerning the Scottish Queen. Probably a

[1] Read, Walsingham, vol. 1, pp. 181-2. P.R.O. S.P. 70/122 f. 30.
[2] P.R.O. S.P. 70/122 f. 30.
[3] Read, Walsingham, vol. 1, p. 205.
[4] Fénélon, vol. 4, p. 406.

rueful knowledge of Elizabeth's caustic tongue, her disconcert-
ing sense of the ridiculous, made him wary of using such
methods at close range.

At any rate, his efforts were unsuccessful, and his interview
with the Queen evidently left him in a bad humour, for he
afterward told the French ambassador with less than diplomatic
discretion that he believed she would never marry unless
disturbed by some new fear for her life or of losing her
kingdom. With a cynicism bred of long experience of the
Queen's vagaries on this matter he remarked that he thought
she simply enjoyed being courted, and that she was now raising
the hopes of Leicester again.[1]

Apart from his concern with diplomatic matters Killigrew
took an active part in the domestic affairs of his country. He
and his brother, William, sat for the Cornish boroughs of
Truro and Helston respectively in the Parliament of May,
1572.[2] Henry was chosen as one of a Committee of Both
Houses which was appointed to consider the best means of
dealing with the Queen of Scotland.[3] As a result of the Committee's deliberations bills were drawn up by Parliament for
Mary's attainder and deprival from the succession to the
English throne. Although the Queen could not be persuaded to
give her consent to these measures she finally allowed the
execution of Mary's fellow conspirator, the Duke of Norfolk.
Norfolk's demise was probably a source of particular satisfaction to Killigrew who prided himself on the part he had taken
in exposing his designs two years earlier.

Killigrew entered the field of diplomacy again in the late
summer of 1572 after the Massacre of St Bartholemew, the
most terrible episode of the religious wars in France and one

[1] *Ibid.*, p. 439.
[2] Willis, vol. 3, p. 89. Killigrew sat in the House of Commons for the
first time in Elizabeth's reign in the Parliament of April, 1571, representing
the borough of Truro. *Ibid.*, p. 79.
[3] T. Vardon and T. E. May ed., *Journals of the House of Commons, 1547
to 1648*, London, 1852, vol. 1, p. 95.

that filled Protestants everywhere with horror and forboding. Killigrew and his co-religionists saw in this wholesale slaughter of the Huguenots by the Paris mob as the culmination of a carefully concerted conspiracy between the Catholic powers.[1] Although this belief was false there was reason to think that the country was confronted by a situation of great peril as a result of the new turn of events in France.

At the court of Charles IX the Guises once more held the upper hand, and this circumstance, as always, boded ill for England. From Paris Walsingham reported rumours of plans for a military enterprise against the English and Scottish coasts, and he strongly advised that steps should be taken to shut up the "postern gate" by way of Scotland.[2] While Elizabeth had no intention of breaking off relations with France, as Walsingham recommended, she was determined to undermine its power in Scotland, and this was one of the primary reasons which caused her to send an envoy to Scotland early in September shortly after word arrived of the Huguenot massacre. The man she chose for this task was Henry Killigrew.

At the time of his departure for Scotland, the country was in the throes of a bloody civil war which had continued with occasional intermissions since the assassination of the Regent Moray nearly three years earlier. Two factions contested for supremacy: one claimed to rule the state by a regency in the name of the child king, James VI. It was predominately Protestant and controlled by a group of nobles of whom the Earls

[1] Fénélon said that this was the view of Killigrew, of his friend, Thomas Wilson, and other men at Elizabeth's court with whom he spoke immediately after the first news of the massacre reached England. The unfortunate ambassador, who was a moderate Catholic and not of that party which was responsible for the murder of Coligny and his co-religionists, found himself regarded with coldness and suspicion on every side. Killigrew, who a short time before had been proclaiming his friendship for France and his support for the Alençon marriage, now told him plainly that there would be a marked change of attitude at court towards this project as a result of the outrages in France. Fénélon, vol. 5, p. 116.
[2] Digges, p. 276.

of Mar and Morton were the chief figures in the autumn of
1572. This party worked for closer connections with England
and looked to Elizabeth for support.

The opposing faction espoused the cause of Mary Stuart and
asserted the right to rule the country until her restoration to
the throne of Scotland. Mary's adherents originally consisted
of a portion of the Scottish nobility and included both Catholic
and Protestant elements. Their leaders were now Maitland of
Lethington and Kirkaldy of Grange who had once been stal-
warts of the pro-English, Protestant party. At first they had
hoped for Elizabeth's backing for their plan to restore Mary,
but her avowed support for this aim grew steadily less as the
Scottish Queen became the centre of foreign and domestic
intrigue. They, therefore, turned to the Kings of France and
Spain for assistance. Disunity and desertion had weakened the
Marian party, but it still remained a potentially powerful force
in the country.

To Elizabeth the presence of a faction in Scotland which
supported her rival and looked to her enemies abroad for aid
in achieving their aims was a real source of danger. It acted as
an incitement to her own Catholic subjects, and it laid her
dominions open to the aggressive designs of foreign powers.
She also knew that the continual civil strife which divided the
country was an added inducement to intervention from over-
seas.

After the discovery of Mary's conspiracy with Ridolphi and
the Duke of Norfolk the Queen gave a stronger measure of
support to the pro-English party and endeavored to establish
peace in Scotland on the basis of obedience to the government
of James VI. In spite of the pleas of her councillors and the
King's party, however, she refused to extend aid in the form of
military assistance.[1] She feared that intervention on her part
would provoke similar action from France, but it became
increasingly clear that the Protestant Regency could not

[1] See Burghley's summary of the inconveniences caused by the Queen's
"forbearing and delays." B. M. Cotton MSS., Caligula C.III, f. 457.

maintain its authority without such assistance, and that the Marian party would never submit without a show of force from England.

But time seemed to be on Elizabeth's side. Aid from France and Spain proved a broken reed upon which to depend, and the Marian faction grew steadily weaker. In the spring of 1572, the governments of France and England had agreed to send a joint embassy to Scotland in order to bring the two parties to a settlement of their differences and to induce the Marian faction to accept James VI as de facto sovereign of Scotland.[1] This endeavor for peace failed, but the Anglo-French embassy persuaded both sides to accept a truce of 'Abstinence,' for two months.[2] For the Marian party agreement to the truce was a disastrous error. According to its terms both factions were to evacuate Edinburgh, but the Regent's forces proceeded to occupy the town, leaving Maitland and Grange with a small garrison isolated in Edinburgh Castle.[3]

At this juncture Killigrew stepped upon the stage of Anglo-Scottish diplomacy; there to achieve the most dramatic success of his career. The official reason given for his selection was that Sir William Drury, who had represented the English government in the negotiations of the preceding spring, could not be spared from his duties as Marshal of Berwick.[4] But there were probably other causes more important than this. Drury, Lord Hunsdon, and Thomas Randolph, the three men who had been most active in Scottish affairs during recent years, had all aroused the hostility of one or the other of the contesting factions.[5]

[1] P.R.O. S.P. 52/22 ff. 47–8, 55, 57, 60, 74–5.
[2] P.R.O. S.P. 52/23 f. 145.
[3] Patrick F. Tytler, *History of Scotland* (3rd edition), Edinburgh, 1845, vol. 6, p. 170. (hereafter: Tytler).
[4] Instructions to H. Killigrew; P.R.O. S.P. 12/134 f. 264.
[5] Randolph was regarded as too favorable to the Protestant party by the Marian faction while the Regent's party distrusted Drury and Hunsdon whom they thought were partial to their opponents. B. M., Cotton MSS. Caligula C.III, f. 356.

Killigrew, on the other hand, had taken almost no part in the concerns of that country and had not earned the dislike of either party.[1] He had kept on especially good terms with the Calvinists and was well regarded by the clergy, but he also had close connections with some of the Marian party.[2] Robert and James Melville, the nephews of Grange, were old acquaintances and Maitland of Lethington had proven a good friend when Killigrew was a prisoner in France ten years before. In attempting to compose the quarrel between the two parties Killigrew could therefore appear as an impartial arbiter.

The fact that he was chosen to represent the English government in Scotland during a moment when the country seemed in great danger following the recent events in France, is an indication of the confidence which the Queen and her ministers placed in his ability. A Spanish agent in London wrote: "Killigrew has been very fully instructed as to how he is to proceed in this mission. He is a very clever man for such negotiations, a brother-in-law of the Lord Treasurer who consequently employs him in delicate matters like this." [3]

Killigrew's instructions directed him to join with Du Croc, the French ambassador in Scotland, in an effort to achieve a settlement between the rival factions. Ostensibly, he was simply to resume the joint Anglo-French peace negotiations which had been suspended on the proclamation of a truce the previous July.

In addition, however, the English government intended that he should arouse Protestant opinion in Scotland to an awareness of their peril as a result of the terrible slaughter of their Calvinist brethren in France. The Queen commanded him to tell the leaders of both parties that the massacre "has been

[1] Burghley noted in his diary that Killigrew was sent to the Regent Lennox in May, 1571. Murdin, p. 771. The nature of his mission is not stated.

[2] Richard Bannatyne, secretary to John Knox, *Memorials of Transactions in Scotland*. 1549–1573, Edinburgh, 1836. (Bannatyne Club, No. 53.), p. 265. (hereafter: Bannatyne, Memorials.)

[3] *C.S.P. Spanish, 1568–1572*, p. 430.

premeditated and minded a long time before, and that it is concluded among them (the Catholic powers) to eradicate and utterly destroy all such as make profession of the true religion..." Elizabeth also ordered him to give warning of similar plans to entrap the Protestant nobility of Scotland. He was to say that the French intended to accomplish this end by poison or by setting the nobles against one another, and that when the country was torn with civil dissension they would send an army to work the subversion of the whole estate. Killigrew was then to call upon the two parties to agree to an accord upon just conditions when they were offered, to take care for the preservation of the young King in safety, and not to give ear to "foreign and subtle practices."[1]

There was another matter of even greater importance entrusted to him. The recent conspiracies on behalf of Mary Stuart and now the massacre engineered by her relatives, the Guises, had at last convinced Elizabeth of the necessity of taking final measures with her prisoner. Since she herself was unwilling to accept personal responsibility for Mary's death a plan was devised whereby she would be delivered into the hands of her Scottish enemies for execution. It was Killigrew's task to set this plan in motion. He was chosen for these negotiations, as Burghley said, because of the "singular trust" which the Queen and her ministers placed in his ability for work of this kind where great circumspection was required.[2] Probably another reason for his selection was his well known enmity towards the Scottish Queen.

Before his departure for Scotland he had a private conference with Elizabeth at her palace of Woodstock, at which Burghley and Leicester were also present.[3] The Queen and her two councillors told him that he was to handle matters in such a way that the proposal for Mary's delivery and execution came

[1] P.R.O. S.P. 12/134 f. 264.
[2] Murdin, p. 224.
[3] Killigrew's secret instructions, drawn up by Burghley, are preserved at Hatfield House. Murdin, p. 224–5.

from the Scots themselves. But Killigrew was warned that he must not, under any circumstances, divulge Elizabeth's part or that of Burghley and Leicester in initiating these proposals. To this warning the Queen herself added the threat that if any inkling of their participation reached the Scots through his carelessness, he would suffer dire punishment, and Killigrew, in turn, gave a solemn pledge that he would guard the secret as he would his life.[1]

His superiors also informed him that if the Regent Mar and his friends asked that Mary be turned over to them, he was to agree only if they gave absolute assurance that "justice" would be carried out immediately "so that no peril should ensue by her escaping and setting herself up again." The matter was to be conducted in strict secrecy and with all possible speed in order to forstall any move by the French to strengthen their position in Scotland.[2]

After taking leave of Elizabeth, Burghley, and Leicester on 7th September, 1572, Killigrew at once set out for Scotland.[3] So urgent was the mission with which he was entrusted that he did not even have time to bid farewell to his wife and children before leaving the country.[4] As he rode swiftly northward —covering nearly 300 miles between Woodstock and Berwick in only three days' time—his mind was heavily weighed with anxiety concerning the difficulties of his task. Indeed he gravely doubted his ability to fulfil the expectations of the Queen and her ministers.[5] The Scottish negotiations in the

[1] Killigrew to Burghley and Leicester, 23rd November, 1572, P.R.O. S.P. 52/23 f. 111.

[2] Murdin, p. 225.

[3] Edmund Lodge ed., *Illustrations of British history, biography and manners from the reigns of Henry VIII, Edward VI, Mary, Elizabeth and James I exhibited in original papers from the MSS. of Howard, Talboth and Cecil*, vol. 1, London, 1838, p. 347.

[4] B. M. Cotton MSS., Caligula C.IV, f. 104.

[5] The probable state of Killigrew's mind at this time can be inferred from the letter he wrote on 23rd November, 1572, asking Burghley and Leicester to procure his recall on account of his "unableness" to fulfill their expecta-

following months proved to be the toughest of his entire career, and at one point brought him to the verge of disgrace.

When Killigrew reached Scotland he went first to Tantallon where James Douglas, Earl of Morton, resided. Morton was the strongest and ablest man in the Protestant party—"a shrewd fellow" was Killigrew's apt comment, an observation in which admiration was mingled with some distrust.[1] Though not its official leader, Morton had held the reins of power in the King's government firmly in his hands since the death of Moray. The English envoy quickly perceived this fact and wrote to Burghley: "Morton is the only man for her Majesty to account for in this realm."[2] During their conversation at Tantallon the Earl assured him of his devotion to the King and to continued friendship with England.[3]

Killigrew then went to Stirling to present his sovereign's compliments to the Earl of Mar, and promptly thereafter began to sort out the several threads of his mission.[4] He first set to work on the plan for Mary's execution. In order to conceal his own hand as well as that of his government in this project he had the matter brought to the attention of the Regent and the Earl of Morton by a Scottish agent named Nicholas Elphinstone—"a trusty and wise instrument," Killigrew called him.[5] Acting in strict accordance with instructions received from the Queen and her two ministers, he caused Elphinstone to suggest the plan to the Regent and Morton and then have them propose it to himself. The two Scottish leaders seemed favourably disposed to the scheme for liquidating Mary but, in spite of urgent pleas for speedier action from Burghley and Leicester, he was unable to bring the matter to a detailed discussion with Mar and Morton until the first week of October.

tions which, he reminds them, he had already done in previous letters. P.R.O. S.P. 52/23 f. 111.

[1] P.R.O. S.P. 52/24 f. 11.
[2] B. M. Cotton MSS., Caligula C.III, f. 390.
[3] P.R.O. S.P. 52/23 f. 86.
[4] *Ibid.*   [5] *Ibid.*

Their conference took place at Tantallon where Morton lay ill.[1] Although the Regent and Morton had at first welcomed the plan, which had been suggested to them, they now began to raise doubts and difficulties.

Killigrew was a patient man, but his patience was starting to crack. Hard-pressed by his own government for greater speed he wondered whether the Scots were deliberately wasting his time. Somewhat angrily, he declared that if they had no serious intentions in the matter he would pursue it no further. In reply the grim-faced Morton raised himself on his couch and roundly assured the English ambassador that he and the Regent desired Mary's death "as a sovereign salve for all their sores." [2]

Nevertheless, it was clear that their cooperation in the scheme would only be obtained at a heavy price. Despite Killigrew's precautions Morton was probably too shrewd not to guess the true source of the plan and the great importance which the English government attached to it. Killigrew put his finger on one of the major weaknesses of the whole scheme when he remarked anxiously to Burghley: "Although I hope I have dealt as secretly in the matter you wot of as I could for my life, yet the secret being in the mouths of others I fear it will not remain so secret but that there will be some misliking of it." As he foresaw, it was just on this point that there was most danger of blame being attributed to himself by the Queen, Burghley, and Leicester.

During his conversation with Morton at Tantallon the latter told him that Elizabeth's past coldness towards the King's party had alienated many of its members, but that if she would now provide money to pay its soldiers, she could easily regain their confidence. Killigrew replied that the Queen was compelled to bear heavy charges for the defence of her own kingdom, but that if he himself could give some assurance to the English government that the King's party would accomplish "the great

[1] P.R.O. S.P. 52/25 f. 90. The negotiations concerning the plan for Mary's execution in Scotland are treated in Tytler, vol. 6, pp. 174–87.
[2] B. M. Cotton MSS., Caligula C.III, f. 394.

matter"—the expression which the ambassador used in his letters when referring to the plan for Mary's execution—he did not doubt that the needs of the Calvinist leaders would soon be satisfied.[1]

Killigrew and the Scots were engaged in a subtle conflict of will and intelligence in which each side strove to exploit the necessities of the other. For the moment the contest was a draw, and he could merely say: "I perceive that they will make their profit of this matter if they may." Quite clearly, with the passing of time, Killigrew was experiencing a growing sense of inner tension and strain. He felt like one who was groping in the darkness, surrounded by dangerous adversaries, where the slightest miscalculation might bring disaster. A few weeks later he revealed his state of mind in vivid imagery. To Burghley he wrote: "These men be so devilled and uncertain in their doings as I cannot tell what to write of them, but of this your honour may be assured, I trust no one no farther than I see with my eyes or feel with my fingers." [2]

In the task of discrediting France, on the other hand, he had much greater success. His reports of the St. Bartholemew massacre were well calculated to inflame popular hatred of Catholicism. Soon the Calvinist clergy, headed by the redoubtable John Knox, were heaping abuse on the heads of Charles IX and the perpetrators of the massacre. The French ambassador, Philibert du Croc, saw the reputation and influence of his country swept away by a tide of Protestant hatred, and he protested in vain against the public denunciation of his sovereign.[3] On the 19th of September Killigrew wrote: "The news of France clean alienates minds here from putting any great trust in that court," and a week later he reported that "every man now cries out to join with England by some straighter league." [4]

1 *Ibid.*, f. 397.
2 B. M. Cotton MSS., Caligula B.VIII, f. 304. P.R.O. P.S. 2/23 f. 108.
3 P.R.O. S.P. 52/23 f. 90. Bannatyne, *Memorials*, p. 273.
4 B. M. Cotton MSS., Caligula C.III, f. 384. P.R.O. S.P. 52/23 f. 90.

While carrying out his diplomatic responsibilities Killigrew had an opportunity to converse with the Calvinist leader, John Knox. The two men had probably gotten to know one another during Killigrew's earlier missions to Scotland. Knox held a good opinion of the Queen's ambassador as a "godly Protestant"—high praise from this vitriolic old Scot to whom invective came far more easily than compliments.[1]

Killigrew's admiration for Knox shines forth in the letter he wrote to Burghley on 6th October, 1572. His account is particularly interesting since it gives a vivid picture of this remarkable personality as he appeared during the last days of his life. Killigrew wrote: "John Knox is so feeble that scarce can he stand alone or speak to be heard of any audience. Yet doth he every Sunday cause himself to be carried to a place where a certain number hear him and preaches with the same vehemence that ever he did."[2] Knox's death took place scarcely more than six weeks after this letter was written. During his final illness he sent a message to his old friend, Grange, warning him that if he did not forsake his evil ways he would be "dragged from his nest (Edinburgh Castle) and hanged from a gallows with his face against the sun"—a prophecy which Knox's loyal followers hastened to carry out at the appointed time.[3]

News of the Massacre of St Bartholemew did not bring the rival factions closer to an accord, as Killigrew and his government had hoped. He held several conferences with members of the King's party and with their opponents in Edinburgh Castle—the Castilians as they were called. As a result of his conversations in the Castle he came to the conclusion that Maitland was the chief obstacle to a settlement. He therefore dropped a hint in the presence of Maitland's friends, Grange and Robert Melville, that it would be a good idea for him to go

[1] See above, footnote p. 132, footnote 2.
[2] B. M. Cotton MSS., Caligula C.III, f. 390.
[3] Robert Pitcairn ed., *The autobiography and diary of Mr. James Melville*, Edinburgh, 1842, p. 34.

to England to recover his health. Grange and Melville both appear to have approved of this suggestion, and Killigrew immediately transmitted it to Burghley and Leicester.[1]

Elizabeth's reaction to her ambassador's idea for removing Maitland's dangerous presence from Scotland is unknown, but even if she favoured it, there is little likelihood that he would have agreed. Maitland, in fact, was desperately sick, but with a blind obstinacy that is strange in a man of such brilliant intellect, he refused to acknowledge the increasing weakness of his political and military position. He continued to resist any thought of compromise with his enemies and though Grange and Melville seemed more conciliatory, their inclinations were overborne by Maitland's dominating personality.[2]

Killigrew, however, realized that there were other factors that hindered an accord. Concerning the Castilians he wrote: "I am persuaded that they run the French course and hope, by that means, to overthrow their adversaries in the end..."[3] Grange's brother, James Kirkaldy, was in France negotiating for aid, and Killigrew believed that the French ambassador, Du Croc, was endeavouring to undermine his efforts for peace in order to prepare the way for French intervention in Scotland. "It appears," he wrote, "that Du Croc's dealings have not been to make peace and concord, but altogether for an abstinence whereby matters might remain in a doubtful state in order that his master might take his advantage thereof..."[4]

Du Croc, however, realized that in the present state of Scottish feeling towards his country, his continued presence there was unjustified. He departed for France early in October leaving the field free for the English ambassador.[5] Thereafter,

[1] B. M. Cotton MSS., Caligula C.III, f. 386.
[2] On Maitland's attitude at this time see: Ernest Russell, *Maitland of Lethington, the minister of Mary Stuart, a study of his life and times*, London, 1912, pp. 484, 505–7.
[3] B. M. Cotton MSS., Caligula C.III, f. 390.
[4] P.R.O. S.P. 52/23 f. 103.
[5] *Ibid.*, ff. 96–7.

Killigrew sought to induce the Marian leaders in Edinburgh Castle to refer their differences with the Regent's party to Elizabeth and to renounce their dependence on the French King. The French had given them little more than promises in the past, and some of the Castilians seemed disposed to follow his advice. But they stipulated that in return for their agreement to the Queen's arbitration and submission to the authority of James VI, reliable assurances must be given for their lives, and for the restoration of their lands which had been confiscated by the opposing faction in the recent war. Moreover, they demanded a guarantee that Edinburgh Castle would be allowed to remain in Grange's hands.

"I am sure," Killigrew wrote, "if Morton would show himself willing ... the peace would grow out of hand on these terms." [1] But the Earl and his friends were extremely reluctant to agree to them, particularly to the condition requiring that the Castle remain in Grange's keeping. Their reluctance on this point was understandable. To permit the fortress to remain under the command of so able and warlike a soldier as William Kirkaldy would leave the King's party at a dangerous disadvantage. Killigrew's own prejudices were on the side of the adherents of James VI because of their declared friendship for his sovereign and their willingness to submit the controversy unconditionally to her judgement, but he realized that they too bore some responsibility for the present impasse. Morton, he said, was determined to bring his adversaries to obedience "per force." [2]

Nevertheless, towards the end of October, the English ambassador believed that he had brought his negotiations within a measurable distance of success. There seemed a good chance that Morton and the Regent would agree to undertake "the great matter," though it was not yet clear upon what terms. Moreover, the two factions were moving slowly towards an accommodation under his guidance. Then disaster

[1] B. M. Cotton MSS., Caligula C.III ff. 394, 397.
[2] *Ibid.*, B.V.III, f. 304.

struck.[1] On the 28th of October the Regent Mar died suddenly after a short illness. The King's government was now without a head, and the way open for a resurgence of the anti-English faction.[2]

On the same day Killigrew received the terms upon which the leaders of the King's party were willing to put Mary to death. They proposed that Elizabeth should take James under her protection in England, that a defensive league be concluded between the two countries, and that 2,000 or 3,000 soldiers be sent by the Queen to accompany Mary into Scotland, that when her execution had taken place, they should assist the Calvinist party in besieging Edinburgh Castle.[3] The ambassador must have realized the disappointment and chagrin which Elizabeth, Burghley and Leicester would feel on learning of these conditions. They negated the features of speed and secrecy which were considered essential to the success of the plan, and they would advertise to the world Elizabeth's personal involvement in the death of her rival.

Morton and the Regent felt no moral scruples about liquidating the Scottish Queen, but they were not so simple-minded as to assume the rôle of Elizabeth's hired assassins without obtaining assurances for their own security. In the event that Mary's death would bring down upon their heads the wrath of her friends in Europe and Scotland, they were determined that the Queen's part in their action should be known. She would then be less able to disown them or, under the terms of the agreement, avoid coming to their assistance.

Killigrew made two serious blunders at this juncture. That he should have agreed to send off these unpalatable terms to his superiors in London was bad enough. Still worse, his letters to Burghley and Leicester gave the impression that he had allowed his sovereign's name to be brought into his discussions with the Scottish leaders. On this point Elizabeth herself had

[1] *Ibid.*, C.III, f. 397.
[2] *Ibid.*, B.VIII, f. 302.
[3] P.R.O. S.P. 52/23 f. 106.

given Killigrew a specific warning and had received from him a solemn pledge of secrecy.

About two weeks later he received a scathing reprimand from Burghley and Leicester that almost reduced him to a state of nervous collapse, and caused him to be severely ill for several days. Their letter also made clear the greatness of the Queen's displeasure with him. In reply Killigrew wrote a grovelling letter that denied the errors with which Burghley and Leicester had charged him, but acknowledged that his despatches had been so hastily and badly written as to justify the interpretation which had been placed upon them.

"I cannot excuse myself," he said, "who by negligence and ill-favoured utterence have given your honours most just cause to conceive as you have done, and therefore do most humbly crave your pardon, and that it would please your honours ... by letting her Majesty understand whence the error proceeded, to procure the continuance of her Majesty's favour without the which and the continuance of your honours' my life shall be rather a heavy burden unto me. And truly my Lords, I was stricken with such sorrow upon receipt of your letters, as I was not able since then to brook anything I took for sustenance. And that in respect of my unableness to answer the expectations conceived of me and the necessity in my judgement of some fitter man for her Majesty's service here, I am a most humble suitor to your Lordships (as I was also before this fault was laid to my charge) to be called home where I may serve in some other vocation more apt for my capacity than this." [1]

Despite this agonizing confession of personal inadequacy Killigrew was determined to make one matter clear in his own defence. "If," he declared, "it shall ever be proved that I used her Majesty's name or passed the bounds of my commission I will never desire more favour of your honours, but rather that you would do justice upon me to the example of others. And

[1] Killigrew to Burghley and Leicester, 23rd November, 1572, P.R.O. S.P. 52/23 f. 24.

this is absolute to the first point whatsoever my Cornish English caused your honours to gather to the contrary..."[1] His explanation was evidently accepted by the Queen, Burghley, and Leicester, for he was allowed to continue his embassy until its successful termination six months later.

Killigrew's mistakes resulted from the fact that he was suffering from a bad case of nerves because of the dangerous and perplexing situation which suddenly confronted him at the end of October, 1572. Mar's death and the answer Killigrew had received from the Scots concerning the plan for Mary's execution temporarily brought his negotiations to a standstill and left him in complete uncertainty as to what his next step should be. To Burghley and Leicester he wrote rather incoherently: "I know not what to write till I see further—neither touching the peace nor the other matter—for God knows what shall become upon this new event (the Regent's death) ... I am so amazed with this news that I know not what to write but leave the accident and the sequel what is fit to be done to your Lordships."[2]

Killigrew was methodical and perfectionist in his work. When his carefully laid plans were suddenly thrown out of gear by unforseen circumstances or when he was subjected to criticism by his superiors, he tended to suffer from extreme depression and anxiety. He lacked that total independence and fortitude which would have enabled him to disregard such pressures.

As always, however, the natural bouyancy and firmness of his personality reasserted themselves. He quickly recovered his presence of mind and set about finding a way out of his difficulties. He felt sure that the Marian faction would turn to their own advantage the uncertainty which now prevailed among the King's party and, to confirm these suspicions, a rumour came to his ears that the Castilians planned to seize young James. Killigrew, at once, consulted the Earl of Morton

[1] *Ibid.*
[2] B. M. Cotton MSS., B.VIII, f. 302.

with whom he had already established a friendly and confidential relationship. He urged him to take order for the security of the King's person and to prepare for a surprise move on the part of his adversaries. The masterful Douglas promptly took command of the situation. He assured the English ambassador that he would handle matters as if the Regent himself were alive.[1]

But the position of the King's government was still in jeopardy, and resentment was growing among its supporters because of Elizabeth's failure to help them. As Killigrew wrote to Burghley and Leicester: "They fear the French aid to the Scottish Queen's faction and see so small and slow comfort come from us." Morton had told him that neither he nor any other nobleman in Scotland would take the Regency because the burden was so great. The ambassador begged his friend, Leicester, to secure assurances of assistance from the Queen for the Protestant party or to have him recalled, since otherwise his presence would be of no further value in Scotland.[2]

As to the "great matter," he said that no further action could be taken for the present. "For the love of God," he wrote, "trust to yourselves and your assured doings, whereof here I cannot make you assured."[3] Killigrew's implied suggestion that Elizabeth and her government should undertake Mary's execution on their own responsibility was the only practical one under the circumstances, but this was a thing to which she would never willingly consent. Although Killigrew brought up "the great matter" with the Scottish leaders on two other occasions, they could never be induced to do it on terms that were acceptable to the English government.

The negotiations for Mary's execution—the cold inhumanity of the bartering over the terms upon which her execution was to be carried out—is an episode that reflects credit on none of the participants. Excuses, of course, can be found for their

[1] *Ibid.*
[2] *Ibid.*, f. 305.
[3] *Ibid.*, f. 302.

behavior. The sixteenth century was a time when the life of the individual counted for little when weighed against the interests of the state, especially when that individual threatened its very existence by making herself a centre of intrigue and disaffection. Judged by the standard of Philip II, Alva, or Catherine de Medici, the English and Scottish politicians concerned in this affair cannot be charged with extreme cruelty. Elizabeth, in particular, only rarely considered the employment of assassination as a means of achieving her aims. Her reluctance in this respect was not generally shared by other European rulers. Mary Stuart, however, was a constant and intolerable threat both to herself and to England's security. Considering the trouble Mary caused it is surprising that she was allowed to live as long as she did.

To extenuate an action, however, is not to justify it. Not all statesmen or diplomats choose to measure their conduct by the prevailing standards of the time. As far as Killigrew is concerned, he was, to his discredit, the perfect agent for such a mission. Though a kindly man in private relationships he entirely lacked that nobility of spirit which enabled a fellow Puritan, Sir Amyas Paulet, to answer the Queen's suggestion that he dispose of Mary by poison by saying that he would not make so foul a shipwreck of his conscience as to shed blood without law or warrant.

Quite apart from the question of morality, the plan for having Mary put to death by the Scots suggests a lack of realism strange in two such masters of the art of real politique as Elizabeth and Burghley. Did they really believe that the Scots could be induced to carry it out on the terms which they had devised, or that their authorship of the scheme could be concealed by the indirect methods Killigrew had been instructed to employ? Of course, the entire plan bears the stamp of Elizabeth's least amiable trait—that of thrusting onto others responsibility for acts which threatened to bring danger and odium upon herself. It also savours of another lesser fault of which she was sometimes guilty—that of being too clever by half.

Possibly the Queen and her ministers allowed their judgement to be affected by the mood of panic which swept the country immediately following the Massacre of St Bartholemew, or they may have hoped that the Scottish leaders could be panicked into prosecuting their plan after Killigrew had regaled them with details of the slaughter of the Protestants in France, and had pointed out that so long as Mary Stuart lived, there was the strongest probability that she and her Guise relations would engineer a like holocaust in Scotland. Viewed rationally, there was little chance of such an occurrence ever taking place, but most Protestants were not in a rational frame of mind in the autumn of 1572, and it was, therefore, not entirely unreasonable to expect that the Scots might be unwary enough to take up the English plan. The only trouble with this expectation was that it put too low an estimate on the sagacity of James Douglas, Earl of Morton, an estimate which Elizabeth and her councillors now had cause to revise.

Killigrew's letters at the end of October brought home to his government the full seriousness of the situation created by the Regent's sudden death. After consultation with Burghley Leicester spoke in strong terms to Elizabeth concerning her delay in helping her friends in Scotland, and to strengthen the effect of his words he showed to her the warnings contained in Killigrew's despatches.[1] Leicester's comments and her ambassador's letters made a strong impression on the Queen's mind, for she acted with unusual promptness. Early in November she despatched a letter to Morton, couched in the most friendly terms, which strongly suggested her desire that he should assume the Regency.[2] Morton, she knew, was the man best qualified to establish a strong government in Scotland, and one that would maintain a close alignment with England.

Killigrew, in the meantime, found that matters were not as desperate as he had supposed. The Castilians made no move to take advantage of their opponents' temporary weakness, and

[1] Murdin, pp. 230–2.
[2] P.R.O. S.P. 52/23 f. 107.

he was able to persuade the two factions to extend their truce
to the end of December.[1] There were rumours of an attempt
on the part of the Marian party to have its old ally, the Earl
of Argyle, made Regent, but when a convention was held to
elect a successor to Mar, the nobility gave overwhelming
support to Morton.[2] It was not certain, however, that he would
yield to the will of his fellow nobles. Elizabeth's avowal of
friendship had not yet been followed by material assistance, and
Morton had warned her ambassador that, unless it was forth-
coming he would not assume the burden of the Regency.

Killigrew knew that Morton was a dangerous man to trifle
with and not one given to making idle threats. When the day
of the election approached and definite assurance of aid had
still not come, the English ambassador hit upon a subterfuge
calculated to secure the aims of his government. On the day
before the election he sent a letter from Elizabeth to the
convention where it was publicly read for the encouragement
of the King's party. It made no definite commitments on the
matter of assistance, and this had a discouraging effect on the
Queen's friends who, as Killigrew informed her, looked for
"some more substantial comfort." [3]

Elizabeth's letter, however, referred the Earl of Morton to
her ambassador for a personal communication directed to himself. The same evening Morton visited Killigrew at his lodging,
no doubt in expectation of receiving the assurances for which
he and his friends were waiting. These, the ambassador could
still not give him. He therefore avoided the necessity of a direct
answer by pleading sickness and by asking the Earl to wait a
few days until his recovery. To assuage Morton's disappointment he told him that the Queen had as great concern for the
King's well-being as she ever had, and added other glib general-
ities of this kind encouraging him to take the Regency.[4]

[1] *Ibid.*, f. 119.
[2] *Ibid.*, f. 107A.
[3] *Ibid.*, f. 117.
[4] *Ibid.*

Killigrew's words produced the desired effect, and on the 25th of November Morton was proclaimed Regent. The following day, not surprisingly, marked the ambassador's complete recovery from his convenient illness.[1] By this timely strategem he had helped to secure for his sovereign a victory which her delays had nearly forfeited. The election of Morton gave to Elizabeth a trustworthy friend for the next six years, and to Scotland one of the ablest rulers of its entire history.

[1] *Ibid.*

CHAPTER VII

SCOTTISH DIPLOMACY,
DECEMBER 1572–SEPTEMBER 1575

KILLIGREW's success in gaining Morton's acceptance of the Regency scarcely lessened the difficulties with which he was confronted. Of all the King's party none was more distrusted by the Castilians than Morton, and his elevation only made them more adverse to compromise. The English ambassador became increasingly certain that they were deliberately dragging out negotiations in order to win time until aid from France enabled them to settle the war on their own terms. Grange openly admitted that he had received 2,000 crowns from this source, and that he expected a still greater sum of money on the arrival of his brother, James, in Scotland.[1]

Despite his misgivings Killigrew was forced to play the part of peacemaker and to restrain the determination of the Regent and his friends to reduce their opponents to obedience by force of arms. He himself believed that this was the only feasible solution to the Scottish problem, but that the Calvinist faction could never achieve it without military as well as financial assistance from England. Elizabeth, however, had no intention of involving herself in war until every avenue of peaceful mediation had been explored. If he allowed the King's Lords to draw his government into military action prematurely he would be in great peril of he Queen's wrath.[2]

Killigrew, therefore, acted with extreme caution. He used every means in his power to compel the Calvinist party to offer acceptable terms to the Castilians. Even when a sum of 2,500

[1] P.R.O. S.P. 52/23 f. 23.
[2] Elizabeth's attitude on this point is reflected in Killigrew's letter to Burghley on 27th March, 1573. He wrote: "By your letters—I see her Majesty's earnest charging of me. Nothing has been left undone that might reasonably be done to end this trouble without the Queen of England's forces." P.R.O. S.P. 52/24 f. 55.

pounds, sent by the English government, reached him late in December he only delivered 1,000 pounds of this amount into the hands of the Regent. The remainder he kept until Parliament was convened in Edinburgh the following month during which there would be a further opportunity for negotiations between the two parties.[1]

But time was running out. The Abstinence expired on 31st December, and when the English ambassador requested Morton to accept an extension of the truce the latter declared that he would agree neither to a longer Abstinence nor to further negotiations unless he saw clear evidence that they would result in a secure peace. Hitherto, he said, the truce had simply afforded time for his adversaries to strengthen their position in the Castle while the power of his own party had been weakened.[2]

Nevertheless, in the final days before the expiration of the Abstinence, Killigrew made frantic efforts to bring about a settlement between the opposing factions. Morton demanded that both submit their differences to an impartial arbiter, and the Castilians replied that they were willing to accept the French King's arbitration. To this the King's Lords made the caustic comment that they would not commit to Charles IX's judgement "a dead horse skin."[3]

Negotiations broke down completely on the Regent's demand that no more victuals should be taken into the Castle while the discussions were in progress. In reply the Marian leaders declared that they would take no further part in the parley until this stipulation was withdrawn. Though the English ambassador went to the Castle and made an eloquent appeal in the interest of peace, his words made no impression.[4]

Early the following morning, with characteristic impetuousity, Grange threw down the gage of battle by firing a cannon

[1] B.M., Additional MSS., 5754, f. 35.
[2] P.R.O. S.P. 52/24 f. 2B.
[3] *Ibid.*
[4] *Ibid.*

from the Castle wall.[1] War had begun, and Killigrew knew that unless his government took more active measures on behalf of the King's party disastrous consequences might follow. The Regent was in an angry and restive mood over Elizabeth's failure to give him fuller assistance. Without it he would be unable to defeat the enemy or even maintain his army in the field. He told the ambassador "that if now, after he had taken such a burden upon him in hope of her favour and support, he should be in danger to be left in the mire, he would surely quit the regiment (Regency) and shift for himself which he thought he would be able to do as well as any here in Scotland."[2]

Morton's words had an ominous ring in Killigrew's ears. He had heard that Marian agents were bringing offers from the French King to the Regent, and, as he warned Sir Thomas Smith, if Morton was driven to carry on the war without English help he might turn to France for support.[3] The English ambassador, therefore, lost no time in bringing to the attention of his superiors the critical situation which had arisen in Scottish affairs. Shortly before the middle of January, either on his own initiative or on instructions from his government, he seems to have paid a secret visit to England. According to Fénélon he stayed several days at the house of his brother-in-law, Lord Burghley.[4]

Killigrew's temporary return to England coincided with and perhaps influenced a marked change in the policy of his government. The change is reflected in an interview which Elizabeth had with the French ambassador about this time. To his expressions of concern over rumours of the intended despatch of military forces to Scotland, she replied: "As regards my army assure yourself that it has not passed the borders of Scotland, and so it will do no harm to anyone except those who

1 *Ibid.*
2 P.R.O. S.P. 52/24 f. 2B.
3 P.R.O. S.P. 52/24 ff. 11, 59.
4 Fénélon, vol. 5, pp. 238, 243.

have offended me." But she added sternly: "…we are not such a fool that we do not know well that this good will between you and the Scots only tends to our evil, and that the Scots do not seek after you except with regard to their own profit…"[1]

Killigrew's reports and those of his friend, Francis Walsingham, at the French court had evidently begun to make a strong impression on the Queen's mind. Walsingham wrote that a Marian agent had sent word to the Castilians that if they could hold out until Whitsun they would receive assistance from the Pope, Spain, and France. A short time later he reported news of an intended expedition of 1,000 men under the Duke of Maine to reinforce Edinburgh Castle. Another army, he said, was to liberate Mary Stuart.[2]

These rumours proved to have no foundation in fact. Charles IX was ready enough to offer aid and encouragement to England's enemies, now that the Guises were in the ascendant at court, but the renewal of civil war in France greatly reduced the possibility of taking effective action on their behalf. The present situation was very similar to the one which had existed in the spring of 1560. Again, however, there was the chance that the French government might soon triumph over domestic opposition and then be free to take advantage of its opportunities. Against this danger the Queen and her ministers now began to prepare themselves.

According to Fénélon, when Killigrew returned to Scotland, he brought with him 10,000 crowns to aid the Regent.[3] At the same time, on Morton's request, Sir William Drury, the Marshal of Berwick, sent two experts in gunnery to make a survey of the Castle. They reported that a battery of cannon could reduce it within twenty days, and soon afterwards Elizabeth commanded the despatch of ordnance to Edinburgh.[4]

[1] B. M. Cotton MSS., Caligula C.III, f. 427.
[2] Digges, p. 296.
[3] Fénélon, vol. 5, p. 243.
[4] P.R.O. S.P. 52/24 ff. 2D, 18. B. M. Cotton MSS., Caligula C.IV f. 15.

On arrival in the Scottish capital the ambassador found military operations against the Castle progressing rapidly under Morton's forceful leadership. Entrenchments were being dug around the perimeter of the fortress, and the sources of water supply upon which its garrison depended, destroyed. Against these activities the Castilians could only maintain an ineffective cannon fire. Meanwhile, on the 26th January, James Kirkaldy landed at Blackness in a French pinnace carrying ordnance, munitions, and money for his friends in Edinburgh Castle.[1] But the ship and supplies were immediately seized by the Regent's men, and Grange's brother was captured.[2]

Under the impact of this disaster and of the increasing evidence of England's intention to aid its supporters in Scotland, the strength of the Marian party began to ebb away. Killigrew's aim now was to complete the isolation of the Castilians by bringing about a reconciliation between the Regent's party and the remaining adherents of Mary Stuart outside Edinburgh Castle. In this work he was strongly supported by Morton, who realized as well as the English ambassador that he could not count on Elizabeth's full support in the war until all means to secure a settlement by negotiation had been exhausted.

The Regent, therefore, asked Killigrew to move him in the presence of the Scottish Lords, who were then assembled in Parliament, to make reasonable offers to the Duke of Châtel-herault and the Earl of Huntly, the foremost members of the nobility still attached to the Marian party.[3] The English ambassador knew that if Morton made overly generous concessions to the King's enemies on his own initiative he would arouse the anger of his followers. For this reason he willingly acceded to his request.

On the 21st January Killigrew made an address before the Parliament on the lines which the Regent had asked. His words were well received. To Burghley he reported: "Though my

[1] P.R.O. S.P. 52/24 ff. 10, 18A.
[2] P.R.O. S.P. 52/24 ff. 16A, 22.
[3] Ibid., f. 17.

eloquence was bare, yet was her Majesty's credit and the reverence borne to her by that company so persuasive, that the intention took good effect, as I trust the sequel shall witness." [1]

Nor was his hope disappointed. At Perth, in February, Killigrew presided over a conference held in his own lodging. There the Earl of Huntly and Lord John Hamilton, acting on behalf of his father, the Duke of Châtelherault, met with representatives of the King's party. As a result of his persuasions they agreed to a pacification under which Huntly and Hamilton submitted to the King's authority on very liberal terms. [2]

Killigrew had good reason to feel satisfaction with what he had achieved. Except for the small band in Edinburgh Castle all Scotland now acknowledged the Regent's authority. As he proudly wrote of the successful conference: "All was done in my house to her Majesty's great honour and credit in this country. I trust that both the Duke and Huntly will prove as much her Majesty's as any of the rest... Now there remains but the Castle, the expugnation of which is looked from her Majesty unless it may be had by treaty, wherein I will omit no reasonable occasion." [3]

The ambassador believed that, in spite of the defection of their friends, the Castilians would never yield unless they were faced by the certainty of siege by an English army, and his eagerness to put an end to "that den of troublers" greatly increased when he learned from captured spies that Maitland and Grange still put their trust in Charles IX. When, as they hoped, his army came to Scotland they intended to deliver the Castle into its possession. He also discovered a plan of Maitland's to have the young King taken from Stirling Castle and sent to France. [4]

At the end of February Killigrew felt confident that his

[1] *Ibid.*

[2] *Ibid.*, ff. 32–4.

[3] B. M. Cotton MSS., Caligula C.IV, f. 26.

[4] P.R.O. S.P. 52/24 ff. 38, 44A. B. M. Cotton MSS., Caligula C.IV, f. 27B.

government would soon despatch an army to Scotland, and he assured the Regent that Elizabeth intended to help him recover the Castle.[1] In consultation with Drury and Morton he was already making arrangements for the transportation of men and supplies to Edinburgh, the exchange of hostages and other matters incidental to the coming operations. His brother-in-law, the Lord Treasurer, was having ships and munitions made ready at Newcastle for the same purpose.[2]

But the plans of English officials once more had to wait upon the irresolution of their sovereign. As Elizabeth considered the cost and danger of the Scottish expedition her mind began to search for means whereby these difficulties could be avoided. Killigrew learned of the Queen's objections from Burghley, and he doubtless recalled with exasperation how closely they conformed to a familiar pattern of rationalization enacted on other critical occasions.

Taking up the various points mentioned in Burghley's letter he said in reply: "As for the charges and hazards of her Majesty's people and munitions, I answer that ... with the example of the journey to Leith, and of the other of the doubt of war with France, adding that I am out of doubt the commodity will far exceed the charges or the doubt of war which can have no ground upon this enterprise, but God's will be done. For my own part, if this Castle be not recovered—and that with expedition—I think I see the beginning of sorrows, and her Majesty's hitherto peaccable reign decaying, as it were, in post—which God of his mercy defend."[3]

The Queen also wished her ambassador to press Morton to make larger concessions to the Castilians. Burghley suggested that Grange be allowed to keep the Castle, if he and his friends

[1] P.R.O. S.P. 52/24 f. 38.
[2] *Ibid.*, ff. 20-1, B. M. Lansdowne MSS., 16, f. 86.
[3] P.R.O. S.P. 52/24 f. 47. In his letter to Burghley of 12th February, 1573, Sir Thomas Smith said that when he had moved the Queen concerning aid for the Regent, she had told him of a device to do this without any such charges. B. M. Lansdowne MSS., 16, f. 86.

would submit to the King's authority, and if Grange himself gave adequate pledges for his future loyalty as captain of the fortress. But Killigrew knew how strongly the Regent felt on this point. He protested to Cecil: "I would rather go to Rome barefoot than deliver that answer. I beseech your Lordship, if there be not good meaning to proceed in these causes, I may be revoked." If Morton, he added, finds that "I begin to halt or wax 'tepidus'—whom hitherto he has found so true, he will smell a rat, and I fear, provide for a 'dear year'." [1]

Despite his apprehensions Killigrew put this suggestion to the Regent. As he anticipated Morton's reaction was a violent one. Angry and amazed he declared that, even if he were willing to agree, the nobility would never consent to Grange's retention of the Castle. The Regent resolved at once to write the Queen for aid, and he asked the ambassador to do the same. Before the letters could be despatched welcome news arrived. A letter from Burghley told of the Queen's definite resolve to assist the King's party without further delay. [2]

Killigrew's forceful letters had evidently stiffened Elizabeth's resolution. He thereupon requested Morton to make one more effort for a peaceful settlement. He urged him to offer the Castilians the same assurances for their lives and lands that had been given to Huntly and Châtelherault. Although the Regent protested that the granting of these terms would endanger the King's estate as well as his own life he finally consented. [3] The English ambassador immediately had these terms delivered to the Castilians. With them he enclosed letters from Burghley which apparently promised that the English government would give the Marian leaders friendship and protection to insure fulfillment of the conditions for their surety, if they accepted

---

[1] P.R.O. S.P. 52/24 f. 50.

[2] *Ibid.*, ff. 54-5. See Elizabeth's instructions to Sir William Drury, whom she appointed to command the army which was to be sent to Morton's assistance. B. M., Additional MSS., 5754, f. 32.

[3] P.R.O. S.P. 52/24 f. 55.

this offer. He also added an eloquent appeal of his own for its acceptance.

He informed the defenders of the Castle that the terms were the very best he could obtain and that if they refused them now, they would never receive the like again. "God grant," he said, "that you may bethink yourselves in time, for there will be nothing added or diminished from these articles for your assurance... If you can like of these conditions for your surety, and render the house to the King, I will promise that you will find no less friendship in England than the Lord Treasurer's letters to me offered. If you dare trust me you shall not be deceived." To this appeal he added the stern warning that if they did not surrender the Castle they would "feel the cannon within eight days...," and that if they did not answer him immediately in writing they need never look to hear from him again.[1]

Killigrew's message made no impression. The two Marian leaders only replied with further proposals for negotiation that were obviously aimed at winning time in expectation of foreign aid.[2] Neither threats nor concessions could shake their resolution. It is difficult to account for the attitude of Maitland and Grange at this juncture. They had no reason now to doubt that an English army was about to march against them. An experienced soldier like Grange might feel confident of his ability to withstand Morton's ill-disciplined levies, but against an English army equipped with heavy artillery there was no chance of successful resistance. Probably he and Maitland still believed that French forces would soon land in Scotland, but in fact the government of Charles IX gave not the slightest indication of taking such action on their behalf.[3]

[1] *Ibid.*, f. 551.
[2] *Ibid.*, f. 59.
[3] The French ambassador in London protested to Elizabeth and Cecil over the despatch of English troops to Scotland, but he said very little concerning possible retaliatory measures by his government if the protests were ignored. Fénélon, vol. 5, pp. 284, 306, 308–10, 322–3. At the end of

Both men seem to have taken their desperate stand for personal reasons. Maitland was dying, his body paralyzed with disease. During recent months he had doubtless come to the conclusion that neither his plans for a union of Scotland and England through Elizabeth's recognition of Mary Stuart as her successor, nor his ambition to play a leading role in Scottish affairs had the slightest chance of attainment. Certainly, if he sanctioned an agreement which acknowledged the authority of Morton's government the end of his hopes was certain. Now, despairing of life itself, he chose to perish in the ruins of the cause for which he had fought so long.

Grange's less complex nature was influenced mainly by loyalty to his friend, Maitland, and by considerations of honour. He had already deserted the King's party. If now, in his hour of peril, he abandoned Mary Stuart's cause as well, he would forfeit the last vestige of his reputation as a man of honour. Almost to the very end Maitland and Grange held their followers to the stern path they had chosen.

To some extent, both men were defenders of an aristocratic social order that was passing away in Scotland. With keen insight Killigrew had already perceived the first signs of this change. On 23rd November, 1572, he wrote to Burghley: "Methinks I see the noblemen's great credit decay in this country, and the barons, boroughs, and such like take more upon them; the ministers and religion increase, and the desire in them to prevent the practices of the papists; the number of able men for service very great and well furnished in both horse and foot; their navy so augmented as it is a thing almost incredible." [1]

On 25th April, 1573, an English army of 1,500 men, including

February, 1573, Maitland and Grange wrote to their former ally, Huntly: "We are assuredly persuaded that the Queen of England will not send forces, nor take the matter plainly on her to meddle openly, for if she do so she is assured to provoke France to do the like." P.R.O. S.P. 52/24 f. 35.

[1] P.R.O. S.P. 52/23, f. 31. For a biography of Kirkaldy see: L. A. Barbe, *Kirkaldy of Grange*, Edinburgh, 1897.

500 arquebusiers and 140 pikemen, under the command of Sir William Drury entered Edinburgh. There they were joined by the Regent's Scottish force, about 500 strong.[1] At the same time 33 guns, transported from Berwick by sea to Leith, were brought to Edinburgh.[2] Against this formidable array the Castilians could muster a garrison of less than 150 soldiers.[3] Nevertheless, when Drury issued a final summons for their surrender, no reply was returned.[4] He therefore began to plant his batteries in preparation for the siege. Killigrew had believed that the Castilians would surrender before the battery and assault were made, but there now seemed little possibility of any other solution than that of force.[5]

Yet the task of diplomacy was by no means ended. As the ambassador well knew the latent Anglo-Scottish hostility might lead to dangerous outbreaks between the allied armies. The two commanders, Drury and Morton, had little love for one another, and Killigrew made every effort to put their relationship on a more friendly basis.[6] Fortunately he had won the Regent's confidence to such an extent that the latter was prepared to make almost any concession he asked. In the provision of men, equipment, and supplies Morton took care to fulfil the obligations he had undertaken with the English government.

Where there were things necessary in excess of the agreement Killigrew was ready to supply them himself out of his own funds. To Burghley he wrote: "For anything our men can want

[1] P.R.O. S.P. 52/25 f. 57A.
[2] Ibid., f. 25.
[3] Ibid., f. 351. When the Castle surrendered there were 200 people in it, but this number included nearly forty women as well as labourers and others who were not trained military men. Ibid., f. 57A.
[4] Ibid., f. 26II.
[5] P.R.O. S.P. 52/25 f. 35.
[6] The distrust of the English for their allies is shown in the letter of Sir Henry Lee, one of Drury's officers, to Burghley in May, 1573. B. M., Cotton MSS., Caligula IX, f. 91. Morton's dislike of Drury is indicated in his letter to Burghley of 26th June, 1573. P.R.O. S.P. 52/25 f. 76.

above the Regent's promise I will see it performed, and if any
have cause to complain for ill-use, either in lodgings or victuals,
let them come to me." [1] Exceptional expenditures of this kind
were a frequent occurrence in a diplomat's experience. He
could not shirk them since they were essential to the success of
his work, but as his ordinary pay was insufficient to cover
them, he could only hope for recoupment by the later grant
of offices or land from the crown.

Of course Killigrew's exertions could not entirely extinguish
the age old distrust between Englishman and Scot, and there
were always troublemakers who were eager to stir the embers.
One of these, an officer in Drury's army, described the Scots
as a people "affected more to particular love than law; in
appearance only religious but in effect traitorous," and warned
Burghley of a rumoured plot by Morton's troops to make a
surprise attack on the English during the coming assault on the
Castle in order to gain undisputed possession of all the ordnance
and treasure within its walls.[2]

Hearing from Burghley of a similar report by another
English officer, Killigrew hastened to assure the Lord Treasurer
that such rumours were without foundation. He said that an
unprecedented spirit of good will prevailed between the rank
and file of the allied armies, and he pledged his word that in
all their doings the Scottish soldiers, gunners, and pioneers were
"arm in arm with ours". When it came to the assault, he added,
the men of the two nations would race one another to see
which should be foremost. His confidence in the success of the
siege was now so great that it produced in him a mood which
was at once humourous, lighthearted, and ironical. Those who
talked of the possibility of Scottish treachery made him laugh
outright. "It might be answered," he scoffed, "that the sky may
fall and we shall catch larks!"

Concerning the individual who had sent this report he could

[1] *Ibid.*, ff. 52, 44.
[2] Sir Henry Lee to Burghley 11th May, 1573. B. M. Cotton MSS.,
Caligula C.IV f. 91.

only growl into Burghley's sympathetic ear: "As for the newly come courtier's writing, as I cannot prevent it so must I bear it."[1] Both men were accustomed to having their efforts undermined by the perversity of people on their own side and, for the most part, they had schooled themselves to endure it philosophically. The sneering reference to the 'newly come courtier' suggests that the ambassador entertained no very high regard for some of the young gentlemen serving under Drury's command. Himself an old soldier, Killigrew probably thought that their capacities were better suited to dancing attendance on the Queen at court than to enduring the rigours of war.

Perhaps he agreed with Morton's judgement that certain of the English officers had become frightened when they contemplated the prospect of an assault on the Castle, and he may therefore have concluded that talk of Scottish treachery was merely an attempt to rationalize their own fears.[2] On their behalf it can be said that the Castle presented a daunting sight to any army that might be compelled to carry its defences by storm. Situated at one end of a long ridge, the fortress is protected on all sides but one by precipices which can only be ascended by skilled climbers. The one feasible approach was through the Spur, a formidable outwork that constituted the normal entry from the town to the Castle, and which was defended by tiers of guns.[3] It should also be added that when the fighting came, the English officers and most of their men displayed both enterprise and bravery.

Possibly the reluctance of some of them was simply due to their mixed admiration and fear of the enemy commander, Kirkaldy of Grange. By many he was considered the "first soldier of Europe." Certainly he was the one Scottish leader whose professional abilities commanded respect among English military men who generally had a low opinion of the standard

[1] P.R.O. S.P. 52/25 f. 42.

[2] Morton to Burghley 26th June, 1573. P.R.O. S.P. 52/25 f. 76.

[3] A good description of Edinburgh Castle at the time of the siege of 1573 is given in Froude, vol. 10, pp. 465–6.

of generalship, organization, and discipline that prevailed in the Scottish forces. But it was more than soldierly skill that counted in their judgement of him. He was equally famed for his chivalry and valour. His nephew, James Melville, described him as "humble, gentle, meek like a lamb in the house but like a lion in the fields." [1]

Gentleness may seem an odd trait to attribute to one, who as a young man, had helped to murder the aged Cardinal Beaton and then to hang his corpse over the battlements of St Andrews Castle by a sheet until the smell of putrefaction compelled the assasins to cut it down—but assasination was then so common in Scotland as to be regarded as scarcely more than a venial sin, except—perhaps—by the victim himself.[2] In any case, Grange was a far more attractive personality than his rival, Morton, whom one English officer called "wise and wily" —not complimentary terms in a soldier's vocabulary.[3] Grange had been on particularily close terms of friendship with Sir William Drury who was now his opponent in the field.

The first battery opened fire on the 16th May, and the accuracy of the gunners was attested by a loud shriek of terror from the women within the Castle, an event which prompted Killigrew to remark with heartless satisfaction: "This day at one o'clock some of our pieces began to speak such language as it made them in the Castle, I am sure, think more of God than they did before." In the meantime the laying of the remaining batteries proceeded with exasperating slowness. This was due in part to a shortage of Scottish labourers and to the hardness of the ground, but as the ambassador admitted, it was also the result of a lack of skill on the part of some of the English gunners.[4]

The apologetic tone of his remarks on this point indicates that these unnecessary delays were causing annoyance and impa-

[1] Melville, p. 136.
[2] P.R.O. S.P. Henry VIII, vol. 5. f. 56 D.
[3] P.R.O. S.P. 52/26 f. 85.
[4] *Ibid.*, ff. 44, 46.

tience on the part of the Queen and her councillors. Undoubtedly their annoyance was directed in part against himself, since
in his zeal to persuade the government to despatch an army
with siege guns to Edinburgh, he had confidently declared that
its mere presence would frighten the Castilians into submission,
that they would never "abide the cannon." That prediction,
to Killigrew's embarrassment, had been proven false. The
army had now been in Scotland for nearly a month, and the
Castle had still not fallen. He must have realized all too well
Elizabeth's state of mind as she tallied up the cost of keeping
1500 men in the field, together with a large train of artillery
for that length of time to capture a single undergarrisoned
Scottish castle! In order to speed up the work on the batteries
he himself laboured two nights in succession as a pioneer with
pick and spade helping to build two gun mounts close to the
Castle and within reach of enemy artillery and small arms' fire.[1]

Fortunately the Castilians were short of powder and shot and
therefore able to employ their cannon only intermittently. On
one occasion, however, the artillery fire became so intense that
in the two gun mounts directly in front of the Spur commanded
by Sir William Drury, the gunners forsook their pieces and
fled in terror. Only Drury kept his head. Seizing a lint-stock
which one of his men had dropped, he lit the charges and fired
the cannon himself. Emboldened by their commander's
example, the gunners returned to their posts, but the shot
continued to drop so close that they were often buried with
earth cascading over the gun mounts, and Drury had to help
dig them out. Despite the accuracy of enemy fire none of the
besiegers was killed, and the only man injured was one whose
head, as Drury reported, "took a knock by a stone." [2]

[1] *Ibid.*, ff. 23, 44.
[2] See Drury's letter to Burghley of 23rd May, 1573; also Thomas
Cotton's letter to Burghley of the same date. P.R.O. S.P. 52/25 ff. 48.
B. M. Cotton MSS., Caligula C.IV, f. 96. Cotton had come to Edinburgh
as a companion of Thomas Cecil, Lord Burghley's eldest son. Both served
as officers in Drury's army at the siege of Edinburgh. Cotton's letter indicates
his apprehensions concerning the difficulty of taking the Castle by assault.

The cannonading from the fortress imposed further delays on the preparation of the gun mounts which still remained unfinished. In addition it became necessary to knock out the enemy artillery before the gunners could concentrate their fire on the fortifications to open up a breach for the assault. Finally, with all 33 guns in position, the battery commenced on the 21st May, and it soon became clear that neither the Castle nor its defenders could withstand the overwhelming fire power which the besieging army brought to bear upon them. In a few days' time nearly 3000 shot were hurled into the fortress—a feat almost unparalleled in sixteenth-century-siege warfare—and the garrison was literally hammered into submission.[1]

David's Tower, one of the principal bastions of the Castle, fell with a crash under the battering of the artillery. On the 26th May the Spur was taken by storm, an action in which twenty English and Scottish soldiers were killed or wounded. That evening the Castilians called for a parley, and the following day a conference was held at which Killigrew, Drury, and Lord Boyd, a representative of the Regent, met with Grange and Robert Melville. Grange requested that those in the Castle be given surety for their lives and livings, that Maitland have permission to reside in England, and that he himself be allowed to remain unmolested in his own country.[2]

Only a few weeks before the Castilians could have had better terms than these, but now the Regent was determined to exact a full measure of vengeance from his enemies. He promptly rejected Grange's conditions. The garrison, he said, would be pardoned if its members came forth singly without armour and submitted to the mercy of the King and Regent, but the leaders must surrender unconditionally. Their fate was to be determined by the Queen of England. [3]

Grange and his friends were ready to die sword in hand rather than accept these terms, but the soldiers had no intention

[1] *Ibid.*, f. 60.
[2] *Ibid.*, ff. 41, 49–50, 54–7.
[3] *Ibid.*, f. 60.

of sacrificing their lives in this fashion, and they threatened to hang Maitland over the Castle wall unless he advised immediate surrender.[1] On the following day Edinburgh Castle capitulated —the "Thermopylae of the Marian cause" had fallen at last.[2]

Maitland and Grange, who were placed in Drury's custody, wrote to Burghley and Leicester asking them to persuade the Queen to intercede with the Regent for their lives.[3] Both men had once been held in high esteem at Elizabeth's court. Burghley, in particular, had been a good friend of Maitland's. Morton, however, was resolved to inflict the ultimate penalty upon them, and Killigrew gave him full support in this matter.

On searching the Castle shortly after its surrender he found letters which proved that the Castilians had been appealing for aid, not only from the French King, but from Spain as well.[4] In the aftermath of St Bartholomew the effect of this further proof of their reliance on the Catholic powers on the mind of a fervent Protestant like Killigrew can well be imagined.

The ambassador perhaps feared that his brother-in-law's old intimacy with Maitland might incline him to recommend leniency on behalf of the two prisoners. He wrote to Sir Thomas Smith: "For my own part I think them now fitter for God than for this world for sundry considerations. They have left many letters and papers in the Castle. I enclose a copy of a letter sent by the Duke of Alva, which I pray you to communicate to my Lord Treasurer, to show his honour that the unthankfullest thing that may come out of England to the Regent and the best Scots here will be any suit in favour of the ... chief prisoners or of any suspending of their execution."[5]

Elizabeth ordered Drury to turn Maitland and Grange over to the Regent, and she made no effort to save their lives. Maitland died shortly after his surrender, as the English ambas-

---

1 *Ibid.*, f. 73.
2 B. M. Cotton MSS., Caligula C.IV, f. 98. Russell, p. 361.
3 B. M. Cotton MSS., Caligula C.IV, f. 58.
4 P.R.O. S.P. 52/25 ff. 62, 74.
5 *Ibid.*, f. 62.

sador wrote, not without some suspicion of poison. Two months later Grange and his brother were hanged in Edinburgh—Grange, "with his face against the sun," even as John Knox had prophesied only a few months before.[1]

In the case of Maitland Killigrew doubtless felt that his recent actions absolved him from any obligation of gratitude for the favour which the latter had done him in France many years earlier. Like Morton he regarded the death of the two Marian leaders as a political necessity as well as an act of justice. He had offered them every opportunity to make peace on reasonable terms, but they had haughtily rebuffed him and refused to yield until the walls of the fortress had been battered down around their very ears. It now seemed only fair that they should pay the penalty of their obstinacy. Moreover, neither had given any indication that they repented their past policies, and their continued existence would have constituted a threat both to England and to the present government in Scotland.

Although he supported the penalties imposed on the principal Castilians it is pleasant to record that in at least one instance Killigrew counselled mercy on behalf of the defeated party. According to James Melville he intervened to save his brother, Robert, from execution.[2] Like James, Robert had been one of Killigrew's close friends, and in his negotiations with the Castle, the English ambassador had found him more disposed towards agreement than his fellows. Elizabeth, who retained kindly feelings towards Melville since the time he had been Mary's ambassador at her court, also took a lenient view of his transgressions and persuaded Morton to save him from the fate of Grange and his brother.[3]

As so often happens in joint allied military operations there was an aftertaste of bitterness and recrimination. According to James Melville, Drury was outraged by the hanging of his old friend, "for he was a plain man of war and loved Grange

[1] *Ibid.*, f. 84, B. M. Cotton MSS., Caligula C.IV, f. 121.
[2] Melville, p. 135.
[3] B. M. Additional MSS., 33,531, f. 115.

well."[1] Towards Drury himself Morton retained a violent hatred which he had only suppressed out of necessity during the recent action against the Castle. Afterwards he accused the general of slackness in the performance of his duties and of being a "secret friend" of the Castilians. He even enlisted the help of an acquaintance at the English court in an attempt to persuade the Queen to dismiss Drury from his post at Berwick and put Killigrew in his place.[2]

There were no just grounds for Morton's charges. Though worn out by long and dangerous service in Scotland and distracted by anxiety for the welfare of his wife and children in England, Drury had conducted himself with energy, competence, and courage. No doubt he felt a personal preference for Grange and his friends as against the "wily" Morton, but there is not the slightest evidence that he allowed such feelings to affect his actions. Certainly he had done nothing to justify the Regent's underhanded endeavour to destroy his credit. This unsavoury episode helps to account for the distrust which Morton aroused in others.

At the end of June Killigrew was at last recalled to England. Indeed, by this time, his impatience to return home was being intensified, not only by the difficult and exhausting labours he had performed, but by a desire to be reunited with his wife and children whom he had not seen since his summons to Woodstock more than nine months before.[3] Always a devoted husband and father, Killigrew had grown increasingly anxious concerning the welfare of his wife, Catherine, and their children during his Scottish mission, and he now had good reason to hope that his recent services would be rewarded by a grant from the Queen sufficient for him to make some provision for his family's future.

Certainly his achievements merited recognition, since he had

[1] Melville, p. 137.
[2] B.M. Additional MSS. 33, 531 f. 113.
[3] Killigrew to Burghley, 1st June, 1573. B. M. Cotton MSS., Caligula C.IV, f. 104.

won great credit for himself and his country in Scotland. The Regent wrote to Burghley shortly after Killigrew's departure: "In my opinion, amongst her Majesty's ministers that were here, I may give the first praise to her Highness's ambassador, your brother-in-law—whom I pray you to thank therefore, and if either my credit with her Majesty or any other ability might serve, surely he shall not want that reward which his truth and honourable service have merited. And even so will I be an earnest suitor that, if any occasion occur whereby her Highness may be moved to send any of her ministers here in time coming, your Lordship will be a mean that he may be employed, for I think none will be able to bring his legation to as good effect, as well for his own experience and dexterity in doing, as for the universal good liking conceived of him and his good behaviour, both by this nobility and the whole people."[1]

Killigrew's hopes were not disappointed. For his success in Scotland and for his long devotion in her service during the past fifteen years, Elizabeth gave him a substantial reward. Prior to his departure into Scotland Killigrew had petitioned Lord Burghley to use his influence with the Queen to procure for him the manor of Lanrake in Cornwall.[2] In forwarding his petition to the Lord Treasurer he enumerated the various missions he had undertaken on her behalf since the reign of her sister, mentioning in some detail the scant wages and rewards he had received for them.

As a result of these services, he said, he had been reduced to the verge of poverty, and that this evidence of the Queen's favour was urgently needed to keep his children from beggary and as a means to enable him to marry his daughter to a near neighbour.[3] Ten days after the surrender of Edinburgh Castle

[1] P.R.O. S.P. 52/25 f. 74.
[2] Killigrew to Burghley 7th April, 1573. *Ibid.* f. 4. It was probably after his return to England when he wrote the longer account contained in Howard's Collection of Letters. Howard, pp. 184-8.
[3] *Ibid.*, p. 188.

Elizabeth wrote a brief letter to Killigrew commending him for his "travail and care" in her service. She explained the brevity of her letter by saying that she intended to let him know how well she allowed of his service on his return to England.[1] The Queen was better than her word. On the 22nd May, 1573, a month before his return to England, she had granted to her faithful ambassador the manor of Lanrake "in consideration of good service." [2]

Killigrew acted as Elizabeth's representative in Scotland twice during the next two years. He continued to be a staunch friend of the Regent Morton, and he ceaselessly urged the Queen and her councillors to give their support to his administration. Even those in the English government who favoured Morton were inclined to regard him as a calculating opportunist who was ready to sell himself to the highest bidder.[3] Killigrew had no illusions about the Regent's character. Harsh, overbearing, avaricious, he lacked the chivalry of Kirkaldy, the charm, wit and culture of Maitland, the stainless private life, or indeed, the subtlety of Moray. Yet Morton was not the treacherous self-seeker he is often said to have been. He maintained certain clear principles of government and public policy:

[1] P.R.O. S.P. 52/25 f. 64B.
[2] P.R.O. C. 66/1117, Part 10, m.l. Lanrake was formerly the property of the dissolved monastery of St Germains, located near the south east border of Cornwall, which paid to the crown an annual rent of 92 pounds eight shillings and one penny. This, however, was only a conventional rent. An astute man of business like Killigrew could undoubtedly derive a considerably larger income by levying fines and raising rents when his tenants died or their property changed hands. At the Cornish County Record Office there is a survey of the manor of Lanrake, drawn up in 1578 by William Samuel, Killigrew's reeve. It is over 20 pages in length and contains the location, acreage and boundaries of each tenement of the manor as well as the name of each tenant, the amount of the annual rent which he owed, and in many cases the day upon which it was due. One suspects that Killigrew put this document to good use.
[3] See Walsingham's letter to Burghley in April, 1574, in which he describes Morton as a man "noted to be over much inclined to his own gain and profit." P.R.O. S.P. 12/45 f. 27.

the consolidation of the Protestant revolution in Scotland, the reduction of both church and nobility to obedience to the King's government, the suppression of brigandage on the Anglo-Scottish frontier, and above all, close co-operation with England.[1]

In the realization of these aims he attained a considerable measure of success for several years, and many of his policies, particularly those relating to the Calvinist Kirk and the nobility were carried forward vigorously by James VI after Morton's death. They were also policies which, for the most part, Killigrew enthusiastically supported even though he realized that Morton's ruthlessness sometimes defeated the very objects he had in view.[2]

The beneficial results of the Regent's administration were everwhere to be seen. In a society that was traditionally lawless and disorderly the English ambassador noted a new respect for public authority. "The obedience is such in Scotland," he wrote, "that a man may ride where he pleases without fear or danger."[3] Morton himself set an example of personal confidence in the rule he had established. Killigrew said that the Regent often went hunting and fishing alone and unguarded in open defiance of his many enemies.[4] By this simple demonstration of fearless-

---

[1] For various estimates of Morton's character see: Tytler, vol. 6, pp. 293–4. P. Hume Brown, *History of Scotland from the accession of Mary Stuart to the revolution of 1689*, vol. 2, Cambridge, 1902, p. 181, John Hill Burton, *The history of Scotland from Agricola's invasion to the revolution of 1688*, vol. 5, 1870, pp. 440–1. T. F. Henderson's article on Morton in the Dictionary of national biography, *D.N.B.*, vol. 5, pp. 1214–27.

[2] Killigrew tried unsuccessfully to mitigate Morton's severity towards the Earl of Argyle and his wife. P.R.O. S.P. 52/26 f. 69. Argyle's wife had obtained from her former husband, the Regent Moray, some jewels, which had belonged to Moray's sister, Mary Stuart. These Morton was determined to obtain possession of, and he threatened both Argyle and his wife with imprisonment if they were not delivered into his hands. B. M. Cotton MSS., Caligula C.IV, f. 274. P.R.O. S.P. 52/26 ff. 18–68 passim. Tytler, vol. 6, pp. 235–6.

[3] P.R.O. S.P. 52/26 f. 85.   [4] *Ibid.*

ness he taught his countrymen that a man had come to govern them. "For anything I can learn," Killigrew wrote to Walsingham, "if he (Morton) were gone they know no more here where to find another for the purpose than you or I do for our weal in England." [1]

By every means in his power the ambassador strove to further Morton's work in those fields which tended to strengthen the good will between his country and Scotland. He assisted in the interrogation of captured English pirates whose depredations were arousing bitterness among the Scottish merchant class.[2] He also supported the Regent in the task of establishing order on the Anglo-Scottish frontiers by instructing English officials there to perform their duties with greater care.[3] Killigrew's efforts won him widespread respect among the clergy and people of Scotland.[4] When he departed for England in August, 1574, following the completion of his first mission, Morton wrote to Burghley and Leicester that no agent of the Queen had ever conducted himself in a way more pleasing to the generality in Scotland. Another Scottish observer later said that the ambassador was "marvellous well loved by all such as fear God and love peace." Only among Border ruffians, who doubtless resented his zeal in the cause of law and order, was he regarded with dislike.[5]

During his visit to Edinburgh in the summer of 1574 Killigrew had some interesting observations to make about young James VI who was now eight years old. While he was paying his respects to the King at Stirling the two royal tutors, Peter Young and George Buchanan, had the boy translate a chapter out of a Latin Bible into French and then into English. So expert was James's performance that the ambassador confessed that few men could have improved on it. Killigrew's comments

[1] Ibid., f. 35.
[2] "Interrogations of pirates." P.R.O. S.P. 53/9 ff. 21–2.
[3] P.R.O. S.P. 52/26 ff. 43–5.
[4] Ibid.
[5] P.R.O. S.P. 52/26 f. 79.

provide one of the earliest revelations of that erudition that was to be such a marked characteristic of James in later life. Perhaps the ambassador's admiration for the King's Calvinist tutors—"rare men"—he called them, would have been less keen if he had realized the bias which their heroic methods would create in the King's mind against men who shared their opinions.[1]

Killigrew's second journey to Scotland in June, 1575, was interrupted, as he was passing through Berwick, by news of an affray between the two chief Border officials, Elizabeth's Lord Warden of the Middle Marches, Sir John Foster, and Sir John Carmichael, the Scottish Keeper of Liddisdale, a personal friend of Morton. The incident took place at a meeting of the Warden's court at Reidswire on the Anglo-Scottish frontier where the English force under Foster took a severe beating. He and 300 of his followers were captured and taken to the Regent's residence at Dalkeith. Morton set most of the Englishmen at liberty, but he kept Sir John Foster and one or two others in polite custody for a few days in order to give their tempers time to cool. He feared, probably with good reason, that if he released them immediately their thirst for vengeance would result in a new outbreak of violence.[2]

Elizabeth, however, was incensed by the Regent's high-handed methods of keeping the peace. She demanded that he set the prisoners free at once and come to England in person to settle the dispute through consultation with the Earl of Huntingdon, the Lord President of the North. Although

---

[1] *Ibid.*, f. 29.

[2] "Notes of the beginning of the disorders at Reidswire and of the reformation and punishment to follow." B. M. Cotton MSS., Caligula C.IV, f. 57. Thomas Thompson ed., *The historie and life of James the sext; being an account of the affairs of Scotland from the year 1566 to the year 1596 with a short continuation to the year 1617*, (Bannatyne Club, no. 13), Edinburgh, 1825, p. 153. Sir John Harrington, *Nugae antiquae; being a miscellaneous collection of original papers—written during the reigns of Henry VIII, Edward VI, queen Mary, queen Elizabeth, and king James*, (Henry Harrington ed.) vol. 2, London, 1769, p. 128.

Morton expressed regret over the incident and offered redress for the injuries inflicted on the Queen's subjects, he refused to accede to her demands, and he put the blame for the dispute on the English officials concerned. He offered to arrange a meeting with Huntingdon in Scotland, not England as Elizabeth stipulated.[1]

That a mere Scottish nobleman, whom she regarded as greatly indebted to her for past favours, should not only presume to detain an officer of the English crown, but attempt to make terms with her as an equal, drove the Queen into one of those magnificent displays of rage that were a terror to her contemporaries but are a delight to the historian. Her frightened councillors feared that she was about to break off relations with the Scottish government or even plunge the two countries into war.[2] Elizabeth's anger must have been heightened by the fact that this unwelcome news arrived just when she was enjoying at Kenilworth those lavish and colourful entertainments provided by the Earl of Leicester which are described in Scott's celebrated novel.

Killigrew, of course, realized that the detention of Foster would anger the Queen. When he heard of the clash at Reidswire he cut short his journey to Scotland and decided to remain at Berwick until the matter had been settled.[3] Early in August, he received a message from his sovereign which he was commanded to send immediately to the Regent.

In cold and measured tones of contempt and hauteur such as one might use to an impudent lackey—which, nonetheless, suggest a rage that might at any moment explode into violence

[1] B. M. Cotton MSS., Caligula C.V, f. 51. The letters and reports pertaining to the Reidswire raid are contained in the Border Correspondence. P.R.O. S.P. 59/13 ff. 174–217.

[2] See Walsingham's letter to Burghley of 3rd August, 1575, in which he said that the Queen had ordered him to draw up a letter directed to Killigrew that was "so seasoned with choler" that he thought it would put an end to friendship between England and Scotland. B. M. Harleian MSS., 1992, f. 13.

[3] P.R.O. S.P. 52/26 f. 75.

—she expressed amazement at Morton's "strange and insolent manner of dealing." His imprisonment of her warden, she said, was an act that "wounds our honour to the eyes of the whole world," and has "given us so just a cause of breach of the treaty with that realm, whereof if we would take advantage by prosecuting that just revenge that we are provoked to, he should then both perceive and learn what it were for one of his base calling to offend one of our quality."

Elizabeth then administered to Killigrew a sharp reprimand for having failed to keep the government sufficiently informed of events in Scotland and for not rebuking Morton for his ill-behavior. "Having done with the Regent," she concluded, "we must not forget to say something of yourself. First we must charge you with your dark and slight kind of advertisement whereby you show yourself not so careful of our service, as in duty you are bound. Secondly you can receive such demands at their hands that so much touch us in honour without making any reply to the same, whereas indeed, if you either weighed our service or your own duty, you would not put up with things in such sort as you do."[1]

On the receipt of this communication the English ambassador was greatly taken aback. He begged Leicester to secure his recall if a policy of hostility was now to be adopted towards the Regent. His own close identification with Morton during recent years, he said, would make it impossible for him to win the confidence of his enemies should Elizabeth plan to build her support on new foundations.[2]

The Queen's displeasure had shaken his confidence, and her command to deliver an insulting message to the Regent confronted him with a task for which he felt the greatest distaste.

---

[1] *Ibid.*, f. 82. This letter is misdated September, 1575, in Boyd's *Calendar of State Papers, Scotland*. It reached Killigrew at Berwick before 8th August. See Walsingham's letter to Burghley, 3rd August, 1575. B. M. Harleian MSS., 6992, f. 13. See also Killigrew's letter to Walsingham, 8th August, 1575. P.R.O. S.P. 52/26 f. 85.

[2] *Ibid.*, f. 87.

From the very first the dangerous possibilities of the border outbreak filled him with foreboding. Soon after his arrival in Berwick, when the first news came of the skirmish, he had written to Walsingham: "Unless this matter be wisely and temperately handled the broken men of the Border, thieves and others that desire nothing but war and trouble, will draw this sudden misadventure to great inconvenience and a dangerous consequence." "Peace or war," he added, "hangeth now by a twine thread, and there be more in this town that profess war than peace." [1]

Upon receiving the Queen's stern rebuke both to the Regent and himself, he protested to Leicester: "...the Lord knoweth whether I did not wish myself at home, yea in prison, for fear of the burden that I doubted would be laid upon my weak shoulders; and my good Lord would it have not amazed a wiser man than I, considering that I was despatched from her Majesty to do good offices for the entertainment of the amity between the two realms, to hear of a matter so contrary to the same." [2]

In addition to these public matters the ambassador had other anxieties of a more personal nature pressing upon him. His house at Hendon had been infected by the plague, which had killed one of his servants and left his wife so ill that he feared for her life.[3] Moreover, the condition of his own health left much to be desired. In one of his letters he complained that he needed a physician to cure a 'grief' that had fallen into his legs. Perhaps it was a touch of rheumatism brought on by the damp Scottish weather, though the physical ailment may have been accentuated by the troubled state of his mind.[4]

Indeed, hardships large and small smote poor Henry in an unending succession during this mission. While he was returning to England a month later his horse trod the nail off his

[1] *Ibid.*, f. 30.
[2] *Ibid.*, f. 86.
[3] P.R.O. S.P. 52/26 f. 35.
[4] *Ibid.*

large toe. As he woefully reported to his friend, Walsingham, this injury caused him so much pain he could not bear to put a boot on his foot.[1] During his three difficult months in the north Killigrew often must have wished himself back in London engaged in the less strenuous employments of a civil servant, as Teller of the Exchequer.[2]

Despite these burdens he manfully strove to repair the damaged relations between England and Scotland. He and the Earl of Huntingdon, who had now been given charge of negotiations with the Regent, decided to deliver the Queen's message in a less acrimonious form. Both men feared that the violence of her words might provoke Morton to an equally heated rejoinder, and that the breach between the two realms would then become irreparable. To Killigrew, who believed that the survival of England and Scotland necessitated their close alliance against foreign enemies, this turn of events would be an unmitigated disaster.

He therefore let Morton know in unmistakeable terms Elisabeth's opinion of his behavior, without, however, transmitting to him the undiluted substance of her letter.[3] Killigrew's combined sternness and tact took good effect. Morton lost no time in acceding to the Queen's demands. He met Huntingdon at the Bond Road near Berwick, as she had stipulated, where the two men quickly reached a settlement. In addition he dismissed his prisoners with many presents and sent Carmichael to England to ask Elizabeth's pardon.[4] The Reidswire Raid, which Killigrew helped to settle, was the last important skirmish on the Borders, and thereby marked the virtual end of the Three Hundred Years' War between England and Scotland.

[1] P.R.O. S.P. 52/26 f. 92.

[2] Killigrew was also concerned over the effect of his absence from his duties as a Teller of the Exchequer. He wrote to Leicester on 14th August, 1575: "I have no deputy in my office. Therefore, for the surety of her Majesty's money, I have need to be home." P.R.O. S.P. 52/26 f. 85.

[3] Ibid., f. 87.

[4] B. M. Cotton MSS., C. V. f. 58.

As in most human altercations all the participants must bear some share of the blame. Certainly Elizabeth's anger was excessive. It was all very well for her to tell Morton in her most lofty manner that no subject of hers "would dare to enter upon a particular revenge to the breach of a public treaty without our knowledge and allowance," but he knew Sir John Foster well enough to realize that this was exactly what he might do unless he were put under restraint.[1]

Nevertheless the Regent's reply to the Queen's initial communication was too unaccommodating. Her warmest admirer would not include a sweet disposition among her virtues, but no sovereign—least of all, Elizabeth Tudor—could allow an official of Foster's importance to be treated thus without requiring instant redress.

Killigrew's own conduct was by no means above reproach. He claimed that by delaying his journey into Scotland while the dispute remained unsettled, he was only acting with diplomatic propriety. That may have been true enough, but the urgency of the situation demanded bolder measures. Instead of dithering in Berwick he ought to have ridden at once to Dalkeith, and warned the Regent of his peril if he did not immediately offer apologies to the Queen and declare himself ready to accept whatever form of mediation she might stipulate. Had the ambassador made this point forcefully enough and in time, Morton would probably have taken his advice, and the whole crisis might have been avoided.

In his own defence Killigrew afterwards said that on meeting the Regent in Edinburgh late in July, his behaviour towards him was "as strange as though it stood on terms of war".[2] By this time, however, more than two weeks had passed. The probability is that this event and his fears concerning its consequences so unnerved him as to destroy temporarily his capacity to act. He was afflicted by that dismal certainty which a subordinate often feels in such a situation—that however

[1] P.R.O. S.P. 52/26 f. 82.
[2] *Ibid.*, f. 85.

matters turn out in the end, most of the blame will fall upon himself. His anxiety seems to have produced what today would be called a psychosomatic illness, for he described himself to Morton as "somewhat crazed and weak by sickness." [1]

The best proof of his personal resilience and diplomatic skill was the speed with which he afterwards brought about a settlement to the satisfaction of all concerned. Probably his recovery was assisted by the help he received from the Earl of Leicester. Early in August, 1575, he wrote an emotional letter of gratitude to Leicester which indicates that the latter had employed his influence to lessen the Queen's wrath against him.[2] Though at times insanely jealous of any person who threatened him as a rival, Leicester was yet kind and generous to his dependents. The readiness he showed to give his help on this occasion is one explanation of Killigrew's devoted loyalty to him over a period of nearly thirty years.

His personal success as an ambassador, however, was not attended by fulfilment of the aims for which he had worked. The Queen refused to adopt the policies recommended by himself and her pro-Scottish councillors. She made no move to capitalize on the triumph she had achieved in 1573. Partisans of the Calvinist government like Killigrew and Walsingham believed that the defeat of the Marian party and the establishment of a strong Protestant administration in Scotland were victories which Elizabeth could neglect only at great peril.

If she failed to bind the Regent and his followers by continued assistance they would look elsewhere for support, and England's enemies among the pro-French element in Scotland would recover their former power. Yet Elizabeth refused to gather in the fruits of her ambassador's achievements. She rejected his recommendations that she enter into a formal defensive league with Morton's government, and insure the loyalty of the King's party by the grant of pensions to the Regent and the chief Protestant nobles.[3]

[1] The Regent's Declaration to Huntingdon, 6 September 1575.
[2] P.R.O. S.P. 52/26 f. 85.   [3] Ibid., f. 38.

As early as the spring of 1574 Killigrew could see the ill-effect of the Queen's indifference. The growing wealth and prosperity of the country, which Morton's strong government had made possible, caused the Scots to become increasingly independent and critical in their attitude towards England. To Sir Christopher Hatton he made this warning observation: "If any man thinks they (the Scots) be in that state of necessity they must depend on England, having offended France so much, I protest to my knowledge he is deceived, for I know that France woos the Regent and the King's faction. I find them lusty, gallant, having almost forgotten their late and dangerous estate." For less than 2,000 pounds a year in pensions, he said, Elizabeth could hold the King's party loyal to her interest.[1]

Before his departure from Scotland in the summer of 1575 Killigrew saw the growth of those elements of discord that were eventually to cause Morton's downfall. The Calvinist clergy and the merchants resented the heavy financial exactions which he imposed upon them, and the anti-English nobles, who had lost power and influence during the Regent's ascendancy, were keenly watching for an opportunity to attack his authority.[2]

Killigrew was not called upon again to perform ambassadorial work in Scotland—perhaps because the Queen felt that he had become too closely attached to Morton's interest to be of further use for her service in that country. He nevertheless continued to keep in close touch with Scottish affairs through correspondence with Thomas Randolph, with the Regent, and with his other acquaintances among the King's party.[3] His fears

---

[1] P.R.O. S.P. 52/26 f. 81. There is no evidence of any real intention on Morton's part to accept French offers at this time although the Queen's failure to grant his requests for aid, in Killigrew's opinion, had somewhat cooled his friendship for England and made him more favourably disposed towards the pro-French faction. *Ibid.*, f. 65.

[2] *Ibid.*, f. 89.

[3] Two of Killigrew's correspondents were the Scottish Protestant clergymen, Alexander Hay and Nicholas Elphinstone. P.R.O. S.P. 52/27 ff. 22, 27.

concerning the dangers resulting from Elizabeth's neglect of Morton and his friends were soon borne out by events.

In the winter of 1577–8 she sent Randolph north in a belated effort to support the Regent against the aristocratic faction which was making preparations to overthrow his government. Shortly after his arrival in Scotland he sent Killigrew word of Morton's downfall, and Killigrew could only write sadly to his friend, William Davison: "Her Majesty, now it is too late, taketh the Regent's part more than before. What practices lieth hidden we shall discover in time. I pray God it will not be to our cost." [1]

Morton managed to outwit his enemies and to recover a considerable measure of his power in May, 1578, but his former ascendancy in the country was broken beyond repair. Three years later the pro-French faction, under the leadership of Esmé Stuart, Count d'Aubigny, gained control of James's counsels. With James's assent d'Aubigny had Morton arrested, tried, and executed for complicity in Darnley's murder. Morton's death removed England's most faithful adherent, a man whose advancement had been, to a considerable extent, the result of Killigrew's astute diplomacy and had constituted his most important contribution in the sphere of Anglo-Scottish relations. The absence of the Regent's controlling influence laid the country open for several years to the renewed threat of Catholic, foreign domination. That threat was removed only when Elizabeth learned how to bridle the King of Scotland by grants of money for his needy purse and by dangling before him the hope of succession to her throne.

[1] P.R.O. S.P. 52/27 f. 33. P.R.O. S.P. 15/25 f. 98.

CHAPTER VIII

RETIREMENT FROM DIPLOMACY, 1575–1585

FOLLOWING his return from Scotland in September, 1575, Killigrew spent over ten years in almost complete retirement from the diplomatic service. The reason for his withdrawal is unknown. Perhaps Elizabeth had lost confidence in him because of his conduct of negotiations at the time of the Reidswire raid. She may have felt that his slowness in rebuking Morton indicated a failing which she attributed to other Protestant envoys—that of placing sympathy with their foreign co-religionists on a higher plane than their obligation of loyalty to herself and to England.[1]

Whatever its cause this period of retirement brought no cessation to the busy tempo of Killigrew's life. Very likely he found considerable satisfaction in being relieved of the onerous responsibilities and financial burdens of foreign embassies. To a friend he wrote: "I follow my old resolution not to deal in matters of state."[2] Without the distraction and expense of diplomatic employment he could devote himself more profitably to personal concerns at home. Most of his time was divided between London where he occupied the active and lucrative office of Teller of the Exchequer, and Cornwall where he was increasing his standing as a man of property by purchasing land from his friends, the Earls of Leicester and Huntingdon.[3]

---

[1] The Queen, for example, denounced Walsingham as a Calvinist and Puritan who was more interested in the cause of Protestantism than in the safety of England. Read, *Walsingham*, vol. 1, p. 370.

[2] P.R.O. S.P. 15/25 f. 68.

[3] Killigrew purchased the manor of Bottlet from the Earl of Huntingdon for 3,600 pounds in May, 1574. P.R.O. Close Rolls, C. 54/974. (hereafter: P.R.O. C. 54).

At Hendon Killigrew also owned an estate, and there he lived the life of a country squire, supervising the planting and harvesting of his crops. In the autumn of 1574 he wrote to Sir Francis Walsingham at the court: "I had thought to see you before now, but my harvest is not all in the barn which causes my absence for a while longer unless you advise me to the contrary". Referring to Sir Francis's wife, Lady Ursula Walsingham, he added in a humourous vein: "If Mrs Ursula be a courtier I greet her after the best manner, though it be out of the country. I pray that all the saints were come that mean to come this year that I might pay her the twenty pounds I owe."[1] Only rarely could Killigrew bring himself to speak so light-heartedly of his debts — usually they were a great source of personal worry.

To this welcome refuge at Hendon he brought his wife and children when London was afflicted by the plague. In December, 1577, he wrote to his good friend and fellow diplomat, William Davison: "I desire you to excuse my long silence which hath chanced by reason my house was infected with the plague, and so I and my wife driven to Hendon where we have remained till now and where my children remain still. My wife I have brought hither again to receive some ease of her weakness. Had not these urgent causes of moving and removing with my wife's sickly estate have letted me, you should not so long have wanted my letters." [2] No doubt Killigrew found the open spaces and country air of Hendon a healthier environment for himself and his family than the crowded plague-ridden streets of London, but as he knew from experience, disease could sometimes strike them as easily at Hendon as elsewhere. At any rate Killigrew thoroughly enjoyed his rôle as a gentleman farmer. Was he himself not a countryman born from the far reaches of Cornwall? He seized every opportunity to escape from his routine duties at court and at the Exchequer to visit his lands in Hendon and Cornwall.

[1] P.R.O. S.P. 52/26 f. 49.
[2] P.R.O. S.P. 15/25 f. 49.

In the City he had a home in St Paul's churchyard next door to the Dean's house. Here he was frequently joined for dinner by relatives and friends in government service. He jovially wrote to Davison on one occasion: "I had half a dozen good fellows with me for dinner." Among them were Thomas Randolph and Henry Knollys, both veterans in the Queen's diplomatic service, his wife's brother, William Cook, and his nephew, Anthony, elder brother of the more famous Francis Bacon.[1] Sometimes he and Catherine rode up to Hatfield where they enjoyed the hospitality of their brother-in-law, Lord Burghley.[2] On other occasions he visited Burghley's splendid palace at Theobalds at which the Queen and her court were often entertained.

Despite his resolve not to meddle in matters of state, Killigrew was not always able to live up to his resolution. Frequently he was summoned to court for consultation on Scottish affairs, to attend the Queen on royal progresses or to help entertain foreign ambassadors. At such times his rôle was not confined to formalities. In December, 1580, for example, he attended a dinner at Cecil House in Covent Garden given for the French embassy which had come to negotiate marriage between Elizabeth and the Duke of Alençon. There were present 371 guests including all the Privy Councillors, six of the leading peers and 21 others. Killigrew had more to do than help consume the magnificent feast which the Lord Treasurer had laid on at a cost of over 300 pounds. Because of his excellent French he was commissioned to act as an interpreter in conversations with the French ambassadors.

[1] P.R.O. S.P. 15/7 f. 65. Both Killigrew and his brother, William, lived in St Paul's churchyard. They may have lived together in the same house. P.R.O. S.P. 52/4 f. 22A. See also Thomas Randolph's letter of 18th November, 1561, addressed to "my loving and assured friend, Mr. Henry Killigrew at his house in St Paul's churchyard." P.R.O. S.P. 52/6 f. 57A.

[2] In Burghley's household accounts at Hatfield there are several occasions mentioned when Henry and his wife paid visits to the Cecils in the summer and autumn of 1576. Hatfield MSS., vol. 226 (entries for 18th–19th July, 5th June and 5th November, 1576.)

Also acting with him in the same capacity were Burghley's son, Thomas Cecil, and Francis Bacon who was then a twenty year old law student at Grays Inn.[1] One wonders how proficiently Burghley's son performed the duties assigned to him on this occasion. His longest stay in France had been as a youth travelling abroad, as his father fondly hoped, to prepare himself for a distinguished career in the diplomatic service. But the young Cecil—to the consternation of his pious father—preferred the delights of pursuing the fair sex to the rigours of instruction by his tutor.[2] Since Thomas had no head for book learning he may have gained a better grasp of the French language through the former occupation than he would ever have done through the latter.

The principal source of information concerning Killigrew's activities during the period of his temporary retirement is a series of his letters to William Davison, an old friend who had served him as secretary on several missions to Scotland. On his last departure from that country Killigrew had recommended Davison as his successor.[3] Although this suggestion was not adopted Davison soon became one of Elizabeth's principal emissaries to the Netherlands and later a Secretary of State. Like Killigrew, Davison was a stiffnecked Puritan. He also proved himself to be a capable, devoted public servant and a man of complete personal integrity. All these virtues, however, did not deter Elizabeth from smashing his career after the execution of Mary Queen of Scots in February, 1587. In her attempt to throw the blame for this act upon her councillors, Davison was made the chief scapegoat. He was stripped of his offices, confined to the Tower for eighteen months, and never restored to royal favour.

Most of Killigrew's surviving letters to Davison occur in

[1] Conyers Read, *Lord Burghley and Queen Elizabeth*, London, 1960, p. 258.
[2] Read, *Cecil*, p. 216.
[3] P.R.O. S.P. 52/26 ff. 37, 87–8. Melville, p. 61. Nicholas Harris Nicolas, *Life of William Davison, secretary of state and privy councillor to queen Elizabeth*, London, 1823, pp. 3–6. D.N.B., vol. 5, pp. 629–32.

1577–8 when the latter was ambassador in the Low Countries; their interest derives from the insight which they give on character and opinions of the writer. Recognizing Davison as a person of ability and one whose views on matters of public policy coincided with his own, Killigrew took considerable pains to further his career. He had no personal influence with Elizabeth, but he possessed a wide acquaintance among the prominent figures about her, and he could enlist their support for Davison's advancement.

Killigrew was careful to communicate the news sent by his friend from the Netherlands to the great ones at court with whom he was intimate, and he advised him to ply with "advertisements and compliments" the Earl of Leicester and his brother, the Earl of Warwick, the Earl of Huntingdon, who was the Queen's cousin, her favourite, Sir Christopher Hatton, Mr Secretary Walsingham, Lord Burghley, and Sir Nicholas Bacon.[1] Of those mentioned, all were members of the Privy Council and all, with the exception of Burghley, belonged to the forward Protestant group in the government.[2]

Killigrew's correspondence with Davison offers many illustrations of his intense Protestantism and of his belief that the aim of national policy should be the service of God and the Protestant faith. In February, 1578, hearing of a plan to send Leicester in command of a body of English troops to the aid of William of Orange, he expressed the fear that "we shall propose but not resolve." "The Lord give us grace," he added, "to do that may be to his glory, our own surety, and the help of our friends in time... The Lord, for his mercy's sake and for his own glory, defend his and his own against the wise politi-quettes of this age. For my part I can but wish well and pray to his Majesty who only works miracles."[3] This passage reveals

---

[1] P.R.O. S.P. 15/25 f. 40. P.R.O. S.P. 83/10 f. 1.

[2] On factions in the Privy Council see: Conyers Read, "Walsingham and Burghley in Queen Elizabeth's council," *English Historical review*, (January, 1912), vol. 28, p. 39.

[3] P.R.O. S.P. 15/25 f. 74.

the ideals which motivated Killigrew and other Englishmen who urged common action with Protestant powers abroad.

When he referred to the "wise politiquettes of our age" one wonders whether he intended this term to include his own sovereign. One of the principal grievances of Killigrew and his fellow 'hot-gospellers' against the Queen was her consistent refusal to equate God's glory with the surety of her own country.

A corollary of Killigrew's fervent Protestantism was his close relationship with the Puritan movement. His support for men of Puritan beliefs dates back to the very beginning of Elizabeth's reign. In February, 1559, he and his brother, John, helped William Ramsay, a prominent west country Puritan minister, obtain the church of Tiverton for which they held the right of presentation.[1] Thereafter he developed close connections with the dominant Presbyterian wing of the Puritan movement, connections that were strengthened by his long tour of diplomatic service in Scotland. There he gained the friendship of a number of the Calvinist clergy, and his letters at that time reveal a warm admiration for such noted Presbyterian leaders as Knox and Buchanan.[2]

At home he and Catherine acquired a wide circle of friends among English Presbyterian divines. While Henry was engaged in Scottish affairs in the summer of 1575 his wife was receiving letters of religious instruction from Edward Dering, the bold Cambridge scholar who dared to lecture Elizabeth to her face on her failure to cleanse the church of corruption and of the forms of Popery.[3] Another of Killigrew's intimates was John Field, the energetic secretary, organizer, and propagandist of the English Presbyterian party.[4]

[1] On William Ramsey see: Patrick Collinson, *The puritan classical movement in the reign of Elizabeth I*, University of London Ph. D. thesis, 1957, p. 22.

[2] For Killigrew's admiring reference to Buchanan see above, chapter seven, p. 172.

[3] See page 9, footnote 3.

[4] P.R.O. S.P. 15/25 f. 74. On Field see Marshall M. Knappen, *Tudor*

The most interesting example of Killigrew's support of the
Puritans occurred in 1578 when he and Davison cooperated to
secure the establishment of an English church in the Netherlands whose services were modelled on reformed lines. The
event which prompted their action was a request by members
of the Merchant Adventurers for a chaplain to conduct services
at the English house, their headquarters in Antwerp.

Killigrew devised a plan to introduce a friend, Walter
Travers, into this position. Travers was a noted Puritan and a
close friend of Thomas Cartwright who was then living in
exile in the Netherlands. Killigrew learned from Walsingham
that there was no chance of obtaining a licence from the government for a man of such opinions to preach abroad. He therefore
suggested to Davison that he invite Travers over to the Low
Countries simply as a friend. After his arrival there Davison
should secure from the Prince of Orange permission for
Travers to give a lecture at the English house in Antwerp.

To forstall any protest against the introduction of Puritan
forms into the services by Travers, Killigrew recommended
that the Prince should be induced to ask that the same cere-
monies be performed in the English church as those in the
reformed churches of the Netherlands so that disputes might
be avoided. As a fitting reply to anyone who questioned these
proceedings he suggested to Davison: "it might serve for
answer ... that you were glad first to obtain to have one read to
our nation the word of God in our own tongue which before
was never yielded unto." [1]

After consultation with Field, the Presbyterian secretary,
Killigrew completed arrangements for Travers' installation in
the English church, and, in April, 1578, he helped to pay for his
journey to the Netherlands.[2] The strategem was successful, and
after Travers was settled in Antwerp, Killigrew continued

Puritanism, a chapter in the history of idealism, Chicago, 1939, pp. 230–497
passim. (hereafter: Knappen).
[1] P.R.O. S.P. 15/25 ff. 68, 74.
[2] Ibid., f. 86.

to show a lively interest in the success of his labours.[1]

Killigrew's concern with the affairs of the Netherlands had a personal side that was only indirectly related to the weightier matters of religion and politics. He wished to secure positions for two members of his family in that country. One was a son of his brother-in-law, John Michell of Truro.[2] He had been living for some time as servant in Killigrew's home in London, and in the winter of 1577–8 he persuaded his uncle to help him obtain a place in Davison's household. The Cornishman wrote to his friend: "My nephew, Michell, hath been very earnest with me to commend him to your service. He can make copies of occurrents, for though his hand be not learned, it is legible, and can I induce to write day and nights. Good Mr Davison, if you accept of him, put him to all manner of service as the least servant of yours, for so shall he profit most and his friends… I have given him the best instructions I could and warning that if he obey you not as myself, that he may never again look me in the face." [3]

The ambassador acceded to Killigrew's request and took the youth into his household. In thanking Davison for his favour he said: "I end with hearty thanks unto you and for my nephew whom I beseech you to keep under and from idleness. He was wont to be called up a morning, being very given to keep his bed over long which will do him no good." [4] One suspects that the boy's 'earnest' petition to go to the Low Countries arose from an understandable desire to escape the stern guardianship of his uncle.

[1] On 23rd August, 1578, Killigrew wrote to Davison: "I pray you to remember me to Mr Travers whose labours the Lord bless with increase of fruit." P.R.O. S.P. 83/2 f. 43. The episode concerning the efforts of Killigrew and Davison to establish Travers in the English church at Antwerp is treated in Read, *Walsingham* vol. 2, pp. 260–2, 265. A. F. Scott-Pearson, *Thomas Cartwright and Elizabethan puritanism*, Cambridge, 1925, pp. 170–3. Knappen, p. 249.

[2] Vivian ed., *Visitation of Cornwall*, 1620, p. 142.

[3] P.R.O. S.P. 15/25 f. 49.

[4] *Ibid.*, f. 74.

Another of Killigrew's young charges was a boy named Harry Caltropt who appears to have been his illegitimate son. In October, 1577, he wrote to Davison: "I have a young boy of sixteen years, fit to be made a soldier of. I mean to give him money to carry him hither and to furnish therewith a fair arquebus, a pistolet, and gilt morion. It is for Harry whom you used to see waiting on me in London..."[1] Later Killigrew placed him in a French regiment commanded by a friend, the Huguenot soldier, Louis de Hangest, Viscount de Argenlieu, which was serving with the army of the States-General against Don John, Philip II's Governor-General of the Netherlands.[2]

The boy seems to have had an unhappy time in his military venture abroad. Like other foreign contingents serving in the Low Countries his regiment suffered severe privation for want of pay. Moreover, he was dissatisfied with his position in a French unit when he would have preferred to be with his friends among the English volunteers commanded by that gallant warrior, Sir John Norris.[3]

On receiving a letter from his boy complaining of these matters Killigrew wrote to Davison: "I understand by Harry Caltropt ... that he hath no pay, and therefore had twenty shillings from your honour which I shall gladly repay, desiring you to bestow so much more on him if you see need for the same." Yet Killigrew was suspicious. He told Davison that he had already given the boy pocket money and had left some more besides with a friend to give him in case of necessity.

Hy wryly commented: "For him to spend all this and twenty more of yours besides considering the style soldiers make for the most part lying out of garrison, I think it much." Concerning Harry's dissatisfaction at being in a French regiment he said: "...I would have him remain with the French for the language's sake and to be acquainted with their order of

[1] P.R.O. S.P. 15/25 f. 40.
[2] In writing to Davison on 28th October, 1577, Killigrew asked to be remembered to de Argenlieu. P.R.O. S.P. 83/2 f. 43.
[3] P.R.O. S.P. 15/25 f. 116.

service, and therefore I beseech your honour to signify so much unto him when you see occasion. I know how hard it is for our youth to live among the French, but I would have him with patience overcome all difficulties for my commandment's sake which, if he observe not, let him take his pleasure." [1]

Two weeks later Killigrew informed Davison that he had heard that many English and Scottish soldiers in Flanders had perished from sickness and poverty. "I pray you," he said, "to cause your servant, Michell, to write unto me ... whether my boy live or die. If he live and that the plague be so great and the service in the field so small I would he were, by your friendly help and means, called from the camp for a time to some garrison or to Antwerp until the cold of winter shall have cooled the heat of the disease yet raging among them..." "But", he added, with pious complacency, "if God have called him already, among so many others, it is best for him, and the Lord be blessed in all his works." [2]

At the beginning of November, 1578, Killigrew wrote to Davison: "I heard by a friend of mine that the boy deserved not that I should have that care of him, for I hear that he was living in Antwerp since the camp marched without leave of his master so, as I mean to leave him to himself, seeing he will not obey me but rather seeks to put me to shame." "Of a bastard vine," he concluded, "seldom came sweet grapes." [3]

These passages suggest a heaviness and severity in Killigrew's personality that probably grew stronger as he advanced into middle age. Like his brother-in-Law, Lord Burghley, he had

---

[1] *Ibid.*

[2] *Ibid.*, f. 117.

[3] P.R.O. S.P. 83/10 f. 1. The fate of young Harry Caltropt is unknown. He does not appear again in Killigrew's correspondence or elsewhere. For want of pay his regiment was driven to mutiny and pillaging. The depredations committed by its soldiers were so outrageous that the Flemish peasants waylaid and killed a considerable number of them in retaliation. Perhaps this was Harry's fate, or he may eventually have died of starvation or disease like many other of his comrades. P.R.O. S.P. 83/10 ff. 18–19, 80, 82. P.R.O. S.P. 83/11 ff. 50, 52.

little sympathy with youthful frailty.[1] Even towards the way-wardness of young Harry, who provides the only evidence of a redeeming folly in his past life, Killigrew's reaction was that of a stern and self-righteous parent.

In other portions of his correspondence Killigrew reveals himself in a more sympathetic light. The bond between himself and Davison extended to their respective families, and the friendly salutations that passed between the two men often mention their wives and children—Davison asking to be remembered to "the three sisters," Killigrew's young daughters, Anne, Elizabeth, and Mary; Killigrew congratulating his friend on "the good news of my gossip, your wife's safe delivery whom I pray God to make a strong woman." "Mine," he added, "lieth yet in the straw" (in child bed). [2]

In August, 1577, while serving as ambassador in the Nether-lands, Davison requested Killigrew's assistance in obtaining transportation for his wife to the Low Countries as speedily as possible. "I pray you, Sir," he entreated, "hasten her forward all you can that she were over ere the season or weather grow too foul. I beseech you give my servant straight charge he omit it not whatsoever it cost." [3] A short time later Davison again wrote anxiously: "I have sent over for my wife, and I think every day a year until I hear of her safe arrival, faring as a merchant who has all his riches in one venture." [4]

Killigrew quickly responded to his friend's requests, and Mrs Davison made a safe journey to her husband in the Nether-lands. Early the following year, perhaps as a token of apprecia-tion, she and her husband sent gifts to Henry and Catherine. "My wife," Killigrew wrote in acknowledgement, "doth earnestly thank Mrs Davison for her great present of silver thread which she cannot yet deserve, and for "Bon" (probably

---

[1] For Burghley's attitude towards his eldest son, Thomas, see: Read, *Cecil*, pp. 212–17.
[2] P.R.O. S.P. 83/10 f. 10. P.R.O. S.P. 83/2 f. 43.
[3] P.R.O. S.P. 70/144 f. 71.
[4] P.R.O. S.P. 70/133 f. 1162.

a hunting falcon) many thanks. She is yet tame and pleasant and will not bite." [1]

In Killigrew's private letters there is little conscious self revelation of his innermost thoughts and feelings, but this is a typically Elizabethan trait. People of that era found the challenge of every day life too absorbing and difficult to enjoy the modern luxury of introspection. Elizabethans were natural extroverts. They expressed their feelings in action, not on paper.

On the other hand his letters give a great deal of interesting information about ordinary life of the upper classes at court. Like other Elizabethan officials corresponding with diplomats living abroad, Killigrew deliberately wrote large portions of his correspondence to Davison in the form of news-letters. In them he set down a resumé of all events at home and abroad which he believed would be useful for his correspondent to know. These included meetings of the Privy Council and such of their decisions as would have direct bearing on Davison's diplomatic work in the Low Countries, the arrival of foreign ambassadors, and the coming and going of the great personages at the centre of government.

Included also, are lesser items of gossip: the brawls and illicit love making that were a constant feature of court life. Killigrew tells Davison how one Abraham, a groom of the Queen's Stable, assaulted the Recorder of London wounding him on the head and arm. For "this ill fact" he was committed to the Marshalsea and subsequently by the Star Chamber condemned to be "set openly in the stocks at the place where he committed the outrage that he might serve for example to the passersby." [2]

On another occasion Killigrew wrote of one of the Queen's maids of honour who had a child by Mr Bowsen, Esquire for the Body. This gentleman fled to avoid arrest, but the unfortunate lady was thrown in the Tower by the Queen's order. Elizabeth, embittered by her own committment to chaste

[1] P.R.O. S.P. 15/25 f. 86.
[2] *Ibid.*, f. 74.

spinsterhood, was prompt to punish such irregularities. Killigrew's reaction was also characteristic. In the same letter, after
enumerating several other sinful occurrences and the heavy
penalties visited upon their perpetrators, he concluded solemn-
ly: "These things be good warnings of God's displeasure." [1]
Perhaps, like many Puritans, Killigrew took almost as much
pleasure in contemplating, and thereby in sharing vicariously,
the fleshly sins of his fellow mortals, as he did in their punishment. But one should give him the benefit of the doubt.
Killigrew was comparatively free from the Puritan vice of
prudery.

As in the case of other Protestant Englishmen of his time,
he was an interested observer of the voyages of exploration
that were opening up a new world of knowledge and adven-
ture to men of the sixteenth century. For Sir Francis Drake
Killigrew had an especial admiration. Writing to Davison in
August, 1578, of Drake's famous voyage around the world in
the Golden Hind, he said: "Drake that went in the spring is not
heard of, but if he do not miscarry, his journey will yield much
light to our navigation. I make no small account of that man,"
he added. [2]

When Killigrew made this prediction Drake had only been
at sea for a few months; he, therefore, could not have known
of his destination-indeed, no one knew except Drake, Elizabeth, and a select few in the Council. Yet the prophecy was
true enough. Drake brought back not only "much light" to
English navigation—on America, the Pacific, and the Far East,
but a half million pounds in specie.

Other voyages, however, were not so profitable from a
financial point of view. Early in October, 1578, Killigrew
reported to his friend, Davison, the return of Martin Frobisher's
third voyage to Greenland, his ships laden with ore. Despite
the optimism that prevailed in certain quarters over the value
of this ore, Killigrew was inclined to be sceptical. "Some," he

[1] *Ibid.*, f. 71.
[2] P.R.O. S.P. 83/2 f. 43.

said, "judge the voyage to be good and profitable. I, for myself, do think it will prove rather of silver than gold."[1] The ore which Frobisher brought back, in fact, proved worthless.[2]

Killigrew's interest in the voyages never became sufficiently enthusiastic for him to loosen his own purse strings in their support. Many of his friends—Leicester, Walsingham, Randolph, were eager to invest their money in these expeditions, but Killigrew's attitude was more closely akin to that of his brother-in-law, the cautious, thrifty Lord Burghley.

Killigrew's letters reveal that he was an enthusiastic supporter of the rebel cause in the Netherlands and an ardent admirer of the heroic William the Silent, Prince of Orange. He may have met William during his mission to the Palatine in 1569 when the latter was a poverty-stricken exile seeking aid from the German princes after his expulsion from the Low Countries.[3] Two of Killigrew's friends in that country were Philippe de Marnix, Sieur de St Aldegonde and Pierre Loyseleur de Villiers, who were intimate advisors of the Prince of Orange, and even after William's death, the Cornishman was known abroad for his devotion to the House of Orange.[4] Killigrew's harsh

[1] P.R.O. S.P. 15/25 f. 116.

[2] A. L. Rowse, *The Elizabethans in America*, London, 1959, p. 24.

[3] Some personal acquaintance with Orange is suggested in Killigrew's letter to Davison on 15th October, 1577, where he asked him to "render my humble service to the good Prince whom I pray God to prosper." P.R.O. S.P. 15/25 f. 40.

[4] Frequent expressions of friendship towards St Aldegonde and Villiers occur in Killigrew's letters to Davison. P.R.O. S.P. 15/25 ff. 49, 63, 74, 78, 86, 117. Villiers was a refugee French Huguenot minister who was chaplain to William the Silent. See, C. Boer, *Hofpredikers van Prins Willem van Orange*, The Hague, 1952. Killigrew's letters reveal that he had a considerable number of acquaintances among foreign Protestants. In addition to those mentioned there was the prominent Huguenot political writer, publicist and diplomat, Philippe de Mornay, Sieur du Plessis-Marly, who was frequently sent to England by Henry of Navarre to request aid from Elizabeth. P.R.O. S.P. 15/25 ff. 49, 117. Read, *Walsingham*, vol. 2, pp. 263, 294, 298–302. Another was a distinguished and widely travelled soldier of fortune named Fremyn who was serving with his Protestant co-religionists in the Netherlands at this time. P.R.O. S.P. 15/25 f. 98. In June, 1590, Louise de

Puritan fanaticism had little in common with the tolerant, humane, outlook of William the Silent, and when he later served in the Netherlands he bitterly opposed the policies of the Dutch merchant aristocracy from whom William gained his chief support and whose tolerant religious views accorded with his own.

But such differences of attitude, even if he were aware of them, would have counted for little with Killigrew in the years, 1577-8. He looked upon William as a great Protestant leader upon whose success England's very existence depended. In the summer of 1577 the struggle between Spain and the revolted provinces had reached a critical stage. Don John seized Namur in July, and war broke out between himself and the States-General. The situation was one of extreme danger because the States were split on the question of whether to follow William's leadership or that of the Catholic Archduke Mathias whom the nobles of the southern provinces supported for the Governor-Generalship of the Netherlands. Moreover the English government feared that France, which seemed on the verge of composing its civil dissensions, was about to send troops to the aid of Don John.

Late in December, 1577, Killigrew reported to Davison: "A courier came yesterday from our ambassador (in France) who brings no news but all of peace and banquetting there which I like not..." As to Archduke Mathias's championship of the revolted provinces he said: "...we cannot yet tell what to judge ... but think as of the Duke of Alençon when he seemed to take part with the Protestants of France. It is very hard for fire and water to mix unless the Lord do miraculously determine it..." He concluded: "God defend the good Prince of Orange from their hollow hearts upon whose life you see what good and evil dependeth. If it were taken from us we

Coligny, wife of William the Silent, wrote to Killigrew asking his help in securing the release of a Dutch Protestant minister who had been kidnapped by the Ostend freebooters. She thanked him for past favours and referred to him as "one of my very best friends." P.R.O. S.P. 84/37 f. 297.

might here in England justly fear all these numbers gathered together, both by Don John and all the others of his religion. I can only pray for his preservation as our quiet at home." [1] Killigrew was entirely convinced of the necessity of sending money and men to William's aid. In the winter of 1577–8, when the Queen was contemplating the despatch of a large force under Leicester to the Netherlands for this purpose, he hoped and expected that he would be chosen to take part in the expedition. [2]

The troops were not sent, however; instead Elizabeth turned to another fruitless attempt to settle the disputes in the Low countries by mediation. Killigrew's impatience with the Queen's failure to adopt the militant policy, which was urged upon her by his friends in the Privy Council, was probably strengthened by the realization that lack of aid from England compelled William to rely on French assistance. Elizabeth and some of her councillors feared that such assistance would result in the domination of the Netherlands by France, a thing which they opposed even more than Spanish control of this territory.

Doubtless that fear lay at the back of Killigrew's mind, but characteristically he chose to emphasize the religious struggle between Catholic and Protestant. In the summer of 1578, when the Prince of Orange had been forced to call in the army of the Duke of Alençon, he wrote to Davison: "…it cannot be driven out of my head that all French semblants are traitorous… because they proceed still in Languedoc and Gascony with all doings of severity against them of the religion." "What hope," he asked, "can the Prince of Orange conceive of them who forget their own profit for to persecute them of contrary religion?" "The Lord defend him against their deep dissembled practise of treachery." [3]

[1] P.R.O. S.P. 15/27 f. 65.
[2] On 22nd February, 1578, Killigrew wrote to Davison: "If my Lord of Leicester come over (to the Netherlands) you shall see me there, God willing." P.R.O. S.P. 15/25 f. 74.   [3] P.R.O. S.P. 83/2 f. 43.

From the modern standpoint Killigrew's indignation towards religious persecution in France would have been more convincing if he had been equally shocked by similar practices by his own government. In this respect, however, he was no more consistent than the majority of his contemporaries. His ideas of toleration may be inferred from the evident satisfaction with which he reported to Davison of the hanging and quartering of a Catholic priest in Cornwall, and of the apprehension of several others in London.[1] To Killigrew toleration was a virtue only when employed for the benefit of Protestants, especially for his friends, the Puritans.

In fact, the persecution of Catholics in England had the added merit, from his point of view, of distracting the authorities from molesting those of Puritan convictions. In February, 1578, he remarked to Davison: "The Papists be so strait and arrogant that one Steward ... being brought before the Bishop of London in his consistory, and so stubbornly behaved himself, as I think the Bishop will show more favour to such as by malice are called by the name of Puritans." [2]

Seven years more passed before the Queen fulfilled Killigrew's hopes of English intervention in the Low Countries. The assassination of William the Silent in July, 1584, and the military successes of the Spanish armies commanded by the Duke of Parma, culminating in the capture of Antwerp the following summer, caused her to adopt the policy of the war party led by Leicester and Walsingham in the Council. Elizabeth placed Leicester in command of a force of 6,000 men to aid the Dutch provinces, and Killigrew was chosen to accompany him as a counciller. The appointment to serve with his friend Leicester in the Netherlands was undoubtedly a source of great satisfaction to Killigrew. In December, 1577, when it had been proposed to send him with Leicester to the Low Countries, he had written to Davison: "I am Sir, though unworthy, a forespoken soldier of his whose journey I honour

[1] P.R.O. S.P. 15/25 f. 49.
[2] Ibid., f. 74.

from my heart, and shall think my life well spent in it." [1]
Moreover, Killigrew's long experience in diplomatic and
military affairs, and his sustained advocacy of the Protestant
cause in the Netherlands were excellent qualifications for the
rôle he was to play in that country during the next three years.

[1] *Ibid.*, f. 40.

CHAPTER IX

COUNCILLOR OF STATE IN THE
NETHERLANDS, 1585-1589

DURING Leicester's two administrations in the Nether-
lands in 1585-6 and again in the following year,
Killigrew was one of his advisors on the Dutch
Council of State.[1] In his capacity as Leicester's councillor he

---

[1] On 16th November, 1585, the Queen informed the States General of
Killigrew's appointment to the Council of State. P.R.O. S.P. 84/5 f. 63.
Among the Dutch sources there are numerous references to Killigrew's
activities in the Council of State in: Hojo Brugmans ed., *Correspondentie
van Robert Dudley, graaf van Leycester, en andere documenten betreffende zijn
gouvernement-generaal in de Nederlanden, 1585–1588*, 3 vols. Werken van het
historisch genootschap, 3rd series, vols. 56–58, Utrecht, 1931. N. Japiske ed.,
Resolutiën der Staten-Generaal van 1576–1609, Rijksgeschiedkundige publicatiën, vols. 47, 51, 's-Gravenhage, 1921–?. There also are a few references
to his work in this capacity in P. J. Blok ed., *Correspondance inédits de Robert
Dudley, comte de Leycester, et de François et Jean Hotman*, Haarlem, 1911, Pieter
Bor, *Oorspronck, begin en vervolgh der Nederlandsche oorlogen*, vol. 3, Amsterdam, 1681, S.P. Haak ed., *Johan Van Oldenbarnevelt, bescheiden betreffende zijn
staatkundigheid en zijn familie, vol. 1, 1570–1601*, Rijksgeschiedkundige Publicatiën, vol. 80, The Hague, 1934, Jean Hotman, *Brieven over het Leycestersche
tijdvak uit die papieren van J. H.*, (R. Broersma and C. Busken Huet, ed.)
Dijdragen en Mededeelingen van het historisch Genootschap, vol. 34, The
Hague, 1913. The information in these sources do not add greatly to that contained in the volumes of the *State Papers Foreign*, for the purpose of my study.
  The most valuable collection of letters for the Leicester period is John
Bruce's *Correspondence of Robert Dudley*. For the general information
contained in this chapter I have relied on John Lothrop Motley, *History of
the United Netherlands from the death of William the Silent to the Synod of Dort*,
vols. 1 and 2, London, 1867. (hereafter: Motley). This work still provides
the fullest and most useful treatment of Leicester's administration in the
Netherlands despite the obvious prejudices of the author. Of the more
recent works, I have employed Peter Johannes Blok, *History of the people
of the Netherlands*, Part 3, *The war with Spain* (Translated by Ruth Putnam),
New York, 1900, pp. 197–240, (hereafter: Blok), P. Geyl, *The revolt of the*

took no personal part in the campaigns against Parma's forces. Perhaps as he beheld the valorous deeds of his countrymen—of Philip Sidney, the Norris brothers, of young Robert Devereux, Earl of Essex, he felt some pangs of regret for those days, many years past, when he had borne arms in the Protestant cause. But Henry was now an aging man nearing the sixtieth year of his life. His eyesight was failing and his health soon began to deteriorate under the strain of hard service in the Netherlands. Very likely, therefore, he was content to let younger men monopolize the glory and hazards of war.[1]

Probably because of his 25 years of experience as an official in the Exchequer Killigrew proved to be of particular value to Leicester on financial matters. The latter consulted him constantly concerning the distribution of government funds to the officers of his army, and on more than one occasion, he assisted in examinations of accounts submitted by the army treasurer for the purpose of checking the widespread waste and corruption in the English military establishment.[2] When Leicester created a Chamber of Finances for the purpose of making a more accurate assessment of the provinces to contribute to the cost of the war he chose Killigrew to be one of its principal members.[3]

Netherlands (1555–1609), London, 1932, pp. 203–17. (hereafter: Geyl), Read, *Walsingham*, vol. 3, pp. 104–77, 235–84, 353–8. There are also excellent brief studies of Anglo-Dutch relations, 1585–1598, by Sophie Crawford Lomas, Allen B. Hinds, and Richard Bruce Wernham in the *Calendars of State Papers, Foreign*, for these years. I found Professor Wernham's treatment of Anglo-Dutch relations in 1588–9 especially valuable—particularly for the light it sheds upon Killigrew's rôle as a councillor in the Netherlands.

[1] In September, 1583, Killigrew wrote to Burghley: "... my sight is so decayed of late that I can neither write nor read without spectacles..." P.R.O. S.P. 12/47 f. 28.

[2] P.R.O. S.P. 84/6 f. 80. P.R.O. S.P. 84/10 f. 23. On 11th October, 1586, Leicester wrote to the Queen: "There is no payment made to captains or colonels, but it is done by the privity of all or most part of the officers of the Finances, whereof your councillor, Mr Killigrew, is one." P.R.O. S.P. 84/10 f. 63.

[3] P.R.O. S.P. 84/8 f. 104.

The zeal and efficiency with which he performed his duties won a prompt tribute from Leicester. He wrote to Burghley in February, 1586: "I have one here whom I take no small comfort in and that is little Hal Killigrew. I assure you he is a notable servant and more in him than ever I heretofore thought of him, though I always knew him to be an honest man and able."[1] Leicester's goodwill can doubtless be explained in part by the fact that his friend took care never to oppose his will. Killigrew lacked the boldness and independence of character which would have enabled him to criticise Leicester's policies when he disagreed with them. He had been dependent on the Earl's patronage for too many years, and he knew his jealous, arrogant temperament too well to allow any cause for antagonism to arise between them.

Killigrew's expressed views were therefore generally a reflection of those of his patron. He never brought upon himself that jealous, vindictive rage which Leicester directed against other able champions of the Dutch cause such as Sir William Davison, Thomas Wilkes, and Sir John Norris. Yet his praise was more than a reward for mere subservience. Leicester was no fool, and when his antipathies were not aroused, he was a keen judge of character. Moreover, he had many years of personal experience upon which to base a judgement of Killigrew's capabilities.

As Leicester's loyal adherent in the Council of State Killigrew was intimately involved in the events which brought his patron into open and violent conflict with his Dutch allies. This conflict arose because of Elizabeth's refusal to accept the sovereignty of the United Provinces offered to her by the Dutch embassy in London in the summer of 1585, and because of Leicester's subsequent acceptance of sovereign powers as Governor-General of the Provinces in violation of her express commandment. The Queen was unwilling to face the hazards and the enormous cost that would have fallen upon her shoulders if she undertook such a responsibility. Under the

[1] P.R.O. S.P. 84/6 f. 112.

Anglo-Dutch treaty of August, 1585, she confined her rôle to that of an ally with limited commitments in both money and men. To assure repayment of her expenditures following the conclusion of the war she secured possession of the "cautionary' towns of Flushing, Rammekens, and Brielle. Leicester was commissioned only as a lieutenant-general of an auxiliary army, and his duties were restricted primarily to the conduct of military operations.[1]

An office of such petty dimensions was not sufficient to satisfy the vanity of Leicester. Both he and the Dutch also realized the urgent need for a strong authority to unite the Provinces for a more effective conduct of war against Spain. Shortly after his arrival in the Netherlands the States-General offered to Leicester the Governor-Generalship of the Provinces.

As Governor-General he was given large powers over the conduct of war by land and sea and over civil and political matters. He exercised executive authority through a Council of State which included several Dutch members and two English advisors: Henry Killigrew and Dr Bartholomew Clark.[2]

Unfortunately for Leicester the Queen was outraged by his acceptance of the Governor-Generalship. At first she demanded that he surrender the office immediately. Though the persuasions of Burghley and other councillors deflected her from this course she heaped a large volume of abuse on Leicester and on the Dutch who had accorded to him a position similar to that which she herself had refused.

Leicester, Killigrew, and the other English officials at the Hague managed to tone down one of Elizabeth's most violent

[1] Read, *Walsingham*, vol. 3, pp. 131–2. Geyl, p. 203, Blok, pp. 206–7. Motley, vol. 1, pp. 301 ff.

[2] See the advice of the Dutch commissioners in London to the Earl of Leicester concerning the establishment of the Council of State and other matters "for the better direction of affairs of the Low Countries." B. M. Harleian MSS., 285, f. 137. Bruce, pp. 15–6. For the history of the Council of State as an organ of the Dutch government see: Robert Fruin, *Geschiedenis der staatsinstellingen in Nederland tot den val der republiek*, 's-Gravenhage, 1922, pp. 197 ff.

messages to her allies, but nearly three months elapsed before Leicester was restored to favour and before the Queen would sanction his assumption of power as Governor-General.[1] By that time his credit in the Netherlands had been greatly diminished. The contempt with which he had been treated lowered his prestige in the eyes of many of the Dutch leaders. Moreover Elizabeth's abusive behaviour towards themselves aroused suspicions concerning the sincerity of her support for their cause. These suspicions were strengthened by her failure to send sufficient pay to keep her troops from starvation and by reports of secret negotiations for peace between the English government and the Duke of Parma.

In this atmosphere of suspicion and distrust relations between Leicester and the Dutch grew steadily worse. The Earl interpreted his powers as Governor-General in the broadest sense while the States General made every effort to restrict his authority. As a member of the Chamber of Finance Killigrew was at the very centre of the rising tension between Leicester and the leading Dutch politicians. The Hollanders, who commanded the most influence in the States General, resented particularly the attempt of the Chamber of Finances, which the Governor-General established in the spring of 1586, to institute a probe into their finances. They opposed even more bitterly the effort of this body to prohibit their lucrative trade with the southern provinces and other territories under Spanish control.[2]

On this issue a quarrel broke out between Killigrew and Paul Buys, the Advocate of Holland. Buys, who had once been the foremost champion of the alliance with England, became an outspoken opponent of Leicester and of the Chamber of Finances. Killigrew was reported to have told him angrily that 'his excellency (Leicester) would establish the Chamber of Finances or hazard his neck.' He also threatened that 'order

---

[1] P.R.O. S.P. 84/7 f. 26. Blok, pp. 210–1. Motley, vol. 1, p. 426.

[2] Geyl, pp. 210–2. Blok, pp. 212–4. Motley, vol. 2, pp. 70 ff. On the Dutch trade with the Spanish provinces see: Johannes Hermann Kernkamp, *De Handel op den vijand, 1572–1609*, Utrecht, 1931, pp. 166–234.

would be taken with Buys, for his course and practices (in opposition to Leicester) were too well-known.' [1]

Leicester's opponents came chiefly from the wealthy merchant class which had exercised political and economic control of the Provinces for the past two centuries. At the head of the political party representing the interests of this class were two able Hollanders Johan Oldenbarnevelt and Paul Buys. Closely allied with them was young Maurice of Nassau, son of William the Silent. There was, however, a considerable degree of discontent with the rule of this party among certain elements of the Dutch population. They included the artisans of the towns and their Calvinist religious leaders, who preached the doctrines of popular government against the oligarchic rule of the merchant aristocracy, and who proclaimed a narrowly Calvinist orthodoxy in opposition to the tolerant views of the dominant party. In the smaller provinces such as Utrecht, Friesland, and Guelderland there was also a strong feeling of resentment against the overweening political and economic power of Holland.

To overthrow his adversaries in the States General Leicester sought to weld together these elements into a cohesive revolutionary faction. It would perhaps be truer to say that he himself fell into the hands of an astute group of politicians—of whom Deventer, Burchgrave, and Reingoud were the principal representatives—who fanned his resentment against the Holland party for their own ends.[2] As head of the "democratic" faction Leicester set about to foment rebellion in some of the chief cities of the Provinces. Once his Dutch partisans had seized power for the assistance of English troops, Leicester would have a formidable independent power at his disposal with which to overawe his enemies. By this means he could also control the destinies of the Dutch state and compel it to wage war or make peace on terms dictated by his sovereign.[3]

[1] P.R.O. S.P. 84/11 f. 109.
[2] Geyl, pp. 209–10. Blok, pp. 215–221. Motley, vol. 2, pp. 115 ff.
[3] On 27th June, 1586, Leicester wrote to the Queen: "... I hope to get

Killigrew seems to have worked enthusiastically for the realization of Leicester's plans. Two of his close associates were Deventer and Herman Modet, who helped to engineer a successful coup d'état at Utrecht which confirmed the authority of the Governor-General in that city.[1] Killigrew's part in this episode cannot be determined with certainty, but Thomas Wilkes, his successor in the Council of State, later reported that Killigrew had strongly supported the actions of the Calvinist rabble-rouser, Modet, at Utrecht.[2] Moreover his threat against Buys gains a sinister significance in view of the fact that the latter was seized and imprisoned by Leicester's partisans in that city in July, 1586.[3]

Killigrew returned to England in November of that year when the Queen recalled his patron to England. Neither he nor Leicester had accomplished much in the Netherlands except to earn the lasting distrust of the Dutch leaders.[4] Killigrew was thoroughly disillusioned by his experiences of the past year, and he had no wish to concern himself further with Dutch affairs, but when Parma's sudden move against Sluys in the spring of 1587 caused Elizabeth to place Leicester in charge of a second expedition to the Netherlands, he was once again appointed as member of the Council of State.

Killigrew's reaction to his new appointment—as one might expect—was something less than rapturous. On taking his leave of the Queen at Greenwich he remarked pessimistically that he

into my hands three or four principal places in North Holland, which will be such a strength to you that you may rule these men, and make war or peace as you list." P.R.O. S.P. 84/8 f. 123.

[1] Geyl, pp. 210-1. Blok, pp. 217-8. Killigrew's close friendship with Deventer is suggested by the appeal which the latter wrote to him after his imprisonment when the Leicester faction in Utrecht was overthrown in the autumn of 1588. P.R.O. S.P. 84/26 f. 195.

[2] P.R.O. S.P. 70/91 f. 23.

[3] Geyl, p. 212. Motley, vol. 2, pp. 83-5.

[4] Thomas Wilkes was appointed to replace Killigrew on the Council of State in October, 1586. Killigrew returned to England about the middle of the following month. P.R.O. S.P. 84/10 ff. 59-60. P.R.O. S.P. 84/11 f. 23.

knew he was about to enter a labyrinth.[1] Only too well did subsequent events prove the truth of that prediction. Robert Beale, an old acquaintance and Walsingham's brother-in-law, was also chosen to serve with him on the Council of State.[2] Leicester was well satisfied with the competence of his two councillors and, indeed, he felt the need of loyal and efficient helpers, for he quickly found that he was the object of widespread suspicion.[3]

During Leicester's absence two of his personal appointees had betrayed the towns of Zutphen and Deventer to the Spaniards.[4] Shortly before his return to the Netherlands certain of Leicester's private papers fell into the hands of Oldenbarnevelt which proved that the Governor-General was continuing his intrigues with the "democratic" party, and that he had been commissioned by the Queen to coerce her allies into joining the Anglo-Spanish peace negotiations. In the eyes of many of the Dutch leaders Leicester seemed merely the instrument employed by Elizabeth in a plan to betray their nation to the enemy.[5]

The tension that resulted from these suspicions made military

[1] P.R.O. S.P. 84/19 f. 32.

[2] Beale had been Walsingham's secretary when Killigrew was chargé d'affaires at the French court in the winter of 1571-2. Read, *Walsingham*, vol. 1, pp. 149, 157.

[3] On 4th August, 1587, Leicester wrote to Walsingham: "I find myself happy for my two colleagues ... There is not a more sufficient man than Mr Beale is, nor quicker, nor of better despatch." P.R.O. S.P. 84/17 f. 16.

[4] Geyl, p. 213. Motley, vol. 2, pp. 171 ff.

[5] One of these documents was a letter from Leicester to Junius, his agent in the Netherlands, dated 15th June, 1587. He ordered his correspondent to inform the people that the Queen had not been treating with the King of Spain. Junius was also to tell the leaders of the "democratic" party that Leicester was returning and that they should continue to support him against the States General. The other document contained Leicester's private instructions from Elizabeth which specifically ordered him to impress upon the Dutch people the necessity of peace. If they were unmoved by these suggestions he was to say that the Queen intended to accept the offers of peace made by Philip. P.R.O. S.P. 84/13 ff. 73, 124.

co-operation between the allies almost impossible. To Killigrew and Beale fell the unenviable task of trying to squeeze contributions of money, men, and supplies out of the States General to aid Leicester in his attempt to relieve Sluys.[1] Killigrew subsequently assisted the Governor-General and his officers in planning the unsuccessful effort to reach the beleaguered Anglo-Dutch garrison by land and sea.[2]

Although Leicester, Killigrew, and other English officials blamed the failure on lack of support from the Dutch fleet, the disaster at Sluys ended the Governor-General's usefulness in the Netherlands.[3] As a general he was unable to match Alexander of Parma. As a politician he proved unequal to dealing with his opponents in the States General. Despite his past support of Leicester's policies Killigrew seems to have gained some awareness of their futility. In October, 1587, he wrote to Leicester with tactful understatement: "Men who wish you best say it is time for a conference between you and the States. I think it is a better way than by striving."[4]

[1] See the letter from Killigrew and Beale in July and August, 1587. B. M. Cotton MSS., Galba DI, ff. 99, 103, 231. P.R.O. S.P. 84/17 f. 24.

[2] "Two papers relating to consultations between Sir William Pelham, Henry Killigrew, and Sir William Reeve etc. concerning the relief of Sluys, 30th June and 23rd July, 1587." See also Killigrew's letter to Leicester, 6th July, 1587. B. M. Cotton MSS., Galba DI, ff. 188, 212.

[3] See the account of the unsuccessful attempt to relieve Sluys given by Killigrew and Beale on 1st August, 1587. *Ibid.*, f. 231. See also: *A briefe and true report of the proceedings of the Earl of Leycester for the reliefe of the towne of Sluys from his arrival at Flushing about the end of June, 1587, until the surrender thereof 16 July next ensuing. Whereby it shall plainlie appear his Excellencie was not in anie fault for the losse of that towne.* Imprinted at London, 1590. This work was undoubtedly written by an English officer who served with Leicester in the Netherlands during the Sluys operation.

[4] B. M. Egerton MSS., 1694, f. 165. A hint of Killigrew's attitude towards Dudley's conduct towards his allies is contained in a letter from the Governor-General to himself on 25th July, 1587. Leicester said that he understood by a previous letter from Killigrew that Count Hohenlohe commander of the Dutch forces, had written to the States of Holland asking them to assemble at Middleberg. Leicester complained that, as his subordinate in rank, Hohenlohe had no right to make this request without first

When Leicester departed from the Low Countries a month later, Killigrew remained behind as the chief English representative on the Council of State. He was weary of his post, and he felt keen disappointment that he had not been allowed to return home with his patron.[1] Towards Leicester he entertained a genuine sympathy for the difficulties he had experienced in the Netherlands.

Perhaps he realized that these difficulties were largely the result of defects in Leicester's character, but he also knew that his friend had devoted himself wholeheartedly to the task which he had undertaken in the Netherlands, and that he had squandered his substance to keep his starving, ill-paid soldiers alive. The limitations under which he had been compelled to work would have baffled far abler men than himself. If his own conduct towards his allies had often been overbearing and deceitful their behaviour towards him had not always been generous or forthright.[2]

---

obtaining his consent. At the end of Leicester's letter Killigrew noted: "This I wrote not, but only that he (Hohenlohe) would be shortly at Middelberg, as he wrote to the Council of State." *Ibid.*, 1694, f. 145. A person of Killigrew's tactful nature must have been aware that Leicester's suspicious and autocratic attitude towards the Dutch leaders, of which there is clear evidence in this letter, only served to increase their antagonism towards him.

[1] On 5th December, 1587, the day before Leicester's departure from the Low Countries, Killigrew wrote to Walsingham that Leicester wished him to remain in the Netherlands for a time, and he added: "I hope this may be no hindrance to my revocation, which I beseech you to hasten, as you love me." P.R.O. S.P. 84/19 f. 134.

[2] Although Motley is too favourable to the Dutch and not always just to Elizabeth, his estimate of Leicester's character and his achievements in the Netherlands is, on the whole, a fair one. See his summary of the results of Leicester's administration: Motley, vol. 2, pp. 331-4. A satisfactory life of Leicester remains to be written. Frederick Chamberlain, *Elizabeth and Leycester*, New York, 1939, is a polemical defence of Leicester against his detractors. More valuable is Milton Waldman, *Elizabeth and Leicester*, London, 1944. This is a brief study which emphasizes the psychological relationship between Dudley and Elizabeth. Since this book went to press,

Shortly after Leicester's departure Killigrew expressed to Burghley a view that was shared by a considerable number of his countrymen who had served in the Netherlands: "My Lord, in my judgement," he wrote, "hath carried himself very honourably among them (the Dutch) while they have in no measure answered, but rather the contrary, which might have tried any man, yea the most patient of those which have borne rule under a monarch."[1]

Killigrew fervently hoped and expected that he would be recalled to England within a short time after Leicester's departure, but in the event, he was compelled to remain in the Low Countries for more than a year longer.[2] The withdrawal of Leicester marked an important victory for the party of Oldenbarnevelt, Buys, and Maurice of Nassau, and for the States-General whose sovereign power they proclaimed. It also resulted in a great diminution of the authority of the Council of State which the Governor General had sought to make an effective instrument of executive authority and of English dominance in Dutch affairs.

Killigrew and other members of this body complained that they were treated as "mere cyphers," and he found his own position to be especially insecure because of his close association with Leicester.[3] Referring to the leading men of the States party he remarked: "I perceive myself not to be the best welcome among them, as one whom they know to be most humbly bounden to his Lordship and always ready to endeavor myself in his service." His unpopularity with the Dutch was increased by the fact that he did not hesitate to tell them

---

another excellent work on the same subject has been published: Elizabeth Jenkins *Elizabeth and Leicester*, London 1961.

[1] P.R.O. S.P. 84/20 f.

[2] When Leicester left the Netherlands he promised Killigrew that he would obtain his recall within a short time. Killigrew mentions such a promise in his letter to Leicester on 7th May, 1588. B. M. Cotton MSS., Galba DIII, f. 160.

[3] P.R.O. S.P. 84/20 f. 106.

to their faces, and in no uncertain terms, what he thought of their behaviour towards Leicester's "well-wishers."[1]

One manifestation of this distrust was particularly irritating to Killigrew. His grasp of foreign languages had one notable deficiency—it did not include Dutch, and he became convinced that members of the States General often spoke in their own tongue in his presence to conceal important matters from him. To Walsingham he wrote: "I am a suspected man, and to avoid my knowledge they commonly speak in their own language, which I cannot understand..."[2] No doubt there was some truth in Killigrew's belief, but his comment savours a little of the injured vanity of an old diplomat who resented an implied slur on his reputation as a "well languaged" man.[3]

Although they had succeeded in curtailing Leicester's power the States proved unable to provide an efficient government themselves. The Provinces remained disunited, and there were many people in the country who continued to look to Elizabeth and to Leicester as the only hope for aid and for the strong authority which the present government seemed incapable of giving.

It was for these people that Killigrew spoke when he wrote to Walsingham: "I can speak to no man among them but is weary of their (the States') manner of proceeding and sorry for his Excellency's departure, as if it were the entrance into their ruin. Some conceived hope in the good success of the King of Navarre, others that the King of Denmark, by yielding to give one of his daughters in marriage to Count Maurice, might have produced means to uphold them. Howbeit, both these hopes are but vain, and their state, in the meantime, for want of authority doth rent asunder not only by the disunion of the provinces, but by the particular hatred grown between some of their best contributing cities; also by the great disorders likely to arise in all their garrisons for want of pay..."[4]

[1] Ibid., f. 131.   [2] Ibid., f. 118.
[3] Leicester to the Queen, 7th July, 1587. P.R.O. S.P. 83/16 f. 18.
[4] P.R.O. S.P. 84/20 f. 106.

Indeed the country was on the verge of civil war in the opening months of 1588. At Medemblik Deidrich Sonoy, the governor of North Holland, proclaimed his allegience to the Queen of England and to the Earl of Leicester. The frontier provinces: Overyssel, Gelderland, and Utrecht, where the Leicesterian faction was strong, preferred the rule of Elizabeth to that of the States General. Even Holland and Zealand, the stronghold of the States party, were threatened by the revolt of the garrisons in important cities such as Gertruidenberg, and Veere and Arnemuiden on the island of Walcheren.

Still more dangerous was the imminence of an outbreak of hostilities between the English and their allies at the very moment when the King of Spain was about to despatch a great invasion fleet against England. The Hollanders continued to believe that Elizabeth intended to make peace with Philip on terms that were unfavourable to themselves, and they suspected that she was prepared to surrender Flushing and Brielle to the Spaniards to achieve this purpose.[1]

Killigrew and other English officials in the Low Countries were equally convinced of the hostile intentions of the Dutch leaders. Killigrew believed that they intended to crush the pro-English faction and to drive the Queen's army completely out of the Netherlands. In confirmation of this belief he pointed to the despatch of troops commanded by Count Maurice to besiege Sonoy at Medemblik and to rumours of plans by Dutch military leaders to wrest the 'cautionary' towns from English control. Repeatedly he warned his government of the likelihood of an attack upon Flushing.[2] He was also convinced that Holland and Zealand intended to disjoin themselves

[1] Blok, pp. 232–3. Motley, vol. 2, pp. 408 ff.
[2] P.R.O. S.P. 84/19 f. 183. P.R.O. S.P. 84/21 ff. 23, 51, 78. Motley's belief in the upright intentions of the Dutch leaders towards their ally at this time is questionable. For example, there is evidence that only the alertness of Sir William Russel and other English officers at Flushing prevented an attack on that city by naval forces stationed at Middelberg under the command of Count Hohenlohe, Motley, vol. 2, pp. 408 ff. P.R.O. S.P. 84/20 ff. 1, 38, 42, 46.

from the other provinces and to make their own peace with Spain.[1]

In order to prevent these dangers Killigrew believed that the Queen must adopt a clearly defined policy, and in his mind there were two possible alternatives. "If," he said, "her Majesty purpose to continue her assistance here and maintain these countries against the Spaniard, it were expedient some one of authority were sent over to unite the provinces among themselves..." If, on the other hand, she meant to continue the peace negotiations which were now in progress with the Duke of Parma she must "bridle those of Holland and Zealand that seek to disjoin themselves from the rest; which may be done by giving heart to those which remain at her Majesty's devotion..." [2]

As a supporter of Leicester's policies and because of his distrust of the States party Killigrew favoured the establishment of strong English control over the Provinces and the encouragement of those who placed their trust in Elizabeth. His advocacy of this line of action was possibly less the result of a personal liking for Leicester's method of 'divide and rule' than of a total disbelief in the ability of the States General to provide an effective alternative government. He was utterly pessimistic concerning the capacity of this body to provide the leadership necessary for the country's defence. He apparently believed that the present insecurity of his country's position in the Low Countries justified actions which threatened to produce open conflict with the Dutch leaders.[3]

[1] P.R.O. S.P. 84/21 f. 51.
[2] Ibid., f. 155.
[3] Despite his frequent complaints concerning the Dutch leaders Killigrew had the honesty to admit that some of their charges against his countrymen were true. He wrote to Burghley, for example, in July, 1588, concerning Dutch allegations that English forces in the Low Countries were below the number stipulated in the Treaty of 1585. He accepted the validity of these complaints, and he put the blame on the lack of pay and ill-discipline among the English troops which resulted in frequent desertion to the enemy. "...These things," he said, "make our nation the less respected of these

Like most other English officials in the Low Countries he urged the necessity of placing those towns which were in revolt against the authority of the States General under English protection. He was especially insistent on this point in respect of Veere and Arnemuiden whose occupation by friendly troops he considered essential to England's control of Flushing.[1]

The Queen, as usual, procrastinated, and for a time she vacillated between two contradictory policies. She commanded Killigrew to make vigorous protests to the States General concerning their hostile actions against men who were loyal to herself, and she issued vague threats of reprisals in case these protests were ignored.[2] Lord Willoughby, Leicester's successor in command of English troops in the Low Countries, wished to break Maurice's blockade of Medemblik by force, and Killigrew desired the Queen to take the entire island of Walcheren under her protection.[3] Elizabeth, however, was entirely opposed to measures of this kind. She was equally unwilling to listen to the appeals of Sonoy and her other partisans for either financial or military aid.[4]

---

people who be watchful enough for these particularities..." P.R.O. S.P. 84/25 f. 120. Professor J. E. Neale has written an enlightening study of Elizabeth's expenditures during Leicester's Governor-Generalship of the Provinces. He contends that the unforseen heaviness of the war costs and the consequent drain on the English treasury made it impossible for her to keep the troops in pay. The severity of the Queen's difficulties was greatly increased by the financial maladministration and corruption in the military establishment. To these reasons, rather than deliberate parsimony alleged by other historians, he attributes the stringent economies which Elizabeth imposed on her starving army during the Dutch campaigns of 1586–88. J. E. Neale, "Elizabeth and the Netherlands," *English Historical Review*, (July, 1930), vol. 45, pp. 373-96.

[1] P.R.O. S.P. 84/23 f. 290.

[2] P.R.O. S.P. 84/21 f. 1.

[3] P.R.O. S.P. 84/23 f. 267. P.R.O. S.P. 84/23 f. 267.

[4] The rebellious Dutch garrisons asked that the Queen provide the pay owed to them by the States-General. Elizabeth's unwillingness to undertake this expense was one of the primary reasons for her refusal to follow the course recommended by Killigrew and other English officials in the Nether-

Finally, in March, 1588, the Queen made a decisive change in policy. She ordered her representatives in the Netherlands to work for an accomodation between the rival factions and to encourage her Dutch partisans to submit to the authority of the States General.[1] During the spring and summer Killigrew and Willoughby succeeded in obtaining the submission of most of the towns in Holland and Zealand which had defied the States General.[2]

This task was by no means a pleasing one to Killigrew. He regretted the abandonment of those who had looked to his sovereign for protection, and he considered himself an unfit instrument to further a reconciliation between them and their opponents, especially since it entailed a virtual surrender by the English government to the claims of the States General. He asked Leicester to consider "how strange a course this is for me to take which it hath pleased her Majesty to direct my Lord Willoughby and me of late, considering my former actions." [3] Indeed the necessity of conciliating men who in his view, had repaid the Queen's generosity by attacking her friends put Killigrew's temper under considerable strain. To Walsingham

---

lands. Concerning the Queen's attitude on payment of the Dutch garrisons see Walsingham's letter to Sir William Russel on 8th April, 1588. P.R.O. S.P. 84/23 f. 56.

[1] P.R.O. S.P. 84/22 ff. 125, 172, 244, 246.

[2] P.R.O. S.P. 84/23 ff. 14, 98, 100, 366, 381. P.R.O. S.P. 84/25 f. 49. A major source of conflict between the English and their allies was removed when Killigrew delivered Leicester's resignation from the Governor-Generalship to the States General on 1st April, 1588. Leicester had signed his resignation in London on 17th December of the preceding year, but for some unknown reason it was not made known to the Dutch until the following spring. The effect of this delay was to prolong the factional conflict in the Netherlands by several months. Killigrew's announcement of Leicester's resignation did much to gain a general acknowledgment of the rule of the States General, since the leaders of the "democratic" party could no longer claim that their allegiance belonged to Elizabeth's Governor-General. P.R.O. S.P. 84/22 f. 26. P.R.O. S.P. 84/23 f. 100. Motley, vol. 2, p. 411.

[3] B. M. Cotton MSS., Galba D.III, f. 160.

he remarked: "…in this time of reconciliation it were meet some graciouser man than myself were employed." [1]

However, as an obedient servant of his sovereign Killigrew adjusted himself to the policy which she had decreed, and he worked hard and successfully to bring to an end by peaceful means the factional strife which plagued the internal affairs of the Dutch state. Doubtless he realized now that if Elizabeth was unwilling to exercise sovereign power over the Provinces or to allow one of her ministers to exercise sovereign power in her name it was necessary that a capable Dutch leader should be chosen to govern the country, and one who commanded the confidence of the States General. He himself believed that William the Silent's dour but able son, Maurice of Nassau, was the man best qualified to assume this rôle. [2]

Moreover, in the late spring of 1588, most Englishmen recognized that co–operation between their country and the Dutch leaders was essential in the face of their common peril. Killigrew devoted his efforts to persuading the Dutch to send naval reinforcements to the assistance of the English squadrons which were patrolling the Channel awaiting the arrival of the Spanish fleet. [3] He also sent home reports of the vast preparations that were being made by Parma in Flanders to join forces with the Armada for the invasion of England. [4]

Killigrew was particularly concerned over the ill–effects of the negotiations with Parma on the very eve of this great assault. The suspicions which they aroused in the minds of the Dutch leaders greatly increased the difficulties of his effort to secure their assistance. [5] The relief he felt when these negoti-

[1] Ibid., f. 93.

[2] Killigrew wrote to Walsingham on 13th July, 1588: "As they (the Provinces) have great need of a governor, and as those of Holland and Zealand bend wholly towards Count Maurice, I wish that the other provinces would also accept him." P.R.O. S.P. 84/25 f. 126.

[3] P.R.O. S.P. 84/24 f. 95.

[4] Ibid., ff. 95, 206.

[5] See Killigrew's letter to Walsingham of 14th May, 1588. P.R.O. S.P. 84/23 f. 265. In order to foment dissension between the allies, the Spaniards,

ations were at last broken off at the end of June is reflected in his letter to Burghley at this time. His letter perhaps also indicates an awareness that his brother-in-law had been a leading member of the peace party in the Council which had pursued the illusory hope of peace with Spain.

On the 31st June he wrote: "...But now I think your Lordship is assured of the Catholic malice towards her Majesty and her domains, which here is confirmed more and more... The place of descent for the Spanish army should seem by most advices to be in some part of Scotland; others say in the west part of Ireland, and the Duke of Parma, some say at Sandwich, others fear Romney Marsh, where the landing is easy, the ground full of cattle and horse and with a small harbour made guardable for a time..."[1]

Killigrew was with the Council of State at the Hague when news arrived of the encounter between the English and Spanish fleets off Gravelines. He reported to Walsingham that Spanish ships had been seen between Calais and Dover to the number of 120 sail on the 30th July. "The same night," he said, "was heard a furious fight between the two fleets. The next morning the Spanish fleet was seen about Gravelines, 45 less in number than before, and her Majesty's navy at their backs." "These news," he added, "have wonderfully encouraged them (the Dutch) to hear that our ships and the Spanish are entered into fight, whereas before they were somewhat dismayed that all this time the two navies have been so near together and no more dealing, which made them conceive some suspicion all was but in show to better the conditions of peace." [2]

The open engagement of English naval forces against the

---

in July, 1588, disseminated garbled versions of the terms of peace put forward by the English commissioners at Bourbourg. According to these terms the Queen had promised to turn over Flushing and Brielle at once to Spain and had offered to lend her own troops to impose these conditions on the "rebels." P.R.O. S.P. 84/25 ff. 78, 79, 110, 126, 165.

[1] P.R.O. S.P. 84/24 f. 206.
[2] P.R.O. S.P. 84/25 f. 162.

Spanish fleet, and the great victory which followed led to a marked improvement in Anglo-Dutch relations. As Killigrew's letter of 30th July suggests, the battle banished for a time at least the fear of the Dutch leaders that Elizabeth intended to desert them and to make peace with Spain. The events of July and August, 1588, gave them a fuller realization of their dependence on English assistance, and their confidence in the Queen's intentions was strengthened by her refusal to countenance further attempts to encourage opposition to their authority. By the end of the year the States General under the leadership of the Oldenbarnevelt party had gained general recognition throughout the Provinces.[1] This was an essential precondition for an effective government of the Dutch state and for successful resistance against Spain.

It was also a necessary step in the re-establishment of good relations between the two allied powers. Equally essential to the achievement of this aim was the removal of those English officials who were identified with Leicester's discredited policy of building a rival power in the Provinces to the States General. Killigrew was one of the principal individuals remaining in the Netherlands who was associated with the disputes and misunderstandings which had poisoned Anglo-Dutch relations during the past three years.

He himself realized that his usefulness as the Queen's chief civilian representative in the Netherlands had long since been exhausted.[2] Despite his good work in settling the internal divisions of the Dutch state he still felt keenly the distrust of the governing faction because of his past connection with Leicester. For a man whose principal talent in former years had been that

[1] In September, 1588, Leicester's old partisan, Deventer, was overthrown by supporters of the States party at Utrecht. This event removed the worst obstacle to a general union of the provinces under the States-General. Blok, p. 239.

[2] As his replacement Killigrew recommended George Gilpin, the English secretary of the Council of State, who had spent many years in the Netherlands as an agent of the Merchant Adventurers. P.R.O. S.P. 84/20 f. 110. Read, *Walsingham*, vol. 3, pp. 133, 354.

of a concilliator this atmosphere of suspicion must have been extremely painful.

Moreover, he was increasingly plagued by sickness, and his appeals for recall on this ground were frequent and pathetic. In May, 1588, he informed Leicester that he had fallen into a "burning ague". "Your good Lordship," he said, "may consider how unfit and unable I am to be employed in this respect of my present sickness, which I find so daily to increase upon me, as I doubt I hardly shall be able now in my old age to shake it off. I have now continued here in this troublesome and unpleasant place of service a long time since your Lordship's departure, not without your ... promise that my abode after you should not be long which I beseech your Lordship to remember..." [1]

The following autumn Killigrew was compelled to absent himself from the Council of State for seven weeks because of sickness, but at last, in October, 1588, he received welcome news from his brother, William, that the Queen was about to recall him. [2] His replacement, Thomas Bodley, arrived at Flushing two months later, and Henry was finally able to return home in January, 1589. [3]

During the last few months of his service in the Netherlands Killigrew became a strong advocate of reconciliation with the States General. He suggested to Burghley that some English envoys should be sent over "for clearing of doubts" between the two governments, and he recommended Lord Buckhurst as a man particularly well qualified to act in this capacity. [4] His recommendation of Buckhurst is significant, for he was an outspoken opponent of Leicester's policy of hostility towards the States General and of inciting factional strife to undermine their authority. As ambassador to the Netherlands in the spring of 1587, Buckhurst's conciliatory dealings with the Dutch

[1] B. M. Cotton MSS., Galba D.III, f. 160.
[2] P.R.O. S.P. 84/26 f. 309. P.R.O. S.P. 84/28 f. 194.
[3] P.R.O. S.P. 84/29 f. 81. P.R.O. S.P. 84/30 f. 133.
[4] P.R.O. S.P. 84/26 f. 235.

leaders had done much to restore their confidence in the good faith of his government. The success of his mission was a damning indictment of Leicester's methods, and for this he earned the latter's implacable hatred.[1]

Killigrew's change of attitude may have been influenced by the death of his patron in September, 1588.[2] Free from Leicester's dominating personality he could undertake the work of conciliation for which he was best suited by temperament and past experience. During the final two months he devoted himself entirely to bringing about a better relationship between his government and the Dutch leaders.[3]

Nevertheless Killigrew's three years of service in the Low Countries were the most frustrating and unsatisfactory of his entire career. For this unhappy experience he received some compensation through the military success which his countrymen achieved shortly before his departure. In September, 1588, the Duke of Parma led his Spanish veterans against the Anglo-Dutch garrison at Bergen-op-Zoom.

[1] On Buckhurst's embassy see Read, *Walsingham*, vol. 3, pp. 238–43.

[2] Leicester died on 4th September, 1588, *D.N.B.*, vol. 6, p. 120. On 1st October, 1588, Killigrew asked Walsingham for an immediate recall "now it hath pleased God to call away my Lord of Leicester, that I may yield him the last service and testimony of my devotion at his funerals." P.R.O. S.P. 84/27 f. 1.

[3] Killigrew induced his successor, Thomas Bodley, to make some modifications in the papers which he presented to the States General in January, 1589. These documents contained Elizabeth's recommendations for changes in the executive machinery of the States General and for the settlement of various grievances between the two governments. Bodley to Walsingham, 30th January, 1589. The supposition that the changes suggested by Killigrew were intended to conciliate the Dutch leaders is strengthened by the advice which he gave after his return from the Low Countries. In March, 1589, Gertruidenberg was betrayed to the Spaniards under circumstances which revived all the old suspicions of English treachery. The following month a letter was sent to the Netherlands, apparently written by Elizabeth, which blamed the loss of the city on the "evil counsel of certain of those countries." A marginal note says "Mr Henry Killigrew thought good that these lines should be strucken out, but her Majesty liketh them and would them in." P.R.O. S.P. 84/32 f. 59. Blok, p. 248.

Killigrew wrote to Burghley an urgent appeal in support of the States' request for English reinforcements. Gone now were the old complaints of Dutch duplicity as he mustered all his eloquence on behalf of his country's valued Protestant ally. "Surely," he observed, "seeing in what good stead the division of these Provinces from Spain has stood her Majesty during the coming of the Spanish navy to join with the Duke of Parma and their value in the future for the common defence, aid should be given lest they should quail before the fiery sword of the Duke of Parma." [1] On this occasion the Queen acted with unusual speed. A considerable force of men was immediately sent to the aid of the besieged garrison, and two months later the mighty Parma was forced to withdraw his army after a humiliating defeat. The English and their Dutch allies had at last acted in unison to achieve a signal triumph, and the legend of Spanish invincibility on land had been shattered just as that of its supremacy on the seas had been destroyed the previous summer.[2]

[1] P.R.O. S.P. 84/26 f. 235.
[2] Read, *Walsingham*, vol. 3, pp. 353-4.

CHAPTER X

FINAL YEARS, 1590–1603

T HE final decade of the sixteenth century marked a
definite break in official and court life. Most of Killigrew's friends were now dead or in retirement.
Leicester had died while Killigrew was in the Netherlands,
Thomas Randolph in March, 1590, and Sir Francis Walsingham the following month. His good friend, William Davison,
was a disgraced man as a result of Elizabeth's displeasure concerning his part in the execution of Mary Stuart.[1]

However, the Lord Treasurer, Burghley, continued to hold
his place as the Queen's first councillor, and he remained as
staunch a friend as ever. The family bond between Killigrew
and his distinguished brother-in-law was strengthened by their
long acquaintance and service under Elizabeth dating back to
the reign of her sister. Henry's brother, William, occupied
the office of Groom of the Privy Chamber, a position which he
continued to hold until his death in 1622.[2] In this place of close
and continual contact with the Queen he afforded an added
bulwark of protection. William was a careful, discreet man,
much like Henry. Probably, of all his brothers, Killigrew felt
the greatest affection for him.[3]

---

[1] D.N.B., vol. 16, p. 723. Ibid., vol. 5, p. 631. Read, Walsingham, Vol. 3,
p. 448.

[2] On 14th March, 1573, while he was ambassador to Scotland, Killigrew
asked Burghley to intercede with the Queen to obtain for his brother the
office of Groom of the Chamber. P.R.O. S.P. 52/24 f. 50.

[3] William had been at court almost from the beginning of Elizabeth's
reign. He and Henry seem always to have been on close terms. During the
early part of the reign they both owned houses in St Paul's Churchyard.
After 1590, they lived close by one another in Lothbury. D.N.B. vol. 11,
p. 110. William also owned a house at Hanworth, Middlesex, where he
founded a junior branch of the Killigrew family. There too Henry doubtless

Nevertheless, Henry must have felt a certain sense of lone-liness and isolation among the pushing, ambitious men—Essex, Raleigh, and the Bacon brothers who were now crowding around the throne hoping for favour and advancement. In matters of policy he shared their militant spirit, but tempera-mentally he was far closer to the hardheaded old Lord Treasurer and his son, Robert Cecil. In the diplomatic service also new men such as Sir Henry Unton, Sir Thomas Edmondes and Killigrew's son-in-law, Sir Henry Neville, were now occupy-ing posts that had formerly been held by old friends.

Yet the new age was not without its compensations. Since the Anglo-Dutch alliance of 1585 and the defeat of the Armada three years later, England had entered upon a period of open war with Spain and the Guise party in France. The Vere brothers were leading English troops to victory against the Spaniards in the Low Countries. Norris, Willoughby, and Sir Roger Williams fought alongside Henry IV against the Cath-olic league and the King of Spain. At court Robert Devereaux, Earl of Essex, assumed the leadership of the pro-war faction, as successor to his stepfather, the Earl of Leicester.

When in March, 1595, Killigrew wrote an essay on England's foreign policy during the early years of Elizabeth's reign citing the instances of intervention on the side of Protestants in France and Scotland, he had the satisfaction of viewing them as the first steps towards the fulfilment of the more aggressive line of action that was now in progress on a wide front in western Europe.[1] Now, in his old age, he saw the implementation of that bold policy of alliance with the Protestant powers which he had enthusiastically and often unsuccessfully advocated in former years.

---

visited him on many occasions. In January, 1598, he informed Robert Cecil that he was about to go to his brother's house to transact some busi-ness. P.R.O. S.P. 12/266 f. 5. In his will William asked to be buried in the church of St Margaret Lothbury. *Somerset House, Prerogative Court of Canterbury*, Savile, p. 96. (hereafter: P.C.C.)

[1] Hatfield MSS. vol. 25, f. 70.

After his return from the Low Countries in 1589 old age and ill-health greatly reduced Killigrew's activities as a diplomat. However, in 1591, he was the oldest and most experienced member of the Queen's foreign service.[1] Despite his infirmities, therefore, she found it impossible to dispense with his services. When she despatched her favourite, the Earl of Essex, to France in command of a force of 3,400 men in the summer of that year, she appointed Killigrew, Sir Thomas Leighton and Sir Henry Unton, English ambassador to the French court as his advisors.[2] Elizabeth's purpose in sending an army to Normandy was to assist Henry IV in capturing Rouen which was held by a garrison loyal to the Guise party in France.

Killigrew and Leighton were particularly well qualified to take part in this operation. Not only were they veterans in the art of war, but both had been leaders of the Anglo-Huguenot relief force which had fought beside the Protestant garrison of Rouen in the autumn of 1562, the last occasion on which English soldiers had been concerned with military operations in connection with that city.[3]

Despite their presence the Normandy expedition proved a

[1] The only diplomat of equal length of service was Thomas Randolph who died in 1590.

[2] Killigrew's appointment to accompany Essex was first reported in July, 1591. P.R.O. S.P. 12/249 f. 93.

[3] For Killigrew's part in Essex's Normandy campaign see: Edward P. Cheyney, *A history of England from the defeat of the Armada to the death of Elizabeth, with an account of English institutions during the later sixteenth and early seventeenth centuries*, London, 1914, pp. 256, 273. (hereafter: Cheyney, vol. 1). Thomas Coningsby, *Journal of the siege of Rouen*, (J. G. Nichols ed.), *Camden Society Miscellany*, vol. 1, London, 1847, pp. 8, 47, 78. (hereafter: Coningsby). Walter Bourchier Devereaux, *Lives and letters of the Devereaux, Earls of Essex*, London, 1853, pp. 234, 239–60. G. B. Harrison, *The life and death of Robert Devereaux, earl of Essex*, London, 1937, pp. 48, 56. Joseph Stevenson, *Correspondence of sir Henry Unton, knight, ambassador from queen Elizabeth to Henry IV, king of France in the years MDXCI and MDXCII from the original and authentic copies in the State Papers and the State Paper Office, the British Museum and the Bodleian Library*, (Printed for the Roxburgh Club), London, 1847, pp. 50–100, passim. (hereafter: Unton Correspondence).

complete failure. Essex and most of his fellow officers were young and inexperienced. They tended to look upon war, not as a serious occupation, but as an exercise in knight-errantry. Killigrew and Leighton had not been commissioned to take part in the actual direction of the army; their rôle was largely advisory. Moreover, both men were so afflicted by old age and illness that they found it difficult even to perform their duties in this capacity. Killigrew fell sick soon after the army landed at Dieppe, and Leighton suffered agonies from the gout.[1]

There is something pathetic and amusing in the efforts of these two tired old men to keep track of the high spirited youth who had been committed to their charge. Elizabeth obviously intended that they should restrain Essex from reckless and dangerous enterprises. When they allowed him to set out on a visit to the French King at Noyon, which carried him through country infested with enemy patrols, she angrily upbraided them like an anxious mother whose favourite son has been endangered by the failure of others to protect him from his own folly.[2] As Killigrew watched the behaviour of the young Earl during the Normandy campaign—his frequent oscillations between schoolboy high spirits and moody petulance when the Queen's wrath descended upon him—one wonders whether the shrewd old diplomat did not suspect the self-destructive traits which underlay his outward brilliance.[3]

But the failure of the 1591 campaign was largely the result of factors that were beyond the control of the English commander. Henry had agreed to pay the Queen's army if its presence in France was required for more than two months.[4]

[1] P.R.O. S.P. 78/25 f. 340.

[2] Elizabeth to Killigrew, Essex and Unton, 2nd September, 1591. *Unton Correspondence*, pp. 55-7.

[3] Killigrew reported to Burghley that when Essex read the Queen's letter criticising him for his visit to Henry IV, "he fell into such a passion that he cast himself on his bed, and all the buttons of his tunic broke, as if they had been cut by a knife." P.R.O. State Papers France, S.P. 78/25 f. 282. (hereafter: P.R.O. S.P. 78).

[4] Rymer, vol. 7, p. 56.

Because of various delays the siege of Rouen did not begin until the end of October, and when the stipulated time ran out the bankrupt King was unable to fulfill his bargain. Within a short time disease, starvation, and desertion reduced Essex's force to 1,500 men, less than half its original number.[1] When the English and French armies at last attacked Rouen their efforts proved vain against the stout defence of the well-provisioned garrison and its able commander, the Marquis of Villars.

In the meantime Killigrew remained at Dieppe because of ill-health. Despite his sickness he was far from inactive. He kept in constant touch with Essex and with his government in England, acting as a medium of communication between Elizabeth, her councillors, and the army before Rouen. His other duties related to matters of military administration: the pay, provisioning, and discipline of the English army. All the endemic problems of sixteenth century military life fell to his charge. Hundreds of sick men remained at Dieppe, and he had to provide for their hospitalization, feeding, and transportation back to England.[2] Hundreds more, sick and deserters, wandered back from the English encampments. Many were simply left to die in the fields along the roadsides or in the streets of Dieppe by the angry local population, who only desired to be rid of the pestilent foreigners who looted their homes and burned their churches.[3]

Towards deserters Killigrew took stern action. On one occasion he acted the part of a sergeant-major by collaring such soldiers as he found wandering through the street of Dieppe after the departure of the army, and delivering them

[1] P.R.O. S.P. 78/26 f. 116.

[2] Killigrew's correspondence with Essex, and Burghley is contained in P.R.O. S.P. 78/25–6, Hatfield MSS., vol. 168.

[3] P.R.O. S.P. 78/26 f. 161. On 14th October, 1591, Leighton wrote to Burghley that the English soldiers under Essex's command were "the most disorderly and ill-governed— that ever I saw in my life, given to all manner of evils as blasphemy, drunkeness, spoil, burning of houses, robbing of churches, disobedience to their commanders—." *Ibid.*, f. 27.

into the hands of the provost-marshal. He directed the city watch to keep a sharp look-out for any English troops who tried to leave the country without licence from the Lord General.[1] Concerning indiscipline and looting Killigrew was equally strict. He advised Essex to deal promptly in all such cases by court-martial.[2] Unfortunately these precautions had little effect, for the officers were as quick as their men to plunder the French populace along their route of march. "Such captains," he sadly wrote to Burghley, "little knew wherefore the fox doth spare his next neighbours' places."[3] He did his best, however, to see that those of the French who complained of theft received recompense for their losses.[4]

But towards the sick and starving soldiers he displayed a creditable humanity. Twice he paid a considerable sum of money out of his own pocket to obtain food for a large number and ships to carry them back to England.[5] For his labour and generosity Killigrew received small thanks. The Queen complained that the arrival of the disease-ridden troops in English ports threatened to spread plague through the country. He was also criticized because of the failure of the captains and mustermasters to keep accurate accounts of the money paid to the troops, though this was not a matter for which he was directly responsible.[6]

However, Killigrew's good work was not ignored by the commander. Late in November he paid a visit to Essex's army which was now battering the defences of Rouen. One of Essex's officers, Captain Thomas Coningsby, wrote in his journal on 20th November: "My Lord General rose very early and went to the King's quarter ... and accompanied with my Lord Ambassador (Unton) and many others, he alighted on a

[1] *Ibid.*, f. 74. Hatfield MSS. vol. 168, f. 58.
[2] P.R.O. S.P. 78/26 f. 121.
[3] *Ibid.*
[4] *Ibid.*
[5] Hatfield MSS., vol. 168, f. 59. P.R.O. S.P. 78/26 ff. 122, 161.
[6] *Ibid.*

fair green and so did many others, not knowing his intent, and
there he knighted Sir Henry Killigrew." [1] A week after the
bestowal of this welcome and well deserved reward Killigrew
returned to England.[2] Early the following January Essex was
recalled by the Queen. His military achievement had been
negligible, but he had proven himself a gallant soldier. On
returning to England, the young Earl was marked down as a
coming man who stood high in Elizabeth's favour, and who was
now ready to assume a leading place in her councils.

For Killigrew the Normandy campaign marked the end of
his services in foreign parts. In the autumn of 1595 he was
selected as an envoy to Henry IV, but illness prevented his
departure.[3] Subsequently he took part at home in negotiations
with the States General and the city of Rochelle for the settlement of debts, but his activity concerning affairs of state grew
steadily less.[4] In March, 1599, he at last surrendered the Tellership of the Exchequer, an office which he had occupied for
38 years.[5]

But Henry had many private concerns to occupy his attention during those years. His first wife, Catherine, had borne
him four daughters: Anne, Elizabeth, Mary, and Dorothy. All
were grown women by the end of Elizabeth's reign, and all
were married off by their father to gentlemen of good family.[6]
Catherine died in childbirth in August, 1583, and seven years

[1] Coningsby, p. 47.

[2] P.R.O. S.P. 12/240 no. 92.

[3] P.R.O. S.P. 78/36 f. 95. P. Laffleur de Kermaingant ed., L'ambassade
de France en Angleterre, mission de Jean de Thumery, sieur de Boissise, (1598–
1603), Paris, 1886, pp. 22–3.

[4] P.R.O. S.P. 12/253 ff. 78, 111. B. M. Cotton MSS., Galba DXI, f. 125.
H.M.C. Report on the historical manuscripts of Lord De L'Isle and Dudley
preserved at Penshurst Place, vol. 2, London, 1934, pp. 161, 225.

[5] Hatfield MSS. vol. 57, f. 72. P.R.O. C. 66/970, Part 8, m. 13.

[6] Killigrew's eldest daughter, Anne, married successively Sir Henry
Neville and George Carleton, Bishop of Chichester. Elizabeth married
first, Sir Jonothan Trelawny, second, Sir Thomas Reynell, third, Sir Thomas
Lower. Mary married Sir Reginald Mohun, and Dorothy, Sir Edward
Seymour. Vivian, Visitations of Cornwall, p. 269.

later Killigrew married a second time to a French woman named Jaél de Peigne.[1] Like Catherine, Jaél seems to have been a person of literary tastes. Many years later, after Henry's death, the famous Genevan scholar, Isaac Casaubon, stayed at her house in London.[2] By his second wife Killigrew had three sons and a daughter, Joseph, Henry, Robert and Jaél.[3] This is a considerable feat for a man over sixty years of age and proof that he was far from decrepit even at this time.

By the last decade of Elizabeth's reign Killigrew had achieved some degree of financial security. Near St Margaret's Church, Lothbury, in the City he owned an expensive house.[4] In Cornwall he had three manors as well as property in Penryn and Truro, including the late Dominican Priory of Truro called "the Friars of Truro." From the income of these lands he left to his wife, Jaél, and his two younger sons life annuities totalling £ 140. From this same course he also gave them gifts which came to a total value of over £ 1,700. [5]

Another source of profit was the Tellership of the Exchequer. The yearly fee of £33.6s.8d. is no indication of the true value of this office. All the revenues paid into the Exchequer, as well as a great part of the sums which issued from it, passed through the hands of the four Tellers of the Exchequer. The money they received remained in their possession. In Elizabeth's reign they even set up offices in their own houses at the Queen's expense where it was kept in strong boxes while they transacted business at home rather than at the Exchequer.

The Tellers were required to render half-yearly accounts to auditors for the sums which had passed through their hands in both receipts and payments. During the intervening period

[1] Harleian Society ed., *Publications, registers of St Thomas the Apostle*, vol. 6, 1861, p. 96. *Notes and Queries*, vol. 11, p. 17.

[2] Mark Pattison, *Isaac Casaubon, 1559–1614*, Oxford, 1892, pp. 301, 304.

[3] P.C.C. 26 Bolein.

[4] In 1599, Killigrew was assessed eight pounds for lands in St Margaret's parish, Broadstreet Ward valued at forty pounds. P.R.O. Exchequer Subsidy Rolls, E. 179/146 f. 390.

[5] P.C.C. 26 Bolein.

considerable amounts of money accumulated in their hands.[1] Some of the Tellers employed this money for short term loans, and though large profits could be made by means of such transactions they inevitably gave rise to serious abuses. Officials who made large loans out of Exchequer funds sometimes found themselves saddled with a number of unpaid debts, and without sufficient resources to settle their accounts.[2]

There is evidence that Killigrew too used this illegal method of supplementing his income, but to what extent it is impossible to say.[3] He lent out a great deal of money during his lifetime, some of which was never repaid. If he employed government funds to finance his loans there is no indication that he was ever unable to render satisfactory account of the sums committed to his charge.

Killigrew was probably as exacting and conscientious in the performance of his duties at the Exchequer as he was in other aspects of his official career. His diplomatic correspondence gives frequent evidence of anxiety lest the office be mismanaged

[1] On the duties of the Tellers of the Exchequer see: F. C. Dietz, "The exchequer in Elizabeth's reign," *Smith College studies in history*, vol. 8, no. 20, (John Spencer Basset and Sidney Bradstreet Fay ed.) Northampton, Mass., 1923. G. R. Elton, *The Tudor revolution in government, administrative changes in the reign of Henry VIII*, Cambridge, 1953, pp. 252-3.

[2] In February, 1578, Sir Thomas Gresham, Elizabeth's financial agent in the Netherlands, wrote to his servant instructing him to borrow 1,500 pounds from Mr Stonely, Teller of the Exchequer, for three days. P.R.O. S.P. 12/122 no. 41. In August, 1586, Lord Burghley was informed that Stonely was unable to make up his accounts by 16,000 pounds and that he had been forced to lay the burden on the other Tellers. P.R.O. S.P. 12/192 f. 9.

[3] Killigrew rejected Anthony Bacon's request for a loan of 200 pounds because of the refusal of his deputy (in the Exchequer), Sugden, to give him the amount required. Bacon was a poor risk, but Killigrew's statement implies that he was willing on occasion to make loans out of Exchequer funds when there was reasonable certainty of repayment. James Spedding ed., *The letters and life of Francis Bacon, including all his occasional works, namely letters, speeches, tracts, writings, not already printed among his philosophical, literary, or professional works*, vol. 1, London, 1861, pp. 349, 353. (hereafter: Spedding, vol. 1.).

during his absence.[1] Even the obligations of friendship took second place when he was dealing with Exchequer affairs. One of the duties of the Tellers was to issue pay to ambassadors, and the close fisted financial practices of the Queen's government compelled them to adopt a stern attitude in this matter.

In the autumn of 1565 Thomas Randolph wrote from Scotland bitter complaints to Leicester and Cecil concerning the privations he was suffering for want of money, and he also gave vent to his annoyance with his friend, Killigrew, who he believed was responsible for the withholding of his pay. "I pray you," he said, "to charge Harry Killigrew who is harder unto me than ever Browne, the Treasurer was." The ambassador evidently received sharp reprimand for his complaints because a few months later he felt obliged to offer a humble apology to Cecil for his "doing touching Mr Killigrew." [2] Apparently it was a risky business for one of Randolph's station to criticize a man who was the brother-in-law of the Queen's Secretary of State and a close friend of her favourite, the Earl of Leicester. Fortunately this incident resulted in no permanent breach between Killigrew and Randolph.

In addition to his other grants Killigrew had the good fortune to receive several wardships. The competition among courtiers and members of the gentry to purchase wardships from the crown was intense because there were exceptional opportunities for profit to be gained from the exercise of the rights of wardship over the person and property of individuals whose parents had died while they were still minors. One of the worst social scandals of the Tudor period arose from the ruthless exploitation of wards for the personal aggrandizement of their guardians.[3]

---

[1] In May, 1588, Killigrew petitioned Leicester for his recall from the Netherlands. He asked him to consider "what accounts I am entangled in in respect of mine office which may fall to my utter undoing." B. M. Cotton MSS, DIII, f. 160.

[2] P.R.O. S.P. 52/6 ff. 7, 11.

[3] For a recent excellent book on the subject of wardships see: Joel

In this competition for wardships Killigrew enjoyed the advantage of being the brother-in-law of the Master of Wards, Lord Burghley. While he was a prisoner in France in 1562–3 Henry was given by Cecil the wardship of John Arundell, a young member of the Cornish gentry. Some idea of the value of this grant can be derived from Killigrew's statement that profits of £697. 6s. 10d. accrued from the wardship during the seven month period of his captivity.[1]

Although Killigrew doubtless took care to get full value out of the wardships which came into his hands, unlike many of his contemporaries, he also showed some concern to discharge conscientiously his responsibilities as a guardian. In the autumn of 1572, while he was ambassador to Scotland, he received the wardship of a four year old boy named Jonathan Trelawny, an offspring of a good Cornish family.[2] As Jonathan grew older Killigrew gained Lord Burghley's favour on his behalf. In November, 1582, when the boy had reached his fifteenth year, Henry's wife, Catherine, wrote to Burghley: "I have understood lately from Mr Killigrew how it hath pleased your Lordship to extend your accustomed favour towards young Jonathan in causes concerning his good..." [3] Perhaps Killigrew was able to place his ward in Cecil House in the Strand which was one of the finest educational centres in England for young members of the aristocracy. Even the greatest nobles of the realm coveted the opportunity of sending their sons to be educated in Burghley's household.[4]

Subsequently Trelawny married Henry's second daughter, Elizabeth, and he seems to have been an excellent choice as a son-in-law; in fact, a man after Killigrew's own heart. Richard

Hurstfield, *The Queen's wards, wardships and marriage under Elizabeth I*, London, 1958 (hereafter Hurstfield).

[1] P.R.O. S.P. 12/235 f. 97.
[2] See the inquisition post-mortem of John Trelawny, P.R.O. Chancery Series 2, C. 142/151 f. 8. Vivian, *Visitations of Cornwall*, 1620. p. 229.
[3] P.R.O. S.P. 12/155 f. 97.
[4] Hurstfield, pp. 255–9.

Carew describes Sir Jonothan as "a knight, well spoken, staid in his carriage, and of thrifty providence."[1] He lived at Poole in Cornwall, a close neighbour of his father-in-law whose manor, Lanrake, was only four miles distant.[2]

In view of the fairly substantial sums which Killigrew left to his wife and children and of the several valuable grants which he received from the crown there may appear to be a certain hypocrisy in his repeated complaints of poverty. Such complaints are a frequent occurence in the letters of Elizabethan officials, and they cannot be taken at face value. Yet, the priory, the three manors, and the few acres in Penryn and Truro do not represent great landed wealth. The income from them can hardly have been sufficient for the heavy financial burdens which Henry had to bear.

Especially onerous were the expenses incurred on foreign embassies which far exceeded the trifling sum of forty shillings a day that comprised the daily wage of an ambassador.[3] Throckmorton and Walsingham, both of whom were wealthier men than Killigrew and more generously rewarded by the Queen, protested against the monetary strain imposed by diplomatic employment. Then there were the costs involved in maintaining 'the port of a gentleman' at court and during numerous attendances on royal progresses. Probably Henry depended to a very large degree on the profits arising from the Tellership of the Exchequer and from the wardships in fulfilling his obligations as a diplomat and courtier. Unfortunately, in assessing his financial position it is impossible to say how much he received from these sources.

During the early part of Elizabeth's reign he seems to have suffered severely from financial difficulties. In the summer of 1560 Throckmorton informed the Privy Council that Killigrew would be compelled to leave the court unless the Queen gave

[1] Carew, p. 135.   [2] Ibid., p. 185.
[3] On the payment of English ambassadors in the sixteenth century see: Arnold Usher Meyer, *Englische diplomatic in Deutschland zur zeit Edwards VI und Mariens.* Breslau, 1900. pp. 9 ff.

him some relief.[1] The grant of the Tellership the following year was probably her response to this application. Killigrew's moving appeal for the grant of Lanrake so that his wife and children would not be forced into beggary after his death may not have been without some foundation in truth.[2]

Even in later years, when his position had greatly improved, Killigrew was by no means free from worry concerning money matters. For this his improvident Cornish relations undoubtedly bore a large share of the blame. Henry's generosity to his elder brother, Sir John Killigrew and to his nephew, John, seems to have been prodigal to the point of folly. Both men achieved great notoriety for their numerous acts of violence and robbery against their neighbours and against ships which frequented the southern shores of Cornwall. As Captains of Pendennis Castle they made Falmouth a haven for pirates. The Castle was used as a storehouse for stolen goods, and buccaneers were offered protection from the law in Falmouth harbour by the Killigrews in return for a share of their loot and of the profits of their voyages. Nor did they disdain to indulge in acts of piracy on their own. On one occasion Sir John the elder, assisted by his wife and servants, plundered a Spanish ship which had been driven by storm into the harbour.[3]

For many years both father and son used their power as local magnates to thwart the inquiries of government commissions directed to curb piracy, and they terrorized their neighbours to such an extent that none dared to give evidence against them. At last, however, the Cornish Killigrews fell upon evil days. The elder Sir John died leaving numerous unpaid debts to his brother, Henry.[4] His eldest son, also John, spent his

[1] P.R.O. S.P. 70/19 f. 11.   [2] Howard, *Letters*, p. 188.

[3] On Sir John Killigrew and his eldest son see: Rowse, *Tudor Cornwall*, pp. 85–385 passim. A. L. Rowse, *Sir Richard Grenville of the Revenge, an Elizabethan hero*, London, 1937, pp. 76, 140, 146, 164–8. David Mathew, "Cornish and Welsh pirates in the reign of Elizabeth," *English Historical Review*, (1924), vol. 39, pp. 337–48.

[4] See the Inquisition post mortem of Sir John Killigrew the elder. P.R.O. Chancery Series 2, C. 142/207, f. 108.

youth at court, and it was said that when he returned to Cornwall he "made numerous promises of large satisfaction for the faults committed by his father." [1] In fact he proved a more reckless and spend-thrift rogue than his father. According to charges drawn up against him in 1595 he had lived for many years as a "professed outlaw," gaining his livelihood by oppressing his tenants and by robbing strangers at Falmouth.[2]

About 1595 Sir John was summoned to London to face charges for the crimes alleged against him and to answer the claims of his many creditors. One of those to whom he owed a very large sum of money was his uncle, Sir Henry Killigrew. Lacking the means to settle his debts John took the line of defence that his uncle's demands were fraudulent, that he had already been repaid in full.[3]

But John reckoned without Sir Henry's exact habits and long memory in financial matters. The latter submitted a detailed account to the government showing that his brother and nephew owed him debts contracted over a period of 37 years which amounted to £1,879.3s.6d. without reckoning one penny interest or one penny forfeiture.[4] In addition he stood bound in recognizance for debts owed by his brother of over 800 pounds. Considering that he declared himself ready to submit the dispute to impartial arbiters, and in view of the well-documented record of his brother's and nephew's dishonest practices one can probably accept Killigrew's statement as accurate.

The debts owed by his Cornish relations seem to have been a source of considerable hardship for Killigrew. "To supply the want of his (Sir John the younger's) debts to me," he said, "I have been driven sundry times to take up money upon use

[1] Hatfield MSS., vol. 37, f. 8.

[2] Ibid.

[3] "A list of debts owing to Sir Henry Killigrew". P.R.O. S.P. 12/235 f. 97.

[4] Killigrew's account was probably drawn up in 1598 since he says that the debts were contracted over a period of 37 years, the earliest of which was in 1561. Ibid.

which hath cost me above £200." [1] On one occasion Henry's generosity to his nephew saved the latter from the consequences of his misdeeds. In the autumn of 1587 John had been charged with robbery by some Danish merchants who had taken refuge in Falmouth harbour to escape a French corsair.[2] "Out of very mere love for my nephew," Killigrew related, "I was constrained to lay down £445 debt to the Dane ... to pacify her Majesty's anger and to save the Castle from forfeiture, and himself from prison which was like to have fallen out for want of payment, of which I am not fully satisfied at this day, being above eight year's past." [3] Despite the ingratitude of his brother and nephew he declared that he was ready to abate a considerable part of the principal debt and to release all forfeitures.[4] Because of John's bankrupt condition it is unlikely that his uncle received more than a very small satisfaction for his claims. During the last years of Elizabeth's reign John paid the penalty of his misdeeds by confinement in a London prison.[5]

Killigrew's long suffering and ill-requited generosity to his brother and nephew is a pleasant contrast to the callousness with which he treated young Harry Caltropt. Perhaps his readiness to help them reflected a strong sense of family obligation rather than genuine affection. At any rate his kindness towards his Cornish relations is only one of a number of instances which suggest that there was more to him than the narrow, inflexible Puritanism apparent in some of his actions.

Throughout his career Killigrew maintained close contact with his native country of Cornwall. There he was a landowner in a small way and his friends were prominent members of the local gentry. Two of the most notable among them were his

---

1 *Ibid.*
2 P.R.O. State Papers, Denmark. (P.R.O. S.P. 75/1 f. 100).
3 P.R.O. S.P. 12/235 f. 97.
4 *Ibid.*
5 *Acts of the Privy Council*, 1598–9, pp. 236, 535.

brother-in-law, Sir Francis Godolphin, a great tin magnate and one of the leading officials of the county, and the historian, Richard Carew.[1] Both were men of culture and learning like Henry.

One of the accepted duties of the court gentry was that of giving assistance and protection to inhabitants of their home counties. Both Henry and his brother, William, were praised by Richard Carew in his *Survey of Cornwall* for their willingness to use their influence at court on behalf of their fellow Cornish-men.[2] Even towards the humbler sort Killigrew proved a kind benefactor. In August, 1598, he wrote to Sir Julius Caesar, High Judge of the Admiralty Court, requesting his assistance for a poor Cornish constable who was being put to charges far beyond his means as a result of prosecution by some Scotsmen who accused him of allowing the escape of a felon.[3]

In his capacity as a landowner Killigrew's character perhaps reveals itself in a less benevolent light and suggests that he was as grasping and aggressive as many of his fellow gentry. At any rate, there was an incident involving assault, riotous assembly, and property destruction which was alleged to have resulted from the actions of certain of his agents in Cornwall. This incident originated in a dispute over a ninety acre farm at Hendra near Killigrew's manor of Lanrake. He occupied the farm as tenant in common with a woman named Amy Hancock, who had apparently become enraged by the attempt of some of his employees to prevent the ploughing and harvesting of her land.

Trouble arose one summer day in 1580 when Amy suddenly appeared on Killigrew's section of the farm with thirty armed men at her back, most of whom came from the nearby town of St Germans. They expelled William Samuel, reeve of the manor of Lanrake, and several other of Killigrew's men, spoiled

---

[1] Carew, who is described as a friend in Killigrew's will, and Godolphin were appointed executors of his estate. P.C.C. 26 Bolein (1603).

[2] Carew, p. 123.

[3] B. M., Additional MSS. 12503, f. 412.

their goods, and took away 100 marks worth of corn. No blood seems to have been spilled, but the whole episode was fraught with a violence characteristic of the Cornish countryside at this period. Amy's chief accomplice, a butcher named William Clemens, thrust a seven foot staff with a pike at the end of it at Samuel, who wisely took the hint and departed. To make matters worse disease had broken out in St Germans and several of Amy's followers "had the sore of the plague on them" at the very moment they were carrying out their assault.

Killigrew promptly had the trespassers hauled before the Court of the Star Chamber. Under interrogation the butcher, Clemens, admitted that he had used a staff against Samuel but claimed that this action was only taken in self-defence. Amy Hancock, he said, had hired him to plough her fields and to protect her property because she feared that Samuel might try to prevent her from working her land. Clemens testified that on the day in question Samuel, presumably acting upon Killigrew's orders, came and forbade him to plough, threatening violence as other of Killigrew's agents had done in the past to those working for Amy.[1]

At court the closing years of Elizabeth's reign were marked by a struggle for power between the Cecils and her favourite, Essex. As in the earlier contest between his patron, Leicester, and Burghley and Throckmorton, Killigrew preserved his policy of non-involvement. At this time his sympathies were probably on the side of Burghley and his son, Robert Cecil. Some indication of his attitude towards the men who gathered around Essex is given by his dealings with Anthony Bacon, the son of his deceased brother-in-law, Sir Nicholas Bacon. When the impecunious Anthony wrote to his uncle asking for a loan of 200 pounds the latter brushed him off with a glib excuse. To his brother, Francis, Anthony drily commented a few days later: "My uncle, Killigrew, hath, as they say, uncled me with a frivolous excuse grounded upon the refusal of his deputy, (in

[1] P.R.O. Star Chamber Elizabeth. (St. Ch. S/1 f. 22).

the Exchequer), Sugden, without whose help he said he could not furnish me." [1]

Henry's reply resembles the Lord Treasurer's treatment of a plea put forward by Anthony's brother, Francis Bacon, to obtain assistance in a plan which he had devised for the advancement of knowledge. Killigrew and Burghley were two eminently practical old men. They had no interest in supporting the extravagances of their nephews or in encouraging vague schemes for intellectual inquiry.

Killigrew was now a long established man at court. He was not prepared to risk his assured connections with the Cecils by fraternizing with the hot-heads and malcontents who backed Essex. Moreover, he was far too wise to involve himself with one so unstable and reckless as Essex. Early in Elizabeth's reign he had warned Throckmorton of the futility and danger of using high-pressure methods with her. The Queen's nature had not changed; indeed, in her old age, she grew more autocratic and imperious than ever. Killigrew's long knowledge of his sovereign's complex character doubtless enabled him to predict the disastrous outcome of Essex's attempts to bully her into submission to his will.

Unfortunately one member of his family was not so perceptive. Killigrew's son-in-law, Sir Henry Neville, allowed himself to become enmeshed in Essex's abortive conspiracy and revolt in the autumn and winter of 1600–1. To so obedient and devoted a servant of Elizabeth as Henry Killigrew it was a grievous blow that a kinsman should have any part in a treasonable enterprise, particularly one whose advancement at court he himself had assisted. Neville was the husband of Henry's eldest daughter, Anne, and Killigrew had taken particular pains to enlist the goodwill of the Cecils on his behalf.[2]

[1] Spedding, vol. 1, pp. 349, 353.
[2] In April, 1597, Killigrew wrote to Robert Cecil asking him "to continue that work of favour that you have begun towards our poor gentleman (Neville) who, I am sure, join us in prayers for your preservation in much honour and happiness...." Hatfield MSS. vol. 153 f. 79.

Now it appeared that his son-in-law was involved in a conspiracy that was directly aimed at Robert Cecil, Essex's chief opponent in the Council.

Neville apparently had been living in Killigrew's house at Lothbury prior to Essex's rebellion. After the collapse of the movement Neville was confined for a time at his father-in-law's residence while his desk and other belongings were examined for incriminating evidence.[1] Henry's displeasure against Neville was so great that he refused to allow Anne in his home, and the Lords of the Council were obliged to send him a letter directing him "to receive her in his house and to use her with that countenance and comfort that heretofore he had done."[2]

Neville had in fact taken no direct part in the conspiracy or rebellion. Essex's friends, the Earl of Southampton and Henry Cuffe, had urged him to join the rising and had revealed their plans to him. Under questioning by members of the Privy Council he said that he had told Southampton he would not approve the enterprise unless the undertakers swore not to attempt anything against the Queen's person or state. He also claimed that he had refused to join in any action against his kinsman, Robert Cecil.

Neville, however, admitted that he had agreed not to actively oppose Essex's plan to place his grievances before the Queen by force.[3] This admission, together with the fact that he had concealed his knowledge of the conspiracy, was sufficient to bring upon him very heavy penalties. Before his involvement with Essex, Neville had gained a place of some prominence in public affairs. He had been elected to the House of Commons on four occasions, had been granted valuable offices at court, and, in 1599, had gone to Paris as resident ambassador at the French court where he became known for his Puritan opinions. He was undoubtedly an able man in his own right, but it is

[1] Ibid., vol. 77, f. 32.
[2] Acts of the Privy Council, 1600-1, pp. 178-9.
[3] P.R.O. S.P. 12/297 f. 11.

equally certain that his advancement was assisted by the influence of his father-in-law and the Cecils.[1]

Now, however, his fall was rapid and complete. He was stripped of all his offices, saddled with a crushing fine of £5,000, and imprisoned in the Tower.[2] Following Neville's arrest his devoted wife, Anne, wrote frantic letters to Robert Cecil and to Thomas Windebank, Clerk of the Signet, appealing for their help to mitigate the Queen's severity towards her husband.[3] She also enlisted the aid of her uncle, William Killigrew.[4] It is not clear to what extent Henry lent his support to these efforts on his son-in-law's behalf. At any rate, his anger towards him lessened. In July, 1601, his brother, William wrote a letter of thanks to Cecil for the help he had given Neville. "I am so bold," William said, "as to send your Lordship's letters to my poor old brother who will take great comfort to see your honour's favourable care towards his poor distressed son-in-law." [5] Cecil's intercession does not appear to have had much effect. Neville remained in the Tower until the accession of James I when he was released by a royal warrant. Subsequently he became a prominent member of the opposition party against the King in the House of Commons.[6]

By the end of Elizabeth's reign Killigrew had achieved for himself a secure position at court as a respected and distinguished servant of the crown. He was especially valued for his close bond with the Cecil family and for his promptness and dependability in helping friends.[7] Many years before Sir

---

[1] *D.N.B.*, vol. 14, pp. 258–9. On Neville's Puritanism see the anonymous letter to Peter Halins of London. Dec. 7th, 1599. P.R.O. S.P. 12/273 f. 46.

[2] P.R.O. S.P. 12/284 f. 7. Hatfield MSS. vol. 182 f. 114.

[3] Hatfield MSS. vol. 77 ff. 57, 90. See also Neville's letters appealing for Robert Cecil's help: *Ibid.*, vol. 77, f. 90. *Ibid.*, vol. 86, ff. 1, 146. *Ibid.*, vol. 87, f. 153. *Ibid.* vol. 90, ff. 124–5.

[4] P.R.O. S.P. 12/279 f. 20.

[5] Hatfield MSS. vol. 86, f. 141.

[6] *D.N.B.* vol. 14, pp. 258–9.

[7] George Gilpin wrote from the Netherlands to Killigrew asking his help in securing some preferment. He asked him to take up the matter with

Thomas Challoner, English ambassador at Madrid, bore testimony to these traits when he wrote: "Your letter requires such thanks as a thankful friend can yield. Many of my court friends promised gaily, but none have acquitted their promises."[1]

Killigrew's warmth and sensitivity as a friend, however, are sometimes most sharply revealed in his letters. He was especially close to William Cecil, Lord Burghley. The two men were alike in many respects. They had the same painful, rather self-righteous sense of duty combined with a streak of religious pessimism, and the same tendency to portray themselves as overburdened men whose services were ill-appreciated. The picture was possibly a true one, but they both took a certain melancholy pleasure in playing the part.

In the autumn of 1588, following the anxious months, which had culminated in the defeat of the Spanish Armada, Killigrew sent his old associate a just and sympathetic tribute. "It grieveth me," he wrote, "who have no means but by prayer to relieve by any service of mine the least part of the cares you have for the steering of that ship, wherein God hath appointed you to be a pilot from the beginning, that so many storms hath threatened shipwreck and to pilot ... against all the power and practice of the wicked, as I trust He will do still, and to bring you and yours long home, even to Himself (in his time), and that in peace."[2]

Despite his long career and his many valuable services Killigrew never achieved greatness or power in the councils of the government. This fact can doubtless be explained by Elizabeth's attitude towards him. Probably he lacked those outward qualities which were most certain to attract her favour. No portrait of Killigrew has survived, but he seems to have been of small stature. His friends sometimes referred to him affec-

---

Lord Burghley, with whom, as he said, "I know you can do as much as anybody." P.R.O. S.P. 84/41 f. 217.

[1] P.R.O. S.P. 70/22 f. 400.

[2] P.R.O. S.P. 84/27 f. 114.

tionately as "little" Harry Killigrew. He also had a permanent
limp as a result of his wound at Rouen in 1562. It is likely,
therefore, that he fell short of the Queen's exacting standards of
masculine perfection.[1]

His Puritan opinions and his personality were perhaps even
more uncongenial to her. Killigrew possessed a certain dry
humour, but his writings show a seriousness and inflexibility
of character which Elizabeth must have found difficult to bear
in her lighter moods. Nor did he have those traits of boldness
and self-confidence which she found so attractive in men like
Leicester, Essex, and Throckmorton.

David Lloyd described him as a "spotless man" one "whose
severe thoughts, words, and carriage so awed his inferior
faculties, as to restrain him, through all the heats of youth...
insomuch as they say he looked upon all approaches to that sin,
then so familiar to his calling as a soldier, his quality as a
gentleman, and his station as a courtier, not only with an utter
disallowance in his judgement, but with natural abhorrence and
antipathy in his very lower inclinations." [2] So virtuous a man
was doubtless regarded by the vigorous, unconventional
Queen as rather a bore. She apparently told Leicester that she
regarded Henry as "dull".[3] He seems, in fact, to have been
"rather a Victorian character," as one historian has described
Burghley.[4]

Killigrew, however, possessed some accomplishments which
merited the admiration of the Queen and her more cultivated
courtiers. Lloyd bestows a glowing panegyric upon his learning
and his literary and artistic abilities. He says that Killigrew
could repeat Cicero's orations to his dying day, and that he was
well read in Aristotle, Livy, Xenophon, and Tacitus. Killigrew

[1] In referring to his part in the relief of Rouen in 1562 Killigrew's
petition for the fee farm of the manor of Lanrake stated: "he carrieth
the witness and work thereof to his grave." B. M. Lansdowne MSS. 106,f. 31.
[2] Lloyd, p. 587.
[3] P.R.O. S.P. 84/16 f. 18.
[4] A. L. Rowse, *The England of Elizabeth*, London 1950, p. 279.

is also credited with expert knowledge in such diverse fields as history, architecture, sculpture, numismatics, and military engineering. In addition to all these talents Lloyd praises him for his skill as a poet and painter.[1]

Unfortunately there is not much evidence to support most of Lloyd's claims. That Killigrew was a learned man, well read in the classics, is attested by his correspondence and by his close acquaintance with numerous men of academic ability. On one occasion he sent some French verses which he had written to his friend, Thomas Challoner. Challoner returned them translated into English, and Killigrew presented the verses to Maitland of Lethington as a token of appreciation for the latter's assistance in securing his release from imprisonment in France.[2]

In May, 1575, he sent detailed plans for fireworks and pageantry, to Leicester, which he had received from an Italian artist, for the purpose of entertaining the Queen during her famous visit to Kenilworth in July of that year.[3] These instances do not shed much light on the extent of Killigrew's accomplishments. Taken together with Lloyd's statements they at least suggest the possibility that he was well grounded in the many sided Renaissance culture of his time and that he possessed wide literary and artistic interests.

Whatever his personal limitations Killigrew was an excellent public servant, and the Queen respected him as such. After Burghley's death in August, 1598, he was the only one left of

[1] Lloyd, pp. 585–6. Lloyd has a poor reputation as a historian. He was criticised in his own time for failing to support his statements by citing authorities. An eighteenth century writer says that among men of learning he had "not only the character of a most impudent plagiary but a false writer and a mere scribble...." Anthony Wood, *Athenae oxoniensis, an exact history of all the writers and bishops who have had their education in the University of Oxford to which are added the fasti, or annals of the said University,* (Philip Bliss ed.), vol. 4, London, 1820, p. 349. After reading a number of Lloyd's biographies in his *Worthies,* my impression is that while he is frequently in error on matters of fact, his personality sketches, though superficial, are generally accurate.

[2] P.R.O. S.P. 70/22 f. 400. P.R.O. S.P. 70/23 f. 792.

[3] Pepys MSS. vol. 2, f. 517.

the men who had served her in those days long ago in Mary's reign when she had been a lonely girl in constant danger of her life.

Perhaps their common memory of that time cemented a certain bond between Elizabeth and her old servant during the closing years of her reign. She had been far from generous in rewarding him for his many services, but that was the Queen's way. She was not a particularly warmhearted or generous person. Her own life had contained too much unhappiness and insecurity to allow the development of these softer qualities in her personality.

Yet Elizabeth could be both gracious and kind in small matters. There is record of one pleasant episode in the spring of 1601 which indicates her good will towards Henry and his family. His French wife, Jaél, applied for English citizenship and was granted a letter of naturalization by the government. This she sent to court for the Queen's signature.[1] Sir Thomas Windebank, Clerk of the Signet, who was a friend of the Killigrew family, wrote to Jaél a few days later: "I have presented to her Majesty the letter to make you an English lady, and she has signed it quickly with many gracious words..." He suggested that her husband should come to court in person to thank the Queen for her kindness. Unfortunately sickness prevented Henry from performing this office. Some time afterwards Jaél wrote to Windebank from her house in Lothbury: "I should not have delayed my reply, but I was waiting for a messenger who, sharing the favour, would have supplied my defects in acknowledging it, but he is too ill to follow your counsel."[2] Elizabeth's kindness to his wife must have been especially gratifying to Henry at a time when he was sick in body and suffering great personal anxiety over the folly and misfortune of his son-in-law, Sir Henry Neville.

During the last few years of his life Killigrew retired to Cornwall. Perhaps he lived in the old Castle of Ince near Lan-

[1] P.R.O. S.P. 12/279 f. 107.
[2] *Ibid.*, ff. 108, 111.

rake where, according to local legend, one of his family was said to have kept four wives, one in each of its four towers, none of whom knew of the others' existence.[1] There is an amusing irony in the possibility that a story of this kind grew up around the person of so respectable a Puritan gentleman as Henry Killigrew. He died on 2nd March, 1603, just over three weeks before Elizabeth whom he had served for nearly half a century.[2] His body was laid to rest in St Margaret's Church, London, near his home in Lothbury.[3]

The high opinion with which Killigrew was regarded during retirement by his fellow Cornishmen was noted by Richard Carew in his *Survey of Cornwall* who wrote: "Sir Henry Killigrew, after embassies and messages and many other employments of peace and war in his Prince's service, to the good of his country hath made choice of a retired estate, and reverently regarded by all sorts, placeth his principal contentment in himself which, to a life so well acted, can no way be wanting." [4]

---

[1] Richard Polwhele, *History of Cornwall, civil, military, &c.*, vol. 4, p. 74.
[2] P.R.O. C. 142/251 f. 40.
[3] See above: footnote 3.
[4] Carew, p. 132.

CHAPTER XI

THE MAN AND HIS CAREER

T HROUGHOUT his diplomatic career in Elizabeth's reign —from the early days immediately following her accession, when he unsuccessfully sought to form an alliance with the Protestant princes of western Germany to the time when he served with the army of the Earl of Essex in Normandy, Killigrew cast himself in the rôle of an ever vigilant sentinal standing guard over the interests of his country and religion. His duty, as he conceived it, was to alert the Queen and her Council to the danger of Catholic aggression and to win them to a policy of assistance and war on behalf of the Protestant powers.

Since the power of decision in the determination of policy resided in Elizabeth's hands Killigrew faced the problem of finding means of putting pressure on her for the realization of his aims. In this respect he operated under certain disadvantages —he was not a personal friend of the Queen like Throckmorton or a trusted councillor like Walsingham. But there were other methods at his disposal, and these he employed vigorously.

He was closely associated by friendship and marriage with several important members of the Privy Council with whom he corresponded during his diplomatic missions. Through them he could be sure that his views would be made known and strongly supported in the Queen's council chamber. On occasion he tried to influence policy decisions through his contacts with foreign ambassadors in London. The most notable example of his activities in this regard was the assistance he gave to Fénélon's efforts to win the Queen's assent to marriage with the Duke of Alençon in the spring of 1572. More indirectly, he added to the weight of forward Protestant influence on the government by helping to advance people in the diplomatic service who shared his political and religious opinions. Two such men were his son-in-law, Sir Henry Neville, and William Davison.

Killigrew's greatest successes in influencing government policy occurred in the autumn and winter of 1559–60 when, as chargé d'affaires at the French court, he worked in conjunction with Throckmorton to bring about intervention in Scotland, and in 1572–3, when his urgent appeals to Burghley and Leicester helped to win Elizabeth's support for Morton.

In the last analysis, however, it was the Queen's independent judgement, not the advice of diplomats or councillors that determined policy. Sometimes she could be swayed in one direction or another by certain individuals or by strong pressure from the Council. When her actions were contrary to the line he favoured Killigrew voiced the suspicion that evilly disposed men had gained control of her mind. Commenting to Davison on Elizabeth's failure to support the Earl of Morton he observed darkly: "Her Majesty hath some that mar more in a day than all her good councillors and servants can persuade in a week." [1] But that belief was merely the illusion of a man who was far from the inner councils of the government. Burghley, who knew Elizabeth better than anyone else, realised how difficult it was to influence or predict her actions.

Yet the despatches of Killigrew, Walsingham, and other Protestant extremists in the diplomatic service had some effect in altering the course of English foreign policy since their communications were one of the principal sources of information from which the Queen and her Council evaluated the intentions of other powers. The constant warnings of such men concerning the hostile plans of the Catholic rulers, especially Philip II, intensified the distrust of English statesmen.[2] When

[1] P.R.O. S.P. 15/25 f. 98.
[2] On the rôle of the diplomat in heightening international tension during the years following the Treaty of Cateau-Cambrésis see Mattingly, pp. 198–208.

Catholic-Spanish intrigues in England and the steps taken by Philip in the Netherlands and France confirmed the truth of these warnings the stage was set for the decision to enter into war against Spain and the Guise party in France.

Killigrew's value to the government was not that of a man who provided guidance in the formulation of policy but of one who excelled in the techniques of diplomacy. In the judgement of his professional associates and superiors he was one of the ablest men in the diplomatic service. Elizabeth's high opinion of his capabilities in this respect is indicated by the numerous times she sent him on missions abroad or to Scotland.

Moreover, the variety of his employment was greater than that of any other diplomat in the Elizabethan period. This fact was undoubtedly due to his exceptionally broad professional training. The experience he gained during Mary's reign as a secret agent and soldier was an excellent schooling for his subsequent work in a diplomatic and military capacity under Elizabeth. His appointment to the Tellership of the Exchequer soon after her accession afforded a thorough grounding in matters of finance that proved especially valuable when he became a councillor of State in the Netherlands.

As a diplomat Killigrew was subtle, adroit, and courageous. During the early years of Elizabeth's reign the government repeatedly employed him as a kind of 'trouble shooter' on difficult missions where the ability to manoeuvre in and out of ticklish situations was an essential requirement—one need only recall his skill in matching wits with that disgruntled old fox, John de Monluc, Bishop of Valence, or the way in which he turned the screws on the Huguenots to secure the admission of English troops into Havre and Dieppe.

His most notable achievements, however, were gained when he acted in the rôle of a conciliator. In Scotland he performed services of great value for his country by winning the friendship and cooperation of the Protestant party during the first years of Morton's Regency. In accomplishing his aims Killigrew displayed a high degree of persuasiveness as well as readiness to employ deception where the interest of his government required.

Killigrew was by no means unwilling to use Machievellian methods. As a realist, however, he recognized the importance of establishing a reputation of honesty and good faith, both for himself and his government, in the minds of the men with whom he had to deal. In the spring of 1569, for example, he sharply reminded Leicester that the failure of the English government to fulfil promises, which he had made on Leicester's assurance, threatened to destroy his credit as ambassador and to undermine the success of his negotiations. He also impressed upon Burghley the necessity of straightforward action if the German princes were to be won over for an alliance with England.[1]

Killigrew's expressed preference for honesty in diplomacy was not simply a matter of expediency. Essentially, he was a straightforward, uncomplicated person who believed in dealing roundly and honestly. Machievellian deception he adopted as a requirement of his profession; it did not reflect a fundamental characteristic of his personality. The discreet, calculating man of affairs represents only one aspect of his character, and it affords but a partial explanation of his success as a diplomat. There was also in him the bluntly sincere Calvinist soldier whose word could be relied upon by England's Protestant allies. This side of his personality explains the confidence and respect with which he was regarded in Scotland.

Though he could be sharp and stern on occasion Killigrew was normally a person of an equable, kindly temper. There is no hint in his career of the quarrels and enmities which were so characteristic of other Elizabethans. A warlike soldier when the defence of his religion and country was at stake, Killigrew's outlook was naturally that of a civilian who preferred the ways of peace. His pacific inclinations are unconsciously revealed in the pleasure with which he noted the signs of material prosperity in Scotland which were the result of Morton's strong and peaceful rule.

1 Pepys MSS. vol. 2, f. 293. Haynes, p. 520.

He was a quiet, self-effacing man. Probably he did not immediately strike people as an individual of marked ability. It was said that the Borderers, who resented his endeavours to curb their lawless pastimes, called him, 'but a letter bearer and my lord basket-maker'.[1] These comments provide a lifelike glimpse of Killigrew as he appeared to his enemies that almost makes up for the lack of a portrait. One can picture these sardonic, hard-bitten ruffians laughing among themselves at the bustling little emissary on his perennial journeys in and out of Scotland—a person who, in their opinion, was only fit to be a message carrier for the rulers of England and Scotland. But their apparent contempt may have masked an uneasy respect. A man who could win the admiration of the shrewd and ruthless Morton is not to be dismissed as a nonentity.

The very reticence of Killigrew's personality, moreover, was a useful quality in a diplomat. Generally speaking he confined himself to acting as an instrument of government policy, and that after all is the principal function of a diplomat. He was much less inclined than an aggressive individualist like Throckmorton to try to impose his judgements on the Queen and her ministers or to cause them embarrassment by taking an independent initiative on his own. Perhaps also, in the cut and thrust of negotiation, there is some advantage for the man who causes others at the outset to form too low an estimate of his abilities.

The impression of the cautious obedient public servant, which Killigrew often conveys, is offset at other times by behaviour which presents his character in a very different light. When his strong political and religious convictions were aroused he wrote in forceful terms to the Queen's ministers. At a dangerously early moment in his career he even dashed off an angry letter to the all-powerful Lord Burghley because of the latter's opposition to his marriage to Catherine Cooke. The picture of Killigrew jeopardizing his future prospects in a matter of the heart reveals an unexpected and amiable facet of his personality.

[1] P.R.O. S.P. 52/26 f. 76.

Little as he was normally disposed to risk Elizabeth's disfavour he accepted just that risk in the autumn of 1562 by taking command with Thomas Leighton of the Anglo-Huguenot relief force sent to Rouen—an enterprise that had been forbidden by her express orders. Killigrew, as Leicester had observed, could be a tough customer when the need arose.

He possessed great physical energy, a most necessary attribute for a diplomat in the sixteenth century. Travel was a difficult, hazardous business under any circumstances during this period. Most diplomats must have suffered from physical and nervous exhaustion resulting from the long and frequently dangerous journeys which they had to undertake. In addition there was the mental strain of conducting negotiations. Due to the slowness and unreliability of communications envoys were often out of touch with their governments for long periods. Situations arose which required prompt action and where misjudgement on their part might entail serious consequences both for their governments and themselves. If the diplomat went ahead boldly on his own initiative he ran the risk of incurring displeasure by exceeding his commission. If he failed to act his timidity might forfeit a unique chance for success in negotiation. There was also the constant possibility that despatches from home would announce a change in policy that would completely frustrate his past efforts, anger those with whom he had to deal, and bring personal discredit and embarrassment upon himself.[1]

Killigrew and other English envoys suffered all these hazards that were a normal part of the diplomatic profession and by no means peculiar to their own period. Their difficulties were only increased by the fact that they worked for a highly intelligent, but infuriatingly capricious woman. In view of the physical and psychological pressures under which they lived it is not surprising that the letters of Killigrew and other diplomats

[1] An interesting discussion of the difficulties that faced an Elizabethan ambassador on foreign service is contained in: Lawrence Stone, *An Elizabethan: Sir Horatio Palavicino*, Oxford, 1956, pp. 120-4.

often contain anguished pleas for recall because of sickness or personal incapacity to carry out their tasks successfully. Killigrew himself became severely sick on several occasions and sometimes under circumstances which suggest that nervous tension was a precipitating factor in his illness. On two occasions, moreover, during the sea journey between Havre and Dieppe, and on the voyage to Hamburg he nearly lost his life. Elizabethans were a hardy lot, and Killigrew must have been one of the hardiest among them. Over a 24 year period of active service under Elizabeth, he went on nineteen missions, a record unequalled in the annals of Tudor diplomacy.[1] After so strenuous a career he still had enough energy left to sire four children in his old age.

Killigrew, of course, had some limitations as a diplomat. Like other forward Protestant envoys his religious zeal sometimes blinded him to political realities. In some cases he was too rash in committing his country to the assistance of the Protestant powers with whom he was negotiating. At times he showed too great a confidence in the political capacities of foreign Protestant statesmen, especially in the case of the German princes. Occasionally his character reveals a curious vein of naivité that was fairly common among men of his time. How else can one account for the readiness with which he accepted the Vidame of Chartres' assurances that diplomatic pressure at Cateau-Cambrésis would cause the French to disgorge Calais? Despite their Renaissance sophistication public men of the sixteenth century were closer, in many respects, to the Middle Ages than to our own time, and their reactions frequently betrayed a credulity characteristic of the Medieval mind.

Killigrew was also inclined to become anxious and depressed

---

[1] In calculating the length of Killigrew's diplomatic service I have included those years in which he was sent on one or more missions during Elizabeth's reign. Some of his missions, however, were extremely short lasting only a few weeks. During this 24 years period he actually spent about seven years abroad or in Scotland.

in the face of difficulties—rather old womanish at times—
especially when his actions were criticized by the Queen and
her ministers. On one occasion in the autumn of 1572, when
he heard of Elizabeth's displeasure at his handling of negotiations with the Scottish Calvinist leaders, Killigrew became so
upset that for some time he was subject to fits of vomiting.[1]
His reaction, though excessive, is not surprising. There were
few who did not tremble when the Queen's temper was
aroused. At such times Lord Burghley was accustomed to beat
a hasty retreat to his bed chamber.

Even when Elizabeth was but a young woman in the first
months of her reign she showed herself a true daughter of
Henry VIII by her capacity to strike terror in the hearts of her
subordinates. At the peace conference of Cateau-Cambrésis the
English delegates allowed themselves to be drawn by the
French representatives into a discussion of the validity of the
Queen's title to the throne. So outraged was she at the timerity
of mere subjects daring to speak of a matter far above their
station and pertaining to her royal prerogative, that she sent
over a trusted councillor, Sir John Mason, to take charge of the
negotiations. With him she despatched a scathing rebuke to her
diplomatic representatives for their presumption. The effect of
Elizabeth's words on Sir Nicholas Wotton and Thomas
Thirlby, Bishop of Ely—distinguished officials who had grown
grey in the service of the crown—was so devastating as to be
almost comic, although the comedy could scarcely have been
apparent to themselves.

Shortly after delivering the Queen's message Mason wrote to
Burghley that as a result of her reprimand: "Dr Wotton is
fallen half into an ague, marry rather an ague of the mind than
of the body. The Bishop of Ely, albeit his health doth
continue, yet is he factus totus stupidus." "For the love of
God, Mr Secretary," entreated the kind-hearted Mason, "help to
salve this sore and move the Queen's Majesty to heal the wounds

[1] Killigrew to Burghley and Leicester. P.R.O. S.P. 52/23 f. 111. 23rd
November, 1572.

which she hath given with some comfortable letter..." Elizabeth was persuaded to write the letter which Mason requested
to assuage the grief of his colleagues, though it was neither as
gracious nor as forgiving as he doubtless would have wished.[1]
Of all Killigrew's acquaintances only that toughest of Puritans,
Sir Francis Walsingham, could maintain his ironic self-
possession in the face of a royal tantrum.

Killigrew often acted independently as an extremely able
diplomatic tactician, but he preferred to occupy a subordinate
rôle supporting the policies of more dominant personalities
like Leicester and Morton. His difficulties in the Netherlands
were partly due to a reluctance to provoke Leicester's hostility
by pursuing a more conciliatory line with the States General.
He possessed both ability and force of character, but his
qualities were not those of the true leader who enjoys the
exercise of power and responsibility.

Killigrew's correspondence reveals a man of good intelligence, but there is no indication of any unusual qualities of
intellect. Though well educated and one of the most widely
travelled men of his time he was no cosmopolitan. In many
respects his mentality was that of the typical Protestant
English gentleman—practical, unimaginative, insular, and with
all the conventional prejudices against Papists and foreigners.
He was, in fact, a good example of what G. K. Chesterton has
called the "plain, shrewd Briton."

Nevertheless, despite his unhappy experiences as an exile, he
probably gained a certain affection for France in later years. He
spent several years on diplomatic service in that country, his
second wife was a French woman, and he had numerous friends
among French Protestant statesmen, soldiers, and men of letters.
He admired many of the Dutch Calvinist leaders though, as a
good English monarchist, he found their methods of government uncongenial. Towards Spaniards, of course, he felt only
hatred.

Killigrew's failure to secure high office or greater personal

---

[1] See above footnote 1, p. 45.

influence with the Queen was doubtless due to the evident limitations of his character and intellect. His personality and his Puritan convictions did not create a favourable impression upon her, but Elizabeth never allowed personal prejudice to debar a really able man from advancement. Burghley and Walsingham were sober staid personalities, cast in the same mould as Killigrew—yet both were quickly promoted to positions of trust in her government. Killigrew, on the other hand, was by-passed on more than one occasion by younger men of less experience who were advanced to the Privy Council.[1]

Elizabeth obviously did not consider him a person of eminent abilities—an excellent diplomat and one who was well qualified to occupy a lesser post in the civil service—but not an individual whose capacities entitled him to share the intimacy of her council chamber. The Queen's judgement was an accurate one, and Killigrew undoubtedly agreed with it, for he had generally been modest concerning his abilities—not that one need always accept the confessions of his own 'unableness' at face value. Certainly he was conscious of his shortcomings; probably he was not overly endowed with self-confidence, but there is no reason to adopt the fashionable terminology of modern psychology and speak of an 'inferiority complex', for he also enjoyed a healthy appreciation of his considerable merits. Moreover, such self-deprecation frequently had a practical end in view—that of persuading the government to recall him from difficult diplomatic assignments which were inflicting a heavy toll, both on his health and his finances.

Killigrew's comments about himself sometimes reveal an amusing mixture of humility together with the rather smug self-satisfaction of the successful man of affairs. In fact, his very ordinariness, his conventional outlook, his ordinary human strengths and weaknesses, make him more representative—

[1] Two such men were Sir Francis Walsingham and William Davison.

indeed, more likeable as a person—than brilliant Elizabethan types such as Raleigh or Drake.

His career is an illuminating example of the importance of patronage in Tudor society. Like all men of lesser stature he was dependent on the favour and protection of the powerful at court. His first grants of office resulted from his connections with John Dudley, Duke of Northumberland. It was natural, therefore, that he should later attach himself to Northumberland's son, Robert Dudley, Earl of Leicester. Leicester's influence was responsible for his appointment to several important embassies, and Leicester's favoured position with the Queen enabled him to protect Killigrew on occasions when his actions as a diplomat aroused her anger.

Other men also played a significant part in advancing his career. Sir Nicholas Throckmorton may have assisted his entry into Elizabeth's diplomatic service, and for several years thereafter he took pains to urge Killigrew's merits on Elizabeth and her councillors. The life of a courtier must have been a severe exercise in discretion for Killigrew. His friends, Throckmorton and Leicester, were bitter enemies at the outset of Elizabeth's reign, and both were frequently at odds with his brother-in-law, Lord Burghley. Yet he never allowed his friendship for either of these men to interfere with his close connection with the Lord Treasurer. That decision was a wise one because Burghley proved a steadfast friend. To his assistance Killigrew probably owed the grants of both the Arundell and Trelawny wardships as well as the manor of Lanrake.[1]

Despite influence exerted on his behalf by powerful patrons Killigrew never received benefits in proportion to the magnitude of his services. He did not acquire great wealth and, like many Elizabethan officials, he was frequently in a state of financial embarrassment. The largest source of his income probably came from the Tellership of the Exchequer and the wardships. In this respect he was typical of the court gentry

[1] The petition for the manor of Lanrake contained in Lansdowne MSS. 106, f. 31 was drawn up by commandment of the Lord Treasurer.

who gained their wealth from offices and other crown grants rather than land management.[1] Killigrew, the prudent courtier and official, offers an interesting contrast to his eldest brother and nephew who lived beyond their means at Arwennack and made up for their extravagance by brigandage and by exploiting Henry's generosity. At the end of his career Killigrew, at any rate, was a richer and better established man than when he entered the Queen's service. His brother and nephew, on the other hand, died heavily in debt and at odds with the law.

Towards Elizabeth Killigrew felt the same mixture of irritation, bewilderment, and admiration that was the common experience of other men who served her. Her cautious nationalism was undoubtedly the course best suited to the interests of country. Had England assumed the leadership of an anti-Catholic crusade, as the Queen's forward Protestant councillors and diplomats desired, the resulting burden would have been too great for its resources to bear. But they were perhaps justified in believing, on some occasions, that a benevolent providence rather than Elizabeth's wisdom had saved the nation from disaster.

Killigrew usually accepted her lukewarmness in the Protestant cause, her indecision and parsimony with an outward show of pious resignation. Resignation, however, is not a common human virtue, and certainly not one that was characteristic of the Puritan. In several instances his despatches reveal the genuine exasperation he must often have felt towards the ways of his sovereign.

Few men were given a better opportunity to observe Elizabeth at close range, in all her varying moods, over so long a period. Killigrew had been a frequent attendant at court for nearly sixty years. Perhaps he had first encountered her there at the end of Henry VIII's reign when she had been a girl of thirteen and he, a young servant of her father's councillor,

---

1 On the subject of the court gentry see: H. R. Trevor-Roper, "The Gentry, 1540–1640," *Economic history review supplement*, London, 1954, pp. 10 ff.

John Dudley. Soon after Elizabeth's accession, in the spring of 1560, he had felt the blaze of her wrath on returning from Scotland following the repulse of the English army at Leith. A few months later he had watched with amused perplexity the young Queen's daring flirtation with his friend, Leicester.

Unfortunately, there are few indications of Killigrew's personal feelings towards Elizabeth in his surviving correspondence. The sixteenth-century Englishman's ingrained reverence for royalty and a courtier's discretion are a sufficient explanation for his reticence. However, there is no doubt that he possessed the wisdom to recognize the greatness which underlay the eccentricities of her character. He knew, moreover, that her rule was an essential condition for the survival of Protestantism in England. His comparison of Elizabeth with the Regent Morton indicates his realization of this fact as well as an awareness of her extraordinary abilities as a ruler. From Scotland he wrote to Walsingham in the spring of 1574: "...if he (Morton) were gone they know no more here where to find another for the purpose than you or I do a successor for our weal in England. The Lord preserve her Majesty."[1] This brief comment tells much concerning the reasons for the devoted service which men like Killigrew and Walsingham gave to Elizabeth despite their disagreement with her on many important matters of policy.

As a man Killigrew emerges, on the whole, in a favourable light. Certainly he was narrow and stiff in his views, and inclined at times to be both harsh and self-righteous. Like many people of his kind he could be tiresomely sententious and sanctimonious—a veritable Polonius in fact! All of these qualities, of course, are typical of the Puritan mentality. However, few men conform to a stereotype, and Killigrew, fortunately, was not one of them.

Although gravity and a rather painful moral earnestness were dominant themes in his personality there was a lighter, more human side as well. If he did not shine among the boisterous

[1] P.R.O. S.P. 52/26 f. 35.

extroverts at court there is no reason to doubt that with his own friends, in the quiet intimacy of an evening conversation, Killigrew was a most engaging companion, for he was a knowledgeable person, a shrewd observer of men and affairs, and possessed of a keen, dry sense of humour. Referring to Killigrew's missions to the German princes Lloyd says that "he had a humour that bewitched the Elector of Bavaria, a carriage that awed him of Mentz, a reputation that obliged them of Cologne and Heidelberg and a fluency of discourse that won them all." [1]

Morever, Killigrew enjoyed the society of his fellow men and took pleasure in the good things of life. In the summer of 1566 he wrote to his cousin, Hugh Fitzwilliam, a glowing account of the feasts provided by the Earl of Leicester for Elizabeth and her courtiers during one of her visits to Kenilworth. With a delightfully naive astonishment he described the great quantities of food consumed at a single meal.: "My Lady Fitzwilliam was there and said she would never look to see the like in her days. Twenty oxen at breakfast was nothing," he declared. "Speak it upon my credit!" [2]

Unlike many Puritans Killigrew was no prude. Indeed, one who had experienced the rough life of an exile and professional soldier was unlikely to have much prudery left in his nature. To Walsingham, on one occasion, he wrote with evident enjoyment of an amorous exploit by two young blades serving with the English army in the Netherlands.[3]

Killigrew also possessed to a marked degree all the virtues characteristic of the best representatives of the Puritan type. His religious convictions were deeply felt and sincere. He had a strong sense of family obligation, and he showed an unusual gift for friendship. These were lifelong, and he managed to win the lasting esteem of some of the most noted men of his time.

[1] Lloyd, p. 587.
[2] Killigrew to Hugh Fitzwilliam, 3rd September, 1566. P.R.O. S.P. 12/40 f. 60.
[3] Killigrew to Walsingham, 6th March, 1588. P.R.O. S.P. 84/22 f. 77.

These men were often in conflict with one another. The fact that Killigrew was able to retain the friendship of all of them is an indication of suppleness and tact, but it also suggests an essential integrity of character. If he had been a mere time-server he would not have held the regard of men like Burghley, Walsingham, and Throckmorton for so long. Killigrew has no claim to greatness, but he was a steady, competent man who gained and deserved the respect of others—"an honest man and able," Leicester had called him.[1] The successful conduct of affairs in all ages depends on the services of such individuals.

[1] Leicester to Burghley, 18th February, 1586. P.R.O. S.P. 83/6 f. 122.

THE KILLIGREW PEDIGREE

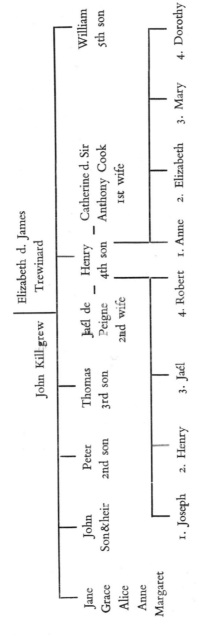

John Killigrew == Elizabeth d. James Trewinard

John Son&heir — Jane Grace Alice Anne Margaret

Peter 2nd son

Thomas 3rd son

Henry 4th son == Jaél de Peigne 2nd wife | Catherine d. Sir Anthony Cook 1st wife

William 5th son

1. Joseph 2. Henry 3. Jaél 4. Robert   1. Anne 2. Elizabeth 3. Mary 4. Dorothy

BIBLIOGRAPHY

I. MANUSCRIPT SOURCES

P.R.O.

1. State Papers, Henry VIII, S.P. 1.
2. State Papers, Domestic, Edward VI, S.P. 10.
3. State Papers, Domestic, Mary, S.P. 11.
4. State Papers, Domestic, Elizabeth, S.P. 12.
5. State Papers, Domestic, Elizabeth, Addenda, 1566–1579, S.P. 15.
6. State Papers, Foreign, Edward VI, S.P. 68.
7. State Papers, Foreign, Mary, S.P. 69.
8. State Papers, Foreign, Elizabeth, S.P. 70.
9. State Papers, Denmark, S.P. 75.
10. State Papers, France, Elizabeth, S.P. 78.
11. State Papers, Holland and Flanders, Elizabeth, S. P. 83–4.
12. State Papers, Scotland, Elizabeth, S.P. 52.
13. State Papers, Mary, Queen of Scots, S.P. 53.
14. Close Rolls, C. 54.
15. Patent Rolls, C. 66.
16. Inquisitions Post Mortem, C. 142.
17. Star Chamber Proceedings, Henry VIII, St. Ch. 2.
18. Star Chamber Proceedings, Edward VI, St. Ch. 3.
19. Baschet, A. ed., Transcripts of documents relating to English history preserved in the public libraries and archives of France 31/33, bundle 24.
20. Exchequer Augmentations Office, Miscellaneous Books, Enrollments of Leases, E. 315.
21. Office of the Auditors of Land Revenue, Miscellaneous Books, L.R. 2.

British Museum

1. *Additional MSS.* 24,127 contains Killigrew's Exchequer accounts for the year 1565. 36294 has an epitaph by William Camden to Catherine Killigrew. 38137 contains Killigrew's correspondence with the Privy Council, 1591.
2. *Cotton MSS.* Julius F. VI, Caligula B. IV, V, C. III, IV have Killigrew's instructions on several of his diplomatic missions. Caligula C. III, IV, V, have many of Killigrew's letters during his Scottish missions, 1572–1575. Nero B. IX, Galba B. XI contain most of his letters during the German embassy of 1569. Galba C. VI, D. I, II III,

have a considerable portion of Killigrew's correspondence in the Netherlands, 1587–1588.

3. *Egerton MSS.* 1694 contains some letters between Killigrew, Beale, Leicester, and Walsingham, 1586–1587. 2790 contains Killigrew's instructions on several of his diplomatic missions. 34,215 has his exchequer accounts, 1576, 1579–1580.

4. *Harleian MSS.* 36, 260, 289 have copies of Killigrew's instructions on several of his diplomatic missions. 138–9 contains some of his letters in the Netherlands, 1587–1588.

5. *Lansdowne MSS.* 106 contains "A note of such voyages as Mr Henry Killigrew made for the service of the Queen's Majesty and her Highness's realm."

6. *Sloane MSS.* 2442 has Killigrew's instruction on several of his diplomatic missions. 4105 contains extracts from several of Killigrew's letters during his mission to France in 1571. 3199 has some of Killigrew's Scottish correspondence, 1572–1573.

7. *Stowe MSS.* 163 has one of Killigrew's letters from the Netherlands, 1587.

8. *Yelverton MSS.* 48083–4 has a number of Killigrew's letters from the Netherlands.

Archives du ministère des affaires étrangères, vol. 9 of the Noailles correspondence contains references to Killigrew, during his exile in Mary's reign.

Bodleian Library, Oxford

1. *Ashmolean MSS.* 1729 contains a letter from Frederick III, Elector of the Palatinate, to Killigrew of 8th September, 1569.

2. *Western MSS.* 28996 has the household book of John Dudley, Duke of Northumberland, which contains entries showing Killigrew's name as a servant in the Dudley household in the reigns of Henry VIII and Edward VI.

Cornish Record Office, Truro

An uncatalogued manuscript survey of Lanrake, drawn up by Killigrew's reeve, William Samuel, in 1578.

Hatfield House, Hertfordshire

Hatfield MSS. volumes covering the years, 1560–1601, contain a considerable amount of Killigrew's public correspondence.

Lambeth Palace Library

Bacon MSS. 650 contains a few letters between Killigrew and Anthony Bacon.

Pepys Library, Magdalen College, Cambridge

> *Pepys MSS.* vol. 2 contains several letters from Killigrew to the Earl of Leicester during the German mission of 1569.

Somerset House, Prerogative Court of Canterbury

> 26 Bolein and Savile, p. 96 contain the wills of Sir Henry Killigrew and his brother Sir William.

II. PRINTED SOURCES

Acts of the Privy Council, volumes covering 1542–1603.

Letters and Papers, Foreign and Domestic, Henry VIII, vols. covering 1536–1546.

Calendar of State Papers, Domestic, Elizabeth, vols. covering 1547-1603.

Calendar of State Papers, Domestic, Elizabeth, 1537–1565.

Calendar of State Papers, Domestic, Elizabeth, Addenda, 1566–1579.

Calendar of State Papers, Domestic, Elizabeth, Addenda, 1580–1625.

Calendar of Patent Rolls, Edward VI, Mary, Elizabeth.

Calendars of State Papers, Foreign, vols. covering 1547–1589.

Calendars of State Papers, Scotland, vols. covering 1560–1583.

Calendars of State Papers, Spanish, vols. covering 1542–1579.

Calendars of State Papers, Venetian, volumes covering 1556–1580.

Anonymous. *A briefe and true report of the proceedings of the earl of Leicester for the relief of Sluys from his arrival at Flushing about the end of June, 1587, until the surrender there of 16th July next ensuing. Whereby it shall plainlie appear his Excellencie was not in anie fault for the losse of that town.* Imprinted at London, 1590.

Bannatyne, Richard, *Memorials of transactions in Scotland, 1549–1573.* (Bannatyne Club, no. 51), Edinburgh, 1836.

Blok, Petrus Johannes ed., *Correspondence inédite de Robert Dudley, comte de Leycester et de François et Jean Hotman*, Haarlem, 1911.

Bor, Pieter, *Oorspronck, begin en vervolgh der Nederlandsche oorlogen*, vol. 3, Amsterdam, 1681.

Bruce, John ed., *Correspondence of Robert Dudley, earl of Leycester, during his government of the Low Countries in the years 1585 and 1586*, (Camden Society Publication, vol. 27). London, 1844.

Brugmans, Hojo ed., *Correspondentie van Robert Dudley, graaf van Leycester, en andere document en betreffende zijn gouvernement-generaal in de Nederlanden, 1585–1588*, Werken van het hist. Genootschap, 3rd series vols. 56–8, 1931.

Coningsby, Thomas, *Journal of the siege of Rouen*, (J. G. Nichols ed.), London, 1847.

Dering, Edward M. *Dering's Works, more at large than ever hath been here-to-fore printed in any one volume, (containing a sermon preached at the tower of London, XXVII, certain godly and comfortable letters, a brief and necessary catechism, and godly and private prayers)*, 4 parts, R. I. James Roberts for Paul Linley and John Flasket, London, 1597.

Dudley Digges ed., *The compleat ambassador or two treaties of the intended marriage of queen Elizabeth of glorious memory comprised in the letters of negotiations of Sir Frances Walsingham, her resident in France, together with the answer of Lord Burghley, the earl of Leicester, Sir Thomas Smith, and others. Wherein as in a clear mirror, may be seen the faces of the two courts of France as they then stood and with many remarkable passages of state, not all mentitoned in any history*, London, 1655.

Dumont, Jean, *Corps universel diplomatique du droit des genes contenant un recueil des traitez d'alliances de paix etc. faits en Europe depuis le règne de Charlemagne jusqu'à présent etc.*, vol. 5, The Hague, 1725.

Ernst, Victor ed., *Briefwechsel des herzog von Wirtemberg im auftrag der kommission für Landesgeschichte*, 3rd vol., 1556–1559, Stuttgart, 1907.

Forbes, Patrick ed., *A full view of the public transactions in the reign of queen Elizabeth or a particular account of all the memorable affairs of that queen transmitted unto us in a series of letters and other papers of state written by herself and her principal ministers and by the foreign princes themselves with which she had negotiation. Published from original and authentic manuscripts in the Paper Office, Cottonian Library and other public and private repositorie at home and abroad*, 2 vols, London, 1735–41.

Haak, S.P. ed., *Johan van Oldenbarneveldt, bescheiden, betreffende zijn Staatkundigheid en zijn familie*, vol. 1, 1570–1601, Rijkgeschiedkundige Publicatiën, vol. 80, The Hague, 1934.

Harleian Society ed., *Publications, registers of St Thomas the Apostle*, vol. 6, London, 1861.

Harrington Sir John, *Nugae Antiquae; being a miscellaneous collection of original papers papers-written during in the reigns of Henry VIII, Edward VI, queen Mary, queen Elizabeth and king James*, (Henry Harrington ed.), vol. 2, London, 1769.

Haynes, Samuel and Murdin, William ed., *A collection of state papers relating to affairs in the reigns of queen Elizabeth from the year 1571 to 1596 transcribed from original papers and other authentic memorials never before published, left by William Cecil, Lord Burghley, and reposited in the library et Hatfield House*, London, 1740–1759.

Historical Manuscripts Commission: *Hatfield MSS.* vols. 4–7, 10, 11, *De L'Isle and Dudley MSS.* vols. 2, 3.

Hotman, Jean, *Brieven over het Leycestersche tijdvak uit die papieren van J. H.*, (R. Broersma and G. Busken Huet ed.), Bijdragen en Mededeelingen van het hist. Genootschap, vol. 34, The Hague, 1913.

Howard, Leonard ed., *A collection of letters from the original manuscripts of many princes, great personages and statesmen together with some curious and scarce tracts and pieces of antiquity, religious, political and moral, London, 1753.*

Japiske, Nicolas ed., *Resolutiën der Staten-Generaal van 1575–1609*, Rijks-geschiedkundige Publicatiën, vols. 47, 51, 's-Gravenhage, 1921–2.

Kausler Ernst von and Schott, Theodor ed., *Briefwechsel zwischen Christoph, herzog von Wurtemberg und Petrus Paulus Vergerius in bibliothek des litterarischen vereins in Stuttgart*, vol. 122, Tubingen, 1872.

Kluckhohn, August ed., *Briefe Freiderick der Frommen, Kurfursten von Pfalz mit verwandten Schriftstücken gesammelt und bearbeitet*, vol. 2, 1567–1572, Braunschweig, 1870.

La Mothe Fénélon, Betrand de Salignac de ed., *Correspondence diplomatique publié pour la première fois sur les manuscrits conservés aux archives du royaume*, vols. 5, 6. (A. Teulet ed.), Paris, 1838.

Powell, Edward ed., *The Travels and Life of Sir Thomas Hoby, Kt., of Bisham Abbey written by himself, 1547–1564*, (Camden Miscellany, vol. 10), London, 1902.

Rymer, Thomas ed., *The Feodora, conventiones, literae et cujuscunque generis acta publica inter reges Angliae et alios quovis imperatores, reges, pontifices, principes, vel communitates ab anno 1101 ad nostra usque tempora habitata aut tractata ... accurante*, vols. 15, 16, London, 1728–1729.

Stevenson, Joseph ed., *Correspondence of Sir Henry Unton, knight, ambassador from queen Elizabeth to Henry IV, king of France in the years MDXCI and MDXCII from the original and authentic copies in the state papers and the State Paper Office, the British Museum and the Bodleian Library*, (printed for the Roxburgh Club), London, 1847.

Teulet, Alexander ed., *Papiers d'Etat pièces et documents inédits ou peu connus relatifs à l'historie de L'Ecosse au 16th siècle des bibliothéques et des archives de France*, (Bannatyne Club publication, no. 107), vol. 1, Paris, 1852.

Thompson, Thomas, *The historie and life of James the Sext; being an account of the affairs of Scotland from the year 1566 to the year 1596 with a short continuation to the year 1617*, (Bannatyne Club publication, no. 13), Edinburgh, 1835.

Vardon, Thomas and May, Thomas E., ed., *House of Commons Journal, 1547–1628*, vol. 1, London, 1852.

Vivian, John Lambrick ed., *Visitations of Cornwall, comprising the Heralds' visitations of 1530, 1573, and 1620*, London, 1874.

Vivian, John Lambrick and Drake, Henry H. ed., *The visitations of the country of Cornwall in the year 1620*, (Harleian Society publication), vol. 60, London, 1884.

Willis, Browne, *Notitia parliamentaria or a history of the counties, cities and boroughs in England and Wales, to which are subjoined lists of the knights, citizens and burgesses with an account of the Roman towns in every shire*, vols. 2, 3, London, 1716–50.

Yorke, Philip, second earl of Hardwicke ed., *Miscellaneous state papers from 1501 to 1726*, vol. 1, London, 1778.

III.   SECONDARY WORKS

a.   Lives of Sir Henry Killigrew

Cooper, Charles H., and Cooper Thompson ed., *Athenae cantabrigienses*, vol. 2, 1586–1609, Cambridge, 1861, pp. 345–9.

Henderson, T. F. art. on Sir Henry Killigrew, *Dictionary of National Biography*, vol. 11, London, 1910, pp. 107–8.

Lloyd, David, *The statesmen and favorites of England since the reformation their prudence, policies, successes and miscarriages, advancements and falls during the reigns of Henry VIII, Edward VI, queen Mary, queen Elizabeth, James I and king Charles I*, second edition with additions, London, 1670, pp. 584–8.

b.   Family and Local Background

Boase, George Clement and Courtney, William Prideux ed., *Bibliotheca cornubiensis, a catalogue of the writings, both manuscript and printed, of Cornishmen and of works relating to the county of Cornwall, with biographical memoranda and copious literary references*, vols. 1, 3, London, 1874–82.

Carew, Richard, *The survey of Cornwall*, (F. E. Halliday ed.), London, 1953.

Drake, Daphne, *St Mawes and Pendennis castle*, (H M Stationery Office), London, 1934.

Hals, William, *The compleat history of Cornwall, general and parochial*, Truro, (1750).

Jeffrey, H. M., "Two historical sketches of the Killigrew family of Arwennack composed by Martin Lister Killigrew in 1737-8 and known as the Killigrew Manuscript." *Journal of the Royal Institution of Cornwall*, vol .9, (1887), pp. 182–216.

Mathew, David, "Cornish and Welsh pirates in the reign of Elizabeth." *English Historical Review*, vol. 29, (1924), pp. 337–48.

Polwhele, Richard, *History of Cornwall, civil, military &c.* vol. 4, 1867.

Rowse, Alfred Leslie, *The England of Elizabeth*, London, 1950.

Rowse, Alfred Leslie, *Sir Richard Grenville of the Revenge, an Elizabethan hero*, London, 1937.

Rowse, Alfred Leslie, *Tudor Cornwall, portrait of a society*, London, 1941.

Tregellas, Walter H., *Cornish worthies, sketches of some eminent Cornishmen and families*, London, 1884.

c.   Public Career

Aird, Ian, "The death of Amy Robsart," *English Historical Review*, vol. 71, (1956), pp. 69–79.

Atkinson, E. G., "The cardinal of Chatillon in England, 1568–1571," *Proceedings of the Huguenot Society*, vol. 3, (1888–1889), pp. 172–85.

Bastard D'Estang, *Vie de Jean de Ferrières par un membre de la société des sciences historiques et naturelle de Lyons*, Paris, 1856.

Black, John Bennett, *The reign of Elizabeth, 1558–1603*, Oxford, 1936.

Blok, Petrus Johannes, *The history of the people of the Netherlands*, Part 3, *The war with Spain*, (translated by Ruth Putnam), New York, 1900.

Brown, Peter Hume, *History of Scotland from the accession of Mary Stuart to the revolution of 1689*, vol. 2, Cambridge, 1902.

Burgon, John William, *The life and times of Sir Thomas Gresham* vol., 2, London, 1839.

Burton, John Hill, *The history of Scotland from Agricola's invasion to the revolution of 1688*, vol. 5, Edinburgh, 1871.

Chamberlain, Frederick, *Elizabeth and Leycester*, New York, 1939.

Chapman, Hester W, *The last tudor king, a study of Edward VI*, London, 1958.

Cheyney, Edward P., *A history of England from the defeat of the Armada to the death of Elizabeth, with an account of English institutions during the later sixteenth and early seventeenth centuries*, vol. 1, London, 1914.

Collinson, Patrick, *The puritan classical movement in the reign of Elizabeth I*, University of London Ph.D. thesis, 1957.

Decrue, François, *Anne, duc de Montmorency et pair de France sous les rois, Henry II, Francis II and Charles IX*, vol. 2, Paris, 1889.

Devereux, Walter Bourchier, *Lives and letters of the Devereux, earls of Essex in the reigns of Elizabeth, James I and Charles I, 1540–1646*, vol. 2, London, 1853.

Dietz, Frederick C., "The exchequer in Elizabeth's reign," *Smith College studies in history*, vol. 8, no. 20, (John Spencer Bassett and Sidney Bradstreet Fay ed.), Northhampton, Mass., 1923.

Dureng, A., "La complicité de L'Angleterre au complot d'Amboise," *Revue Historique Moderne et Contemporaine*, vol. 6, (1904–5), pp. 249–56.

Ehrenberg, Richard, *Hamburg und England im zeitalter der Königin Elizabeth*, Jena, 1896.

Elton, G. R., *The Tudor revolution in government*, Cambridge, 1953.

Froude, James Anthony, *History of England from the fall of Wolsey to the defeat of the Spanish Armada*, London 1875.

Fruin, Robert, *Geschiedenis der staatsinstellingen in Nederland tot den val der republiek*, 's-Gravenhage, 1922.

Fuller, Thomas, *The history of the worthies of England, endeavored by Thomas Fuller*. A new ed., with a few explanatory notes, London, 1811.

Garrett, Christina Hallowell, *The Marian exiles, a study in the origins of Elizabethan puritanism*, Cambridge, 1938.

Geyl, Pieter, *The revolt of the Netherlands, (1555–1609)*, London, 1932.

Harbison, Elmore Harris, *Rival ambassadors at the court of queen Mary*, Princeton, 1940.

Harrison, G. B., *The life and death of Robert Devereux, earl of Essex*, London, 1937.

Hinds, Allen Banks, *The making of the England of Elizabeth*, London, 1893.

Hurstfield, Joel, *The Queen's wards, wardship and marriage under Elizabeth I*, London, 1938.

Hume, Martin, *The courtships of queen Elizabeth, a history of the various negotiations for her marriages*, London, 1904.

Irwin, Margaret, *That great lucifer, a portrait of sir Walter Raleigh*, London, 1960.

Jenkins, Elizabeth, *Elizabeth and Leicester*, London 1961.

Kernkamp, Johannes Hermann, *De handel op den vijand, 1572–1609*, vol. 1, Utrecht, 1931.

Knappen, Marshall M., *Tudor puritanism, a chapter in the history of idealism*, Chicago, 1939.

La Ferrière-Percy, Hector De La,*Le xvi siècle et les Valois d'après les documents inédits du British Museum et du Record Office*, Paris, 1879.

Laffleur De Kermaingant P., *L'ambassade de France en Angleterre, mission de Jean de Thumery, sieur de Boissise, 1598–1603*, vol. 1, Paris, 1886.

Mattingly, Garrett, *Renaissance diplomacy*, London, 1955.

Melville, Sir James, *Memoirs of his own life, 1549–1593*, (With an introduction by W. Mackensie), London, 1922.

Motley, John Lothrop, *History of the United Netherlands from the death of William the Silent to the Synod of Dort*, vols. 1, 2, London, 1867.

Neale, John E., "Advice to the Queen", *English Historical Review*, vol. 65, (1950), pp. 91–7.

Neale, John E., "Elizabeth and the Netherlands," *English Historical Review*, vol. 45, (1930), pp. 373–96.

Notes and Queries, second series, vol. 11, p. 17.

Pattison, Mark, *Isaac Casaubon, 1559–1614*, Oxford, 1892.

Pearson, Andrew, Forret, *Thomas Cartwright and Elizabethan puritanism*, Cambridge, 1925.

Read, Conyers, *Mr Secretary Cecil and queen Elizabeth*, London, 1955.

Read, Conyers, *Lord Burghley and queen Elizabeth*, London, 1960.

Read, Conyers, *Mr Secretary Walsingham and the policy of queen Elizabeth*, 5 vols., Oxford, 1925.

Read, Conyers, "Walsingham and Burghley in queen Elizabeth's council," *English Historical Review*, vol. 28, (1912), pp. 34–58.

Ritter, Moritz, *Deutsche Geschichte im Zeitalter der Gegenreformation und des Dreiszigjährigen Krieges (1555–1569) im Bibliothek Deutscher Geschichte*, (Johannes Zweidineck-Suedenhoff ed.), Stuttgart, 1889.

Rowse, A. L. *The Elizabethans in America*, London, 1959.

Rowse, A. L., *Raleigh and the Throckmortons*, London 1962.

Russell, Eynest, *Maitland of Lethington, the minister of Mary Stuart, a study of his life and times*, London, 1912.

Sixt, Christian, *Paulus Vergerius, päpstlicher nuntius Katholischer bishof und vorkampher des evangelicus, eine reformation geschichtliche monographie*, Braunschweig, 1855.

Smith, Sir Thomas, *De republica Anglorum, or a discourse on the commonwealth of England*, (L. Alston ed.), Cambridge, 1906.

Stählin, Karl, *Sir Francis Walsingham und seine zeit*, vol. 1, Heidelberg, 1908.

Stephen, Leslie and Lee, Sidney ed., *Dictionary of National Biography*, London, 1885–1900.

Stowe, John, *A survey of the cities of London and Westminster containing the original, antiquity, modern estate and government of these cities written at first in the year MDXCVIII*, vol. 3, London, 1720.

Strype, John ed., *The life and acts of John Whitgift, D.D., the third and last Archbishop of Canterbury in the reign of queen Elizabeth*, vol. 1, Oxford, 1822.

Waldman, Milton, *Elizabeth and Leicester*, London, 1944.

Waldman, Milton, *King, Queen, Jack, Philip of Spain courts Elizabeth*, London, 1931.

Ward, A. W., Prothero, G. W., Leathes Stanley eds., *The Cambridge modern history*, vol. 2, *The Reformation*, Cambridge, 1907.

INDEX

Alençon, François, Duke of, 127, 183, 196

Alva, Don Fernando Alvarez de Toledo, Duke of, 102–3, 115, 117, 145, 165

Amboise, Tumult of, 55–6

Antwerp, 105, 197

Anville, Henri de Montmorency D', 88–9, 92

Argyle, vide Campbell

Arran, vide Hamilton

Arundell, John, 231

Arwennack, 4, 7

Ascham, Roger, 13

Aubigny, vide Stuart, Esmé

Augsburg Confession, 32, 36

Augsburg, Peace of, 31

Augustus, Duke of Saxony, 112–3, 115, 119

Bacon, Anthony, 183, 222, 237–38

Bacon, Francis, 183–4, 222, 238

Bacon, Sir Nicholas, 3, 98, 187, 237

Beale, Robert, 206–7

Beaton, Cardinal David, 162

Bedford, vide Russell

Bertie, Peregrine, Lord Willoughby, 213–14, 222

Blois, Treaty of, 124

Bourbon, Anthony de, King of Navarre, 21, 54, 74

Brandon, Charles, Duke of Suffolk, 12

Brandon, Charles, the Duke of Suffolk's younger son, 12

Briquemault, M. de, 91

Buchanan, George, 171, 186

Buckhurst, vide Sackville

Burchgrave, Daniel de, 204

Burghley, vide Cecil

Buys, Paul, 203–5, 209

Caesar, Sir Julius, 236

Calais, 2, 23, 29, 31, 38, 40–5, 76, 78, 93, 105, 252

Caltropt, Harry, 189–190, 235

Cambridge, 10

Camden, William, 97

Campbell, Archibald, Earl of Argyle, 147

Carew, Sir Peter, 16–19, 21, 89

Carew, Richard, 4–6, 232, 236 245

Carey, Henry, Lord Hunsdon, 131

Carmichael, Sir John, 172, 176

Casaubon, Isaac, 228

Casimir, Duke John of the Palatinate, 37, 101, 104–6, 109–10, 112–15, 117–121

Cateau-Cambrésis, 40–7, 78, 252

Catherine de Medici, 74, 88, 125, 145

Causin, Captain, 87

Cecil, Mildred, Catherine Cooke's sister, 96, 99

Cecil, Robert, W.C.'s younger son, 237, 240

Cecil, Thomas, W.C.'s elder son, 184

Cecil, William, Lord Burghley, at the court of Edward VI, 13; attitude towards Vergerio, 34–5; Scottish policy, 1560, 57, 59, 62, 64, 66; attitude towards Robert Dudley, 1560, 68, 71; and K's French mission, 1562, 75, 77, 81–3, 88, 92; opposition to K's marriage to Catherine Cooke, 99; and K's German mission, 1569, 107, 110, 114, 118, 249; and K's Scottish mission, 1572–3, 132–7, 141–6, 151, 153, 155–6,